ERRATUM: Ch

by D. H. THOMAS

THE SOUTHWESTERN INDIAN DETOURS

The story of the Fred Harvey/Santa Fe Railway
experiment in 'detourism'.

Hunter Publishing Co.
Phoenix, Arizona

Library of Congress Catalog #77-94331
ISBN #0-918126-11-8 Paperback
ISBN #0-918126-12-6 Clothbound

CONTENTS

DEDICATION

To Les, without whose idea it would
never have been started, and without
whose help it would never have been
finished.

INTRODUCTION

The writing of the Indian Detours began as an idea for a magazine article; it swiftly became a challenge for a book. The fact more than 50 years had passed meant many participants could no longer be contacted. Over the years, misstatements had been repeated often enough they became facts that had to be disproven.

Time had dimmed memories. Natural disasters had eliminated photographs and written memoirs. Useless trivia often got in the way of important recollection.

Hundreds of phone calls and letters with countless hours of research led to a confusion of contradictory details. Only the unselfish cooperation of participants and their families made the final results possible.

The project became a gigantic jigsaw puzzle with the missing pieces found in dusty scrapbooks, shredding newspaper clips, old photo albums, chance remarks in an interview, neglected archives and carefully catalogued files.

Historically, the book is as correct as it can be 50 years later; emotionally, to those who made the Indian Detours significant, it is a fruition of a conviction that the whole undertaking left an indelible impression upon the history of the American Southwest.

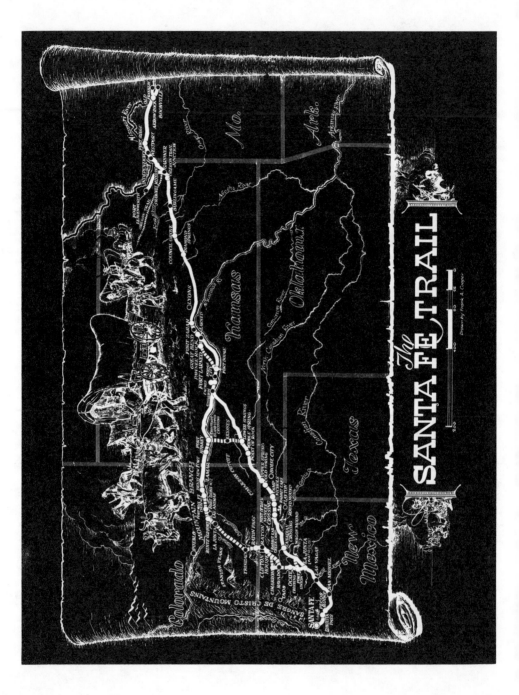

1

THE BEGINNING

The Santa Fe Trail! One of the most romantic phrases in Western history. A phrase, a place, an experience, an adventure.

Santa Fe. A town, a railroad spur line, heart of the Southwest, gateway to an unexplored enchanting region, last two words on the sides of cars of an Iron Horse that panted smoke into the clear blue skies of an unspoiled vastness. Santa Fe, whose Inn was an oasis in a sooty journey, whose covered patio of the Governor's Palace held a frozen mound of blanket-clad Indian squaws patiently crouched before their offerings of fine turquoise jewelry and symmetrical pottery bowls.

The Atchison, Topeka and Santa Fe Railway tracks had followed, as closely as possible, the Santa Fe Trail marked out by the unshod horses of Cortez and his men, blazed by the feet of mountain men on their trapping and trading journeys, pounded smooth by the wheels of westward-bound wagons. The smoke-stacked engines labored up the grades and braked down the slopes, carrying not only the wealthy vacationers, who even then were restless in their fine Eastern homes, but the farmers, miners and laborers who would settle the West.

The farmers, miners and laborers were lured by the tales of opportunity and riches; the wealthy were lured by the tales of California sunshine and a chance to see early civilizations closer to home than Greece, Egypt, and Rome, civilizations that in some cases pre-dated much of what they had seen while cruising the oceans of the world.

Although rail lines had crossed the Southern United States in the middle of the 19th Century, gulping great mouthfuls of territory in jumps from Chicago to Missouri, to Kansas, to New Mexico, to Arizona and finally to California, train travel was mainly a matter of getting from point A to point B in a minimum amount of time; and, until Fred Harvey entered the scene, with a maximum amount of indigestion.

Trains were scheduled for three stops a day, for breakfast, lunch and dinner, a twenty minute horror that saw train-purchased tickets exchanged for cold greasy food, literally thrown onto dirty plates at a station restaurant that was little more than a bare counter with uncomfortable wooden stools. At many stops, since the tickets were purchased ahead of time to facilitate speedy service, the restaurant owners and the train conductors split the proceeds when the twenty-minute stopover was shortened to ten minutes, with strident blasts of the train whistle announcing immediate departure. The uneaten food was then served to the next trainload of passengers in the same customer-swindling plan.

It took an enterprising transplanted Londoner, Fred Harvey, to change the nightmarish meal into a pleasant experience. Taking over the station beaneries, he instituted a chain of Harvey Houses, station restaurants, that served good food, properly prepared, served hot and already on the counters or tables by the time the train pulled into the station. A system of train whistle signals advised the upcoming meal stop operator how many of each entree had been ordered, so when the passenger alighted, the food was ready to be eaten, leaving only beverage orders to be taken by the bright, clean Harvey waitresses. To be sure the food was hot, palatable and a good value, Harvey would make unannounced rides on the train, charging through the depot restaurant like an avenging angel, prepared to fire a lackadaisical chef, an inefficient waitress, throw a plate of

MAY 23 1908

SANTA FE DINING CAR SERVICE
BY FRED HARVEY.

ASSORTED FRUIT, 20

STEWED PRUNES, 20   ORANGE MARMALADE, 20

PRESERVED FIGS, 25

SHREDDED WHEAT BISCUIT WITH CREAM, 25
ROLLED OATS WITH CREAM, 25

TENDERLOIN OR SIRLOIN STEAK, 85
WITH MUSHROOMS OR FRENCH PEAS, 1.00   WITH BACON, 95
WITH BORDELAISE OR BEARNAISE SAUCE, 1.00

EXTRA SIRLOIN STEAK (FOR TWO), 1.60
WITH BACON, 1.85   WITH MUSHROOMS OR FRENCH PEAS, 1.85
WITH BORDELAISE OR BEARNAISE SAUCE, 1.85

MUTTON CHOPS, 60: WITH BACON OR TOMATO SAUCE, 70

BROILED OR FRIED BACON, 40   BROILED OR FRIED HAM, 40
BACON AND EGGS, 50   HAM AND EGGS, 50
VEAL CUTLET, PLAIN OR BREADED, 45
CALF'S LIVER AND BACON, 45

BOILED, FRIED OR SCRAMBLED EGGS, 25: SHIRRED EGGS, 30
POACHED EGGS ON TOAST, 45
PLAIN OMELETTE, 30: WITH HAM, CHEESE, OR JELLY, 45
SPANISH OR MUSHROOM OMELETTE, 45

POTATOES—BAKED, 10, FRENCH FRIED, 15
HASHED BROWNED, OR LYONNAISE, 15   AU GRATIN, 25

HOT ROLLS, 10   CORN MUFFINS, 10
WHEAT CAKES WITH MAPLE SYRUP, 20
DRY TOAST, 10   BUTTERED TOAST, 10   MILK TOAST, 25

COFFEE, PER POT, FOR ONE, 15: PER POT, FOR TWO, 25
COCOA OR CHOCOLATE WITH WHIPPED CREAM, PER CUP, 15

TEA—CEYLON, YOUNG HYSON, ENGLISH BREAKFAST, OR SPECIAL
BLEND, PER POT, FOR ONE. 15: PER POT, FOR TWO, 25
MILK, PER GLASS, 10   MALTED MILK, PER CUP, 15

GUESTS WILL PLEASE CALL FOR CHECK BEFORE PAYING AND COMPARE
AMOUNTS CHARGED

A CHARGE OF 25 CENTS IS MADE FOR EACH EXTRA PERSON
SERVED FROM A SINGLE MEAT OR FISH ORDER

Harvey Girls at Rosenberg, Texas, 1908

cold food through a window, sweep dirty silverware onto the floor. Unlike our later day Continental Airlines pilots, who warned ahead of time that company head Bob Six was on board by radioing, 'this is flight #107, testing, 1, 2, 3, 4, 5, SIX', the Harvey chain had no advance knowledge of Fred Harvey's impending inspection; so they did it right every time, just in case.

The story of his Harvey Girls, the clean, fast, honest and efficient food service at the depots as the Atchison, Topeka, and Santa Fe line wound its rhythmic clacking way across endless miles of the unsettled West, has been told in book and film. His expansion into the hotel business that helped civilize the West has been told. His innovation of gourmet dining service aboard the speeding trains in 1888, when time did not permit station stops, has been chronicled. But his hard sell of the beauties and attractions of the Southwest he had such a deep feeling for, his successful venture into promoting Southwestern tourism on a grand scale in cooperation with the Santa Fe Railway, has not been told.

This is the story of the Indian Detours.

2

THE WHY OF IT

The Indian Detours were born, as many successful enterprises are, in a roundabout way. With the completion of the rail lines through Arizona, a demand for tourist transportation to the Grand Cañon of the Colorado (as it appeared on maps of the 1870's) was satisfied at first by inaugurating a stage service from two points on the Santa Fe Railroad line in 1892. One choice was to leave Eastbound trains at Peach Springs, 120 miles west of Flagstaff, and visit the South Rim. The more spectacular scenery of the South Rim was viewed by those passengers who left the Westbound trains at Flagstaff, and traveled north to Grandview Point via Fort Valley, past the San Francisco Peaks to the rim, a trip of unsurpassed wilderness. Neither of these trips gave the finest view of the Canyon, but both had one thing in common; each route was long, slow and uncomfortable.

The stages were not the usual conveyance that is pictured crossing the country in the 1800's, but rather a big wagon with wooden seats holding 18 people. Even the best-upholstered tourist sat down to dinner carefully after the eleven hour lurching, rocking drive to the Canyon rim.

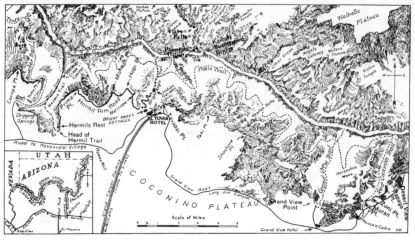

Map of Grand Canyon showing projected spur line

Flyers advertising the Santa Fe Trail trips did little to promote the Canyon sidetrip until 1893, when the head of the passenger department, C. A. Higgins, assembled a booklet extolling the beauties of the trip, and assuring interested travelers that the trip, made three times weekly, was worth every discomfort. There was no rush to sign up for the excursion, perhaps because Mr. Higgins fitted his enthusiasm into only three pages of the 150 page booklet. But the people who did take the trip told friends, and the increasing demand for the detour resulted in the final push needed to provide an easier means to put people on the rim of the Canyon.

Obviously, the Santa Fe Railway was planning ahead for the comfort of the travelers in Arizona, for a small item appeared in the Flagstaff Coconino Sun of February 4, 1899 as follows:

Railway to Operate "Horseless Carriages" Here to Grand Canyon

The contract for the horseless carriages to be operated by the Santa Fe road between Flagstaff and the Grand Canyon calls for three large coaches to cost $4,000 each, and six smaller ones. These will be constructed by the Everette-King Manufacturing company of Chicago.

The vehicles are to be used in transporting sightseers from the Santa Fe station at Flagstaff to the Grand Canyon of the Colorado river.

The first of three larger automobiles is now under construction at the machine shops of the Everette-King company. The work is under the immediate supervision of A. W. King, the designer, whose trackless engines will, he claims, ascend the steep mountain grades with the greatest ease.

The body of the coach will be about the size of an ordinary carette, with a seating capacity for eighteen persons, including the driver. It will seat twelve passengers inside, while six more can be accommodated on top. A fourteen-horsepower gasoline engine will furnish the motive power.

The venture must have proved unworkable, and indeed, even with the difference of rating horsepower in antique automobiles and trucks, the 14 HP engine would hardly have been able to carry 6 passengers in a touring car, much less 18 passengers in a double-decker bus. At least there are no records available to the author proving the vehicles were ever made, and there is no listing of the manufacturing company in automobile encyclopedias. Another way had to be found.

For more than 15 years, the feasibility of building a spur line from Williams to the Canyon had been discussed. The road was fairly level, no mountains had to be crossed no gorges to be bridged. A mining company whose activities included a copper mine at Anita, some 15 miles to the south of the Canyon, agreed to build the roadbed, looking at it as an investment to help move more ore from the mine. It was not destined to be a long term investment for the company, for just as the line reached the mine, the ore ran out. The Atchison, Topeka and Santa Fe took one look at the number of visitors to the Canyon, and in a bankruptcy action against the mining company got possession of the Grand Canyon spur line.

The last 15 miles extending the line to the Canyon, were completed in 1901, and on September 18th, the first scheduled passenger-carrying train stopped at a bare spot by the tracks at the South Rim. Passengers climbed down to set foot on dirt that would be part of the depot and resort hotel complex by 1905.

The travelers of 1901 were hardy individuals. The fact the accommodations at the Canyon's only hotel, the Grand View, were more rough than rustic, did nothing to discourage them. They would come in increasing numbers now the train had replaced the wagon, and some would drive their own cars. In fact, the first private car to drive to the Grand Canyon, arrived only a year later than the first train.

Fortunately for the Santa Fe Railway, the death of Fred Harvey in 1901 caused little ripple in the efficient operations he had started. A smooth transition within the family avoided any delay in completing planned expansions and many people today reading about Harvey operations are unsure when the senior Harvey died. The Fred Harvey Corporation was frequently referred to in newspaper releases as simply 'Fred Harvey', even though management had passed into the hands of his son Ford.

At the Grand Canyon, the Corporation proceeded with the building of what they claimed would be a hotel unsurpassed anywhere in the Arizona Territory, El Tovar. Announcement of the proposed construction had first appeared in the Coconino Sun on June 6, 1903.

First train to the Grand Canyon, Sept. 18, 1901

Begin Construction Bright Angel Hotel

Plans submitted by Charles F. Whittlesey, of Albuquerque, for the new hotel near the head of the Bright Angel trail, Grand Canyon of Arizona, have been finally approved. Work will begin at once. The location selected is in the pine forest 200 yards east of the present temporary structure, but further back from the rim. At this point the gorge is 6,000 feet deep and thirteen miles wide.

Bright Angel tavern, as the new hostelry may be called, will cost about $100,000. It will be under the management of Fred Harvey.

The Swiss style of architecture has been adopted, native stones and logs being used as far as practical. A hotel of this kind has been made necessary to the rapidly-increasing travel since the railroad was extended from Williams.

While today, $100,000 would pay for little more than the excavation, the sum was large enough to impress readers — the hotel would indeed be first class. Almost 18 months later, another item appeared (Oct. 1, 1904) in the same paper revealing what the name of the hotel would be but not promising when it would be ready for tourists.

El Tovar Hotel Is Nearly Completed

The new Harvey hotel on the brink of the Grand Canyon is nearly completed. As the work progresses it becomes more and more evident that for novelty of architecture and design and convenience for the tourist public, the new building will be unsurpassed.

It has been decided to name the new hostelry El Tovar, instead of Bright Angel tavern. Pedro del Tovar is traditionally credited with being the first white man to penetrate into the mysterious depths of the Titan of chasms, and consequently the name will not be without historical significance. The naming of the hotel after the Spanish will be in line with the Alvarado, Castañeda and Cardenas, given to the other elegant Harvey hotels.

"El Tovar" has been under construction for some months. It is modeled after the old Swiss taverns. Its appearance is that of an immense house.

El Tovar opened with a flourish in 1905, and in the folder racks of the Santa Fe Railway stations across the country, a medium-sized booklet was offered for the taking. Pictures of El Tovar showed a solid building of rock and wood, with a circular drive for the horse-drawn coaches, still making their trips up from Flagstaff one day and back the next to accommodate Westbound travelers who didn't want to return to Williams, Arizona.

The brochure mixed descriptive text with assurances

that the tourist would find all the niceties he had left at home.

> "El Tovar is a long, low, rambling edifice, built of native boulders and pine logs from far-off Oregon. The width north and south is three hundred and twenty-seven feet and from east to west two hundred and eighteen feet.
>
> Its lines are in harmony with the simplicity of the surroundings. The architect has combined in admirable proportions the Swiss chalet and the Norway villa. Here are expressed a quiet dignity, an unassuming luxury, and an appreciation of outing needs. Not a Waldorf-Astoria — admirable as that type is for the city — but a big country clubhouse, where the traveler seeking high-class accommodations also finds freedom from ultra fashionable restrictions. You may wear a dress suit at dinner or not. You may mix with the jolly crowd or sit alone in a quiet nook. You may lunch at almost any hour of the day or night. You may dine with other guests or enjoy the seclusion of a private dining room."

The brochure went on to describe the building in detail, getting slightly flowery along the way, concluding with the basics of how much it cost to experience all this luxury on the brink of the Canyon.

> "The hotel is from three to four stories high. It contains more than a hundred bedrooms. The main building and entrance face the east. Ample accommodations are provided for 250 guests. More can be comfortably housed in the annex at Bright Angel Camp.
>
> Outside are wide porches and roof gardens. Boulders and logs for the walls and shakes for the roof, stained a weather-beaten color, merge into the gray-green of the surroundings.
>
> The inside finish is mainly peeled slabs, wood in the rough, and tinted plaster, interspersed with huge wooden beams. Triple casement windows and generous fireplaces abound. Indian curios and trophies of the chase are liberally used in the decorations. The furniture is of special pattern.
>
> El Tovar is more than a hotel; it is a village devoted to the entertainment of travelers. Far from the accustomed home of luxury, money has here summoned the beneficent genii who minister to our bodily comfort. Merely that you may have pure water to drink, it is brought from a mountain spring 120 miles away! And that is only one of the many provisions for unquestioned excellence of shelter and food.
>
> The hotel is conducted on the American plan. There are twenty rooms at $3.50 a day; about forty rooms at $4.00 a day; the remainder are $4.50 and upwards."

The Grand Canyon had finally achieved top billing in places to vacation in the Southwest, thanks to the high rating of El Tovar.

Ten years later, in 1915, El Tovar was still the place to go. But the tourist picture at the Canyon was changing. The

Ready for a Rimdrive at Grand Canyon. El Tovar, 1911

spur line from Williams now made two trips a day. The wagon trips from Flagstaff had been discontinued as being too tedious. If tired transcontinental travelers didn't want to climb off one train and onto another the same day, a Fred Harvey hotel at Williams, the Fray Marcos, rather snobbishly described as 'adequate' offered an overnight stay and good food under the Harvey Girls' ministrations. And the next day, a completely rested tourist could make the three hour train trip to the Canyon, looking forward to the comforts of El Tovar and the beauties of the rim.

El Tovar had changed little in ten years. The circular drive was a little wider, the outside walls a little more weathered, the 100 plus bedrooms available for guests had dropped to 93 since some private baths had been added. Each room now had a telephone connected to the main switchboard, and as the conveniences had gone up, so had the rates. Bathless rooms were $4 to $6; with bath they were $2 more. Where guests had been promised fresh spring water in 1905, they were now treated to fresh milk and cream from a Harvey farm at Del Rio, near Prescott, Arizona. And for those on a limited budget, cottages and tents were both available.

The tent rooms near El Tovar had been added as private automobile touring increased, and charges were $1 and $1.50 a day per person. The cottages were a bit more comfortable with electric lights, toilets and steam heat.

Both types of accommodation were under the watchful supervision of Fred Harvey management, and the driving tourist could eat a la carte at a nearby Harvey cafe.

The motorists who drove their open and sometimes unreliable horseless carriages to the Canyon in 1915 were undoubtedly encouraged to make the trip by the Harvey name on the folders. Crossing the country was still a rugged undertaking with few surfaced highways, and the economy of the country was such that, for the general car buying public, the Model T Ford ($490 for the roomy touring model in 1915, with a $50 rebate because the company reached a sales peak quota) was a far better seller than the bigger, heavier and more expensive American cars. Accommodations along the better-traveled roads were little more than shacks, mostly without any of the amenities, and eating was more of a gamble than Russian roulette. Near big cities, car travel was easier as people in need of an extra bit of egg money took the travelers in, put them up overnight in spare bedrooms and fed them hearty breakfasts the next morning before sending them on their way. But in the wide open spaces of the Southwest, cities were few and distances were far, and the only restaurants to be trusted were Harvey Houses.

It would have been justifiable and natural if the Santa Fe Railway folders had ignored the needs of the adventuresome automobilists, as they were referred to, but in the happy marriage of the Harvey Corporation and the Santa Fe, there was something for everyone, even the less affluent family on a Model T vacation. And, keeping up with the budding love affair between Americans and the automobile, El Tovar had its own motorcar transportation company and a modern (for the day) garage had been built on the grounds to house the cars as well as provide service and parts to private cars. Car storage was available at $1 a day. Not that the coaches had been scrapped and the horses retired. In 1915 autos were not permitted on the narrow Hermit Rim road, nor on the road to Yavapai Point. Because of their scant width, it was felt the roads to these outlooks should be restricted to horse-drawn vehicles solely. The two means of transportation cohabited happily, so while Hermit Rim and Yavapai were to be seen only by those who climbed into the modified wagons of 1905,

The Fray Marcos Hotel at Williams, Ariz.

Early Motorists exploring the Grand Canyon

regular automobile trips were now offered to the guests of El Tovar.

Besides the regularly scheduled tours, the hotel kept cars available for hire, with chauffeurs trained not only in driving the rim roads, but in the history of the area. Seven different routes radiated out from El Tovar, covering from 13 to 66 miles. For a flat fee of $4, a tourist was taken through pine forests to view rock formations, to natural springs, wells and waterfalls, and to visit ranches. For $30, a 66 mile round trip included Aztec ruins, dams and lakes, and a lunch stop in the forest to catch glimpses of wildlife.

If the tourist had a week to spend, trips were made to Flagstaff to show the spur line traveler the scenery he had missed now that the slow wagons no longer made the journey. Muleback excursions down the Bright Angel Trail were offered and an overnight camping trip gave city folk a taste of roughing it easy.

For tourists staying only overnight, the brochures suggested different trips. For $3, the coach visited Hermit Rim Road to the head of Hermit Trail, a 15 mile round trip that took 3 hours. For only $1, the coach would visit Yavapai Point, two miles away, and for $1.50 go to Hopi Point, also two miles from the lodge. A short auto trip to Grand View via Long Jim Canyon, cost $4 for the 16 mile 2½ hour jaunt. Many of these trips were made twice a day, at 9:30 in the morning and 1:30 or 2:00 in the afternoon.

The same fee paid for a mule trip down Bright Angel Trail as far as the plateau, or clear to the river for $6. For the tourist spending two days, combinations of these trips were offered. Particular mention was made in the brochures of Hermit's Rest, where light refreshments were served in a room carved from solid rock and chilled winter visitors warmed themselves at a huge fireplace built into the back wall. A porch hung over the gorge below for summer gazing, and a glass front was provided on the building for lunching in comfort in the Spring and Fall seasons.

This wasn't the only shelter. At the head of Bright Angel Trail, an observatory and resthouse had been built of native stone. It, too, had a large fireplace and was steam-heated as well. Big picture windows looked out on the Canyon, and there was a small library of geological and astronomical subjects. Named 'The Lookout', it had elec-

De Luxe

· MENU ·

DEC 12 1911

OYSTERS—BLUE POINTS 25   FRIED 40   BROILED 40   MILK STEW 35

SARDINES 40   CAVIAR 40   CHOW CHOW 15   OLIVES 20

BROILED OR FRIED BACON 50   BROILED OR FRIED HAM 50
BACON AND EGGS 60   HAM AND EGGS 60

BOILED, FRIED OR SCRAMBLED EGGS 25   POACHED EGGS ON TOAST 45
SHIRRED EGGS 30   PLAIN OMELETTE 35; WITH HAM, PARSLEY, OR TOMATO 50
MUSHROOM OR RUM OMELETTE 50

TENDERLOIN OR SIRLOIN STEAK 90
WITH FRENCH PEAS 1.00   WITH MUSHROOMS 1.10   WITH BACON 1.00
WITH BORDELAISE OR BEARNAISE SAUCE 1.10

EXTRA SIRLOIN STEAK, FOR TWO 1.75
WITH FRENCH PEAS 2.00   WITH MUSHROOMS 2.00   WITH BACON 2.00
WITH BEARNAISE OR BORDELAISE SAUCE 2.00

BROILED YOUNG CHICKEN 65   FRIED YOUNG CHICKEN 65

MUTTON CHOPS 60
WITH BACON 70   WITH TOMATO SAUCE 70

POTATOES—FRENCH FRIED 15   AU GRATIN 25
HASHED, BROWNED, LYONNAISE OR JULIENNE 15

COLD OX TONGUE 40   COLD HAM 50   BOSTON BAKED BEANS, HOT OR COLD 30

LETTUCE SALAD 30   POTATO SALAD 25   CHICKEN SALAD 60

VIENNA BREAD 10   TEA BISCUIT 10   BOSTON BROWN BREAD 10
DRY TOAST 10   BUTTERED TOAST 10   MILK TOAST 25
SHREDDED WHEAT BISCUIT WITH CREAM 25

ASSORTED FRUIT 20   PRESERVED STRAWBERRIES 25   PRESERVED FIGS 25
ORANGE MARMALADE 20

ROQUEFORT CHEESE WITH WATER CRACKERS 25

COFFEE, PER POT, FOR ONE 15; PER POT, FOR TWO 25   DEMI-TASSE 10
COCOA OR CHOCOLATE WITH WHIPPED CREAM, PER CUP 15
TEA—CEYLON, YOUNG HYSON, ENGLISH BREAKFAST, OR SPECIAL BLEND
PER POT, FOR ONE 15; FOR TWO 25
MILK, PER BOTTLE 15   MALTED MILK, PER CUP 15

ONLY PURE SPRING WATER SERVED

GUESTS WILL PLEASE CALL FOR CHECK BEFORE PAYING AND COMPARE AMOUNTS CHARGED
A CHARGE OF 25 CENTS IS MADE FOR EACH EXTRA PERSON SERVED FROM A SINGLE
MEAT OR FISH ORDER

SANTA FE DINING CAR SERVICE
BY FRED HARVEY

Santa Fe Depot at the Grand Canyon

tric lighting so evening trips could be made to enjoy the deepening colors at sundown.

The Santa Fe made no charge for stopovers to enjoy the attractions of the Grand Canyon. In much the same arrangement as an open airline ticket today, the passengers simply paid for the extras they wanted — the spur line trip, the stay at El Tovar, the coach or auto excursions — and then climbed back on the California Limited or The Missionary and resumed their journey across the country. The fare from Williams to the Grand Canyon was only $7.50 for the round trip, and the experience was priceless.

Rim Tour cars leaving El Tovar

Hermit's Rest

Easterners even had a chance to visit with Indians. When Fred Harvey was establishing his Harvey Houses, he traded with the Indians — at Santa Fe, Albuquerque, Williams, Flagstaff, on the reservations he passed through, in the town squares where they came to peddle their wares. With unerring good taste, he collected fine examples of the best of Indian handicrafts. When he died, the corporation built a large hogan opposite El Tovar, half storehouse, half museum, and exhibited the collection to Canyon guests. A small band of Hopis lived on the grounds, and the Supais

Route 1088—Flagstaff to Grand Canyon, Ariz.—83.0 m.

Route map, page 798   Reverse route, No. 1089

Road Conditions—For the most part excellent road, some of it being very fast. There are only a few miles that have not been graded to some extent and all improvement work is likely to be completed for 1914. Most of the way is through a pine forest.

Be sure to take sufficient supplies for the whole run as there is no habitation of any sort soon after leaving Flagstaff except one or two water holes.

MILEAGE
Total Intermed.

0.0 0.0 **FLAGSTAFF.** From station on right go east along tracks; cross branch RR. 1.1; pass right-hand road 3.4; cross RR. at big saw-mill 4.9.

5.9 5.9 Prominent fork; bear left (right is Route 1110 to Winslow). Keep ahead on fine road; pass road to right 6.9; cross RR. 8.7 and 9.0.

12.0 6.1 Fork at foot of hill, fence on right; bear left, shortly curving right upgrade between pines. From here on road is quite winding and a little hilly, but through beautiful pine forest.

19.7 7.7 Fork—sign in angle, open country ahead; bear left downgrade (right is to Lees Ferry). Road is almost straight on new grade; pass left-hand road 20.7; disregard any intersections where old road crosses and recrosses the new grade; go through cedars for some distances 26.0. Coming out into open country 29.5, go down long grades. Road is a little rocky in places.

35.3 15.6 Pass small pond over to right and water hole (on left—35.7).

36.1 0.8 **Caution** for water bars, going down steep grade.

39.3 3.2 Fork; bear right with travel up winding grade.

40.3 1.0 Fork; keep left, following sign, shortly going up small, narrow valley between rocks.

46.6 6.3 Go upgrade, curving around end of sparsely constructed dam for reservoir. Road may be a little rutty through here. Coming into pines again 53.4, pass big signboard at **Moqui tank** 53.2 (water); curve around fence corner 53.6; pass reservoir off to right 55.7, following beautiful road through pines.

67.0 20.4 Fork; keep main road straight ahead, passing numerous trails to Hall's tank. Road is winding but direct through forest.

69.8 2.8 **Grand View,** hotel on right.
First glimpse of one of the side canyons can be had here.
Keep straight ahead past cottages; avoid road to left 70.2.

70.7 0.9 Prominent 3-corners; bear left for Grand Canyon.
Note—Right-hand road is direct to Grand View Point, about 1¼ miles.
After curving left follow good road, winding through forest with rim of canyon at varying distances off to the right, but for the most part a half to a mile away. At one or two places a glimpse can be had of the great chasm through the trees.

72.8 2.1 Keep ahead, passing right-hand road leading to Hammer Point.

79.3 6.5 Fork; bear right. Go through gate 1.1.

82.8 3.5 Station ahead; bear right upgrade on macadam to Circle Drive in front of hotel.

83.0 0.2 **GRAND CANYON**—El Tovar Hotel on left, canyon straight ahead.

Page 816

Blue Book page on Flagstaff to Grand Canyon route.

occasionally came up from the Canyon bottom to bring their finest work to sell to the tourists. Many present day priceless collections were started by Canyon vacationers.

Aware that motorists were not candidates for the guided car tours, the Santa Fe brochures gave explicit directions for duplicating most of the tours. In those days before road maps, direction signs and mileage markers, most motorists traveled with a guide called the Blue Book. Published by a Chicago/New York firm, such major undertakings as a trip from Flagstaff to the Grand Canyon was carefully detailed but the Santa Fe Railway brochures detailed the side trips.

Side trips were constantly being improved. In 1915, two well-maintained dirt roads led to the Canyon, remnants of the wagon roads from Flagstaff and Williams. Motorists traveling the National Old Trails Highway across Arizona were promised in the 1915 Santa Fe folder that by 1916 a new road would be opened up and they would be given a choice of two ways to approach the Canyon from Williams. The new road would go through scenic Wildcat Canyon to

El Tovar stable and garage

Outing party leaving El Tovar Hotel

Hirsch's Ranch, then through Echo Park to a junction with the main Grand View road. This alternate route would be slightly longer, 35 miles in all, but would open new scenic treats.

By 1923, the Canyon was a National Park (proclaimed so on Feb. 26, 1919), and the brochures stressed the importance of the 'big gully'. Prices were much the same as they had been in 1915, with the exception of the mule trips which had been increased by $1 and had a minimum of 3 people. Cars were available on a charter basis, but the minimum fee was 6 full fares regardless of the number of passengers, and the trips were becoming so popular the brochure noted that if the demand for regular trips filled all the cars, private tours were unavailable.

While all this activity was going on in Arizona, another side trip was being offered to transcontinental travelers on the Santa Fe. The railroad had a twofold purpose in planning side trips for passengers. First, the train trip was long and tiring, and any break in the routine of sleeping, eating, through-the-window watching was welcomed. Second, the trips were a means of extra revenue for both the railroad and the Harvey Corporation, whose contract made the two corporations seem one and the same body politic.

By the time the train from Chicago had reached New Mexico, the passengers were ready for a change of pace, and the terminal at Lamy was a natural, as was the opportunity to see the old city of Santa Fe. Daily trips from Lamy to Santa Fe, 18 miles to the North, were made on a spur line. The trains carried day trippers, as well as overnight travelers who could stay at the De Vargas Hotel in Santa Fe. There was no penalty for the stop over and there was no charge for the trip into town and back. An 18 page brochure had been prepared by the railroad in 1916 and passed out to transcontinental travelers in hopes they would find the text irresistible. And a lot of them did.

Liberally sprinkled with photos of not only the city itself, but of all the natural as well as man-made wonders surrounding Santa Fe, the brochure gave readers a capsule history of the region, a detailed rundown on climate, educational facilities, business opportunities, and the delights of choosing Old Santa Fe for their permanent residence. With apologies for even suggesting the passengers might want to get off their green plush seats, the brochure promised, and the author must have crossed his fingers on this one, that rain would undoubtedly not fall to spoil their expedition. The sales pitch concluded redundantly:

"The average traveler is reluctant to leave his comfortable train, even for so short a side trip as that of 18 miles to Santa Fe. Santa Fe hasn't been advertised much, even though written about extensively, and is worth while in every sense of the phrase. It is unspoiled; the tourist is not pestered for baksheesh, and the cringe for a tip is unknown. There are no admission fees to its sights, which are as free as the air, and the glorious sunshine that prevails 325 days in the year. Rain or shine, Santa Fe is an attractive place. Of the trust of this assertion, this booklet seeks to give you a glimpse."

SANTA FE, N.M.
AND VICINITY
"THE MOST WONDERFUL 50 MILE SQUARE IN AMERICA"

The railroad was not averse to appealing to the travelers who had been everywhere, touting the fact the healthful climate of Santa Fe was superior to that of the Nile, the Riviera, or the Adirondacks. The cool nights and comfortable days were stressed, for many of the Easterners and the Midwesterners who traveled the train chose the summer months in order to avoid the sticky weather of East Coast cities and Midwest lake areas.

The section urging day trippers to take walking tours before resuming their westward journey listed the sights that would enchant the pedestrian, such as

". . . the unique adobe flat-roofed houses; the quaint crooked streets; the burros loaded with wood; the mingling of the Indian and Spanish-speaking native and the frontiersman, and the many evidences of ye olden days on every side."

The spur line ended close to the Plaza, and the tourists were encouraged to visit the Lamy Foundation, the Soldiers' Monument, the Kearny Monument, the End of the Santa Fe Trail Monument, the Masonic Building and Hall, the First National Bank Building and the Capitol Bank Building wherein the weather bureau saw to that unending sunshine. For tourists who were busy snapping away to preserve their memories, mention was made of the New Mexico Camera Club welcoming visitors.

The brochure was heavy on architecture, recommending the adventuresome stroller walk away from the Plaza and take in the Public Library, the National Guard Armory, the Elks Theatre and Clubhouse, the Federal Building and the Forestry Building. The listing was partly to impress Easterners that the Southwest was not as wild as they might have heard, but enjoyed the gracious patina of an old civilization, and partly to call the sightseers' attention to the Spanish architecture, not found in their home towns where steep roofs were designed to dump snow and clapboard and brick houses marched in stately rows along paved or cobblestone streets.

The diversions went on. Ten minutes' walk would allow time to visit the old Spanish fortress, the Garita, and gaze at the Capitol and the Executive Mansion, while five minutes more would allow time to at least give a passing glance at the various churches and schools as well as the State Penitentiary. With something for everyone, even sanitariums and cemeteries were included in the walking tours. The day trippers returning to Lamy too late to make connections were put up at Harvey's El Ortiz Hotel at Lamy, catching the early train the next morning.

Having taken care of the day trippers, the brochure went on to take care of those who would stay overnight at the De Vargas Hotel in Santa Fe, naturally a Fred Harvey hostelry. Chauffeur-driven cars stood at the ready in front of the hotel, waiting for those who wanted to see the surrounding areas out of walking distance.

By 1916, automobiles were pretty reliable teenagers. Bigger engines with six cylinders were put in 7-passenger touring cars, perfect for hauling eager sightseers around the New Mexico scenic points. With more power than the 1915 models, they could climb hills slowly but smoothly

Left: End of the Santa
Fe Trail Monument

Right: The Soldiers'
Monument at Santa Fe

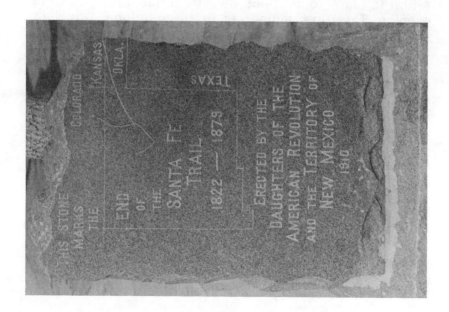

Old Palace of the Governors at Santa Fe

even when fully loaded, and trips of varying length were offered to train-weary tourists.

A choice of several different one-hour drives were offered, designed mostly for the day trippers who would return to Lamy to continue their train ride later that same evening. The trips fanned out in all directions. One went North of the city to see the mineral springs at Aztec and the lake formed by the Water Company's reservoir. Another went South to the Arroyo Hondo; there the tourists could walk along the banks of a canyon, exploring, very briefly, the Pueblo ruins. Back to the North, other prehistoric ruins were visited in the Tesuque Valley and this one-hour trip was a circle drive. Those interested in the religious history of the area could take a trip to the chapel used by Archbishop Lamy, and see the ranch he lived on when he was Santa Fe's spiritual leader.

There were only short stretches of good highway leading out of Santa Fe at this time. A scenic road had been built by convict labor over the 9,600 foot Dalton Divide and down into Macho Canyon. It was a courageous undertaking without heavy machinery for this was the most rugged part of the Sangre de Cristo Range. The road connected with a forest trail for hikers and horseback riders that led to the

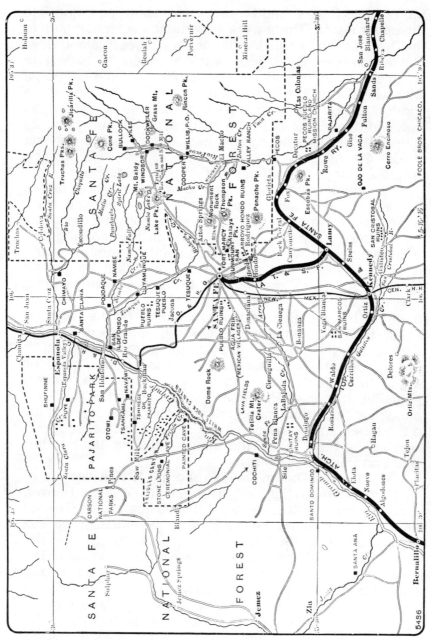

Santa Fe and vicinity routes in 1916

top of Lake Peaks, and there were other trails going into the upper Pecos. There were 13 switchbacks leading up to the Divide, each turn giving flatlanders a breathtaking view. The Automobile Blue Book warned drivers to expect to have to back up to make the hairpin turns if the car had a long wheelbase. Certainly many of the tourists felt more comfortable on the return trip which reached the De Vargas Hotel through cool dense pine forests. At that time, 22 miles of road had been built East out of Santa Fe, and almost 20 miles West out of Las Vegas, each moving toward a planned junction point on the Pecos River.

For tourists with more time to spare and more desire to explore, the auto trips could be combined with horseback riding or wagon trips to the more remote areas not accessible by car. Leaving early in the morning and returning (hopefully) at sundown, a combination tour could be taken to the turquoise mines where Tiffany bought all their raw stones for many years; to the house where Gov. Lew Wallace wrote part of 'Ben Hur'; to examine pictographs, those prehistoric newspapers scratched on rock faces; to visit numerous excavated Indian ruins and historic churches, the tourists changing from tour cars, to wagons, and finally to horses. If the thought of a six hour wagon trip each way didn't discourage the visitor, Bandelier National Monument was suggested, and arrangements could be made to camp out rather than return to the hotel, and so go on to see more remote attractions such as the Puyé Ruins, the Alamo Canyons, the Painted Cave and Pajarito Pueblo.

Besides the Dalton Divide road, by 1916 a section of the Camino Real Highway, destined to connect Denver, Colorado, and El Paso, Texas, had been completed. Twenty miles South of Santa Fe, La Bajada Switchbacks gave a superb view of the Rio Grande Valley. Continuing on South, Albuquerque could be reached by way of Domingo and Bernalillo in four hours, barring flat tires, flash floods, and engine trouble, so the visitor could stay at the De Vargas in Santa Fe and visit Albuquerque all in a long day's time.

If it hadn't been for World War I, the popularity of the Southwestern tours would have kept on growing, but as early as 1915 shortages were being felt as materiel for car manufacturing was diverted for defense machinery use. On

The Santa Fe depot at Lamy in 1917

July 11, 1916, President Woodrow Wilson had signed the first Federal Law which would be the foundation for a nation-wide system of interstate highways. Primarily the act was meant to establish roads which could be used by postal trucks and cars, using matching funds from States and the Federal Government. Then, as now, the States looked at the cost of doing it themselves at their own pace, and jumped on the subsidy bandwagon. But the formal declaration of war on April 6, 1917, called a halt to road building and changed a lot of American habits, among them the taking of trips both by rail and by car for the duration.

All car and truck companies were suddenly pledging their output for the war efforts, and the personal motorcar took a backseat; the railroads were suddenly needed for moving men and machinery from farms and factories, from cities and key plants to the East Coast where ships could transport the needs of a European war. The tourist on the train was subject to delays as passenger trains were shunted to sidings to let military freight trains rumble by uninterrupted.

Gasless Sundays were urged by a President who less than a year before had eagerly signed a bill to build highways for motorists, albeit mailmen on their appointed rounds. And the automobile industry curtailed production of the family car to concentrate on building ambulances,

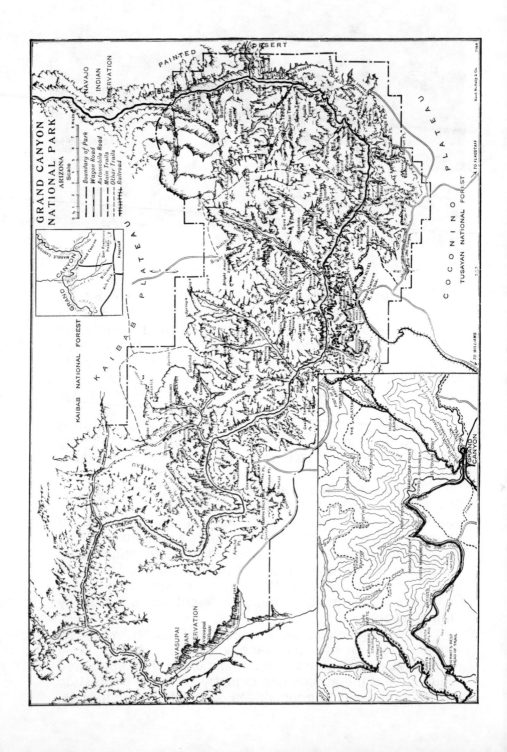

El Tovar from the Hopi House

war trucks and gun carriers. The family car might not be replaceable for years, for who could say with certainty when the war would be over, so it was not subjected to the tortures of a long journey to see the Southwest.

The end of the war in November 1918, was not a magic end to shortages. The railroads had neglected their handling of pampered travelers; equipment was untidy from the

El Tovar at Grand Canyon

demands put on it. The temporary closing of many non-essential services meant a brand new beginning to play catch-up. Even the Harvey Houses had felt the pinch as soldiers on their way to war had not needed the crisp linen, shining silver and gourmet-type meals. The time had been only a short 18 months, but the accelerated period had left decelerated conditions and the touring American public had to sort out their disrupted lives before they could indulge in the diversions they had enjoyed before the War.

Slowly the lure of train travel, the building of better roads, the availability of new and better cars, the upsurge of economy brought the country back to normal, and once more the attractions of the Southwest were touted by the Santa Fe Railways. But it was a lukewarm period for seeing America first. Undoubtedly, part of this was because the War had made Americans acutely aware of Europe, and stirred a desire to visit it 'while it was still there.' European travel was a more enticing siren than the Southwest.

Then suddenly, by the early 1920's, the drought was over; the interest was revived. There remained only the mechanics of the plan to be worked out.

The Indian Detours were about to be born.

3

THE WHEN OF IT

The continued enthusiasm of train travelers for exploring the American Southwest in the early 1920's merited increasing attention from both the Santa Fe Railway and the Fred Harvey organization. But it took one man in the Harvey office to see the possibilities of greatly increasing the numbers of visitors who came from the East and West Coasts, climbed off the trains in New Mexico at Lamy or Albuquerque, and in Arizona at Flagstaff or Williams and either climbed onto a spur line train or into a motorbus to reach points the mainlines didn't touch.

The man was Major R. Hunter Clarkson, who like Fred Harvey had been born in the British Isles. A native of Edinburgh, Scotland, he was educated at George Watson's College in his home town. When he graduated, he was a gentleman farmer, concerned with the breeding of sheep and cattle. A year of this left him restless and eager for more worlds to conquer, and he returned to school to spend the next three years studying banking, insurance and law.

When war was declared in 1914, he volunteered for service in a heavy artillery battery. He was made a Major serving both in the artillery and the Royal Flying Corps. In September of 1914, he was sent to France and served with

Harry Lauder's son. There began a friendship that would span two continents. A few months later he was posted to the Gallipoli Peninsula where he saw action against the Turks.

In 1916 he was transferred to Egypt where his action in the Suez Canal campaign earned him the Military Cross. When British forces were sent to occupy Russia, he was one of the first to go and finally in 1919, he was assigned to duty in Italy.

The Italian campaign was not to his liking, and he retired from service to resume farming in Scotland. In a Glasgow pub one night after chores were over, he met a liquor salesman from the United States whose customers included the Harvey organization. The man found Clarkson likeable and asked him why he didn't come to the States to live, adding that if he ever did, he could get him a job with Harvey.

Less than a year later, Clarkson sold his farm, bought a boat ticket to the States and landed with nothing more than an address to contact. But the contact was made, the salesman was still impressed with the Major, and gave him an introduction to the powers that hired at Harvey. The Major was put in charge of transportation at Grand Canyon.

His duties were all-inclusive. He was assigned to scheduling the motor buses that traveled the rim, the mules that made the trip to the bottom, and the buses that met the trains in Flagstaff and Williams. The routine was to his liking, and the vastness of the Canyon kept him from being homesick for the lonely moors of Scotland.

It was usual for officials of the Santa Fe Railway to vacation at the Grand Canyon, and the following summer, Arthur G. Wells, vice-president of the Santa Fe passenger traffic division, brought his two daughters along to enjoy the view. One of them, Louise, enjoyed the view as long as it included Major Clarkson, and before the year was out, they were married.

Clarkson's charm alone would have advanced his position without the advantageous marriage, and added to this was his liking for hard work and a head for innovative ideas. By the time he had spent four years with the company, he was deep in a study he had initiated to improve the handling of the growing traffic to the Southwest. He knew the

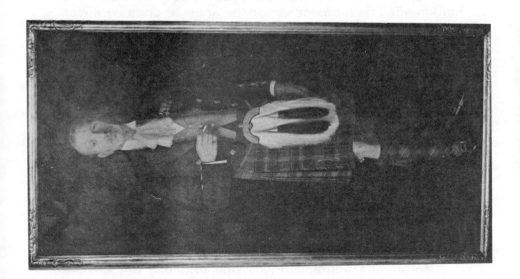

Above: Major R. Hunter Clarkson

Left: a painting of Major Clarkson in kilts by Theodore Van Soelen.

tours at the Grand Canyon were well received, but what about more tours? longer tours? to more points of interest than just Arizona?

His active mind pictured big touring cars, carrying relaxed sightseers to all the historical points in the Southwest. New Mexico had Indian ruins in abundance, the oldest city in the United States, and a wandering river whose name was synonomous with romance.

Clarkson's business-trained mind made him realize the dream was financially too big for him to handle, although he would rather have opened his own transportation company. So he took his idea to Ford Harvey, his boss and his friend. He outlined his plans for two stops that would be practical as disembarkation points, Las Vegas and Albuquerque. From these depots, cars carrying the Fred Harvey insignia would take tourists to Old Santa Fe, to the Indian pueblos both inhabited and long deserted, and deliver them to the trains after three days of luxurious sightseeing, to continue their journey or return home.

Ford Harvey was impressed. Being both visionary and hard-headed as a businessman, he knew at once here was the solution to filling the Harvey Houses, the trains and the till of the Santa Fe/Harvey enterprise. Excellent Harvey Hotels were already at the junction points, the Alvarado in Albuquerque, built in 1882, but constantly being updated, and the Castañeda in Las Vegas, built in the same year was just as tourist worthy. The heart of the tours would logically have to be located in New Mexico; Clarkson was posted to Santa Fe.

For several weeks the plans were charted, changed, charted again. Options were gotten on transportation vehicles. Maps were poured over to see where the tours would go. Clarkson's financial brain was assigned the task of working out costs. Timetables were figured out to the minute. And finally the idea was far enough along to make a public announcement.

Before the announcement was officially released, a name had to be found that would be used in all releases, printed on all folders. The conversation on the point was not recorded. Had it been, it would probably have shown that a discussion of previous side trips that had been promoted since 1901 pointed out they were really detours off

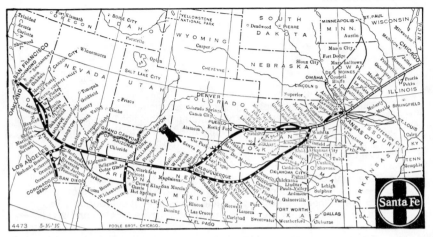

The Santa Fe rail lines

the main line. This would be a detour, a detour to see the Indian pueblos, the Indian ruins; why not call it the Indian Detour? Agreed.

The Albuquerque Morning Journal of August 20, 1925 carried the first release:

Santa Fe Will Establish Bus Detour
Through Indian Pueblos

Railroad Announces Three-Day Journey Between Las Vegas And Albuquerque For Sight-Seeing Trip.

Most Interesting Country in America

New Service Means Hundreds of Tourists Will Visit State Yearly; New Departure in Railroading.

The Santa Fe Railway system announced here Wednesday the establishment of an Indian detour rail and motor way which will enable rail tourists from Chicago to California to see points of historic and scenic interest in this state and at the same time to travel on a fixed schedule. This move on the part of the Santa Fe means that thousands of tourists who have hitherto rushed through the state on the limited and other fast trains and who have missed the best New Mexico — or the entire continent, for that matter — has to offer in the way of interest to the sightseer and student, will spend three days traveling by auto bus through the mountains, valleys, canyons and Indian pueblos of this section of the southwest.

The announcement, which was authorized in Chicago by W. J. Black, passenger traffic manager for the Santa Fe system, was made here by R. H. Clarkson of the Santa Fe-Fred Harvey system, who has spent considerable time in arranging tours for the big project. The Indian Detour will be established next year in time for the spring and summer travel.

The Indian Detour offers three days of unusual motoring through oldest America, in the New Mexico Rockies between Las Vegas and Albuquerque and provides a pleasant break in the cross continent rail trip the year 'round. It will be the last word in transcontinental journeying, both in equipment and skill in handling.

The three-day personally conducted educational tour will comprise visits to old Santa Fe, to the inhabited Indian pueblos of Tesuque, Santa Clara, San Juan, Santa Domingo and other points in the picturesque valley of the upper Rio Grande, as well as to the huge communal ruins of Puyé, a cliff pueblo 20 centuries old.

It will be an all-expense motor trip, under Santa Fe-Fred Harvey management, covering nearly 300 miles of auto transportation, as well as meals and hotel accommodations en route. Special autos of new design are to meet Santa Fe main line trains at Albuquerque and Las Vegas, at which points important station hotels are located and local sightseeing will be done.

The announcement is considered one of the most important ever made in modern railroading in that for the first time in history a transportation system will be operating a rail and bus system in parallel lines over a great part of its territory. It is looked upon as a great step forward in the developing of the section of New Mexico served by the Santa Fe system and especially included in the present plan. When completed it is expected that bus and private auto service will be available with Santa Fe railroad tickets from Raton, N.M. to the Grand Canyon of Arizona.

Numerous optional side trips to other well known but little seen places in the Indo-Spanish southwest, off the beaten path, are being arranged; and in addition a series of exclusive tours in private cars, in charge of trained couriers will be operated.

This was followed on August 21, 1925, by an editorial in the same paper. As they put it:

Santa Fe Auto Tours

The announcement by the Santa Fe railway of plans to make the historic and scenic places of interest in New Mexico available to the tourist through a series of auto bus lines is the best piece of good news the state has had since oil was found. The arrangement which will be put into effect next spring will make all northern and central New Mexico and Arizona to the Grand Canyon accessible to the sightseer. That it will be under the management of Fred Harvey insures the highest degree of comfort to the traveler and that the tours will be kept on the highest plane.

It was the genius of Fred Harvey that recognized the historic interest of the land traversed by the Santa Fe and the unique character of the Indian and old Spanish customs and industries. His influence was seen in the architecture of the stations and in the museums which he made a part of them. He collected vast quantities of objects almost priceless and thus saved them from destruction. So far as he could he brought historic New Mexico to the transcontinental traveler. It is appropriate therefore that his company is connected with the latest development of taking the tourist away from the railway directly to the places of scenic, historic or archaelogical interest.

Fred Harvey had in fact the true spirit of the collector and antiquarian. He insisted on authenticity. He discouraged the fairy stories that too often passed current to astonish the gullible tourist. If Fred Harvey showed an old Spanish bell there was no doubt of its age. If one of his agents related an historical incident or an Indian legend, its veracity could be relied on. Because of the insistence on authenticity which Mr. Harvey drilled in his organization, we may be sure the planned tours will not be vulgarized. The tourists will not be regaled with fanciful stories and amused with "fake" objects of interest. They will have presented to them the life of New Mexico both as it has been and as it still is.

The most interesting part of the announced plans is the one for the tourists to leave the train at Albuquerque or Las Vegas and by automobile traverse the two sides of the Albuquerque-Santa Fe-Las Vegas triangle. More objects and places of interest may be found in and about this section of the state than in many other of equal size. The roads furthermore are excellent. But this triangle does not exhaust the varied and novel items of interest which New Mexico has for the visitor. From almost any station on the Santa Fe trips may be taken that will well repay the traveler. The difficulty in the past has been the uncertainty as to whether means could be procured to reach these places and the nature of the hotel accommodations. All these will now be provided for. A prospective tourist in Boston, New York or Chicago may plan a vacation in New Mexico and know in advance the time schedule and the costs.

These arrangements for tours will induce thousands of visitors to the Grand Canyon to see New Mexico also. They will bring thousands more to the Southwest who have thought the only thing worth seeing here is the Grand Canyon and have hesitated to make the long trip for this single objective. Now they may plan a trip, varying the time to be devoted to it at their pleasure, and be sure each day will bring them something novel, strange or beautiful.

Literally hundreds of thousands of dollars will be expended in advertising to make the Southwest known to the rest of the world. This does not include the large amount that will be spent on the equipment to make travel here easy and agreeable.

On the same day, the front page carried a more detailed coverage of the plans, including an explanation of why the plums would go to the Santa Fe/Harvey combination:

Fifty Thousand Tourists Will Traverse State

Santa Fe-Harvey Bus Lines Expected to Handle Large Crowds; Will be Advertised on Large Scale.

The return from Santa Fe of R. H. Clarkson, assistant to Ford Harvey of the Fred Harvey system, with additional details of the Indian Detour Rail and Motorway, to be inaugurated by the Santa Fe railway and Fred Harvey next spring, only adds to the significance and importance of the step from an Albuquerque and New Mexico viewpoint. The service will operate every day in the year.

Although the amount to be appropriated for launching the undertaking was not given out by Mr. Clarkson, it is believed that it will reach in the hundreds of thousands of dollars for advertising and equipment. In offering a three-day all expense Indian Detour trip as part of the regular ticket sold on Santa Fe transcontinental trains, it is opening the section between Albuquerque and Las Vegas up to the ordinary traveler who has always been of the impression that New Mexico was solely what he could see from the train window.

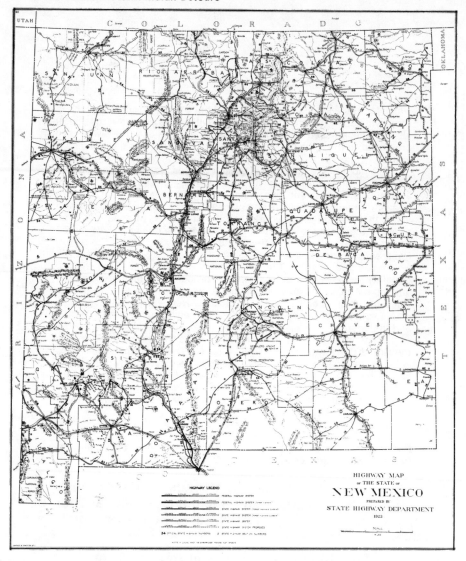

The full plan contemplates the taking of passengers from Santa Fe trains at Raton and bringing them to Albuquerque by way of Taos and Santa Fe. This will not be in the regular bus system, but will be handled by specially adapted touring cars of the larger type. The regular three-day all expense tour will operate solely between Albuquerque and Las Vegas, with Santa Fe, as the central point of access, used as head-quarters and repair depot. On this tour will be employed busses of new design which will as closely resemble a Pullman car on wheels as modern motorway manufacture has been able to accomplish. Busses will have a capacity for approximately 12 persons, it is said, with each passenger having a revolving cushioned seat such as in parlor cars and with the busses built for highest visibility from all sides.

In addition to the special service from Raton to Albuquerque it will also be carried out from Albuquerque west toward the Grand Canyon,

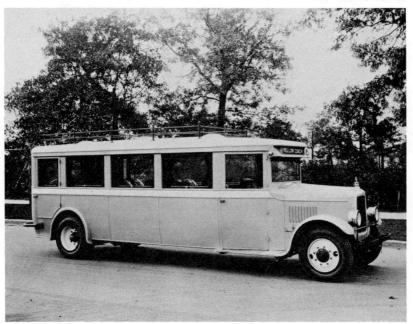

Type X Yellow Coach

Type Y Yellow Coach

which is considered locally of even more importance. These trips will take in Acoma, Laguna, Inscription Rock, the Ice Caves, side trips to Mesa Verde and Pueblo Bonito, etc. etc. and then on from Gallup to connect up with the Grand Canyon busses.

The regular bus service between Albuquerque and Las Vegas will carry local and inter-city passengers, as well as persons bearing the Indian Detour tickets.

Tentative arrangements for this tour are as follows: In coming from Las Vegas, passengers will arrive in Albuquerque about 11 o'clock in the morning, leaving on train No. 9 at 12:20 at night or on the limited west next morning. Since side trips from here are optional under the plan, it means that passengers will have practically an entire day in which to see and shop in Albuquerque. Passengers coming from the east and desiring to take the trip from Albuquerque to Las Vegas will get off here on No. 2 at 2:15 or No. 4 at 5 o'clock in the afternoon and will go out on the bus next morning.

The announcement of the Santa Fe/Fred Harvey plans comes after years of effort by local and state organizations to interest them in just such a plan. The continued reluctance of Ford Harvey to remain out of a plan which local interest might rather handle was only overcome by a petition from local organizations including over 200 Albuquerque businessmen nearly a year ago in which they asked that he should personally take the initiative in the matter. Previous to that there had been intermittent efforts along that line culminating about a year ago in a dinner at the Franciscan when it was attempted to organize a transportation line along the same plan but on a smaller scale than the one now announced.

The organization failed, less for want of capital than from fear that there would not be found locally the proper management for such a huge undertaking. Also it was obvious that no local enterprise could provide the comprehensive regular transportation service, wide publicity and well organized relations with ticket and tourist agencies throughout the United States and abroad, coordinated under one head in order to assure uniform service and provide tickets on an all-expense basis indispensable if ultimate success is to be attained in developing the attractions of New Mexico for the best class of tourist travel. This entails wide contact with the traveling public, a heavy and increasing investment for equipment and advertising and calls for proportionate resources to meet inevitable losses in operation during the pioneering period, all of which are obviously beyond the scope and means of local enterprises.

Private individuals in Albuquerque figured on forming such a corporation but were held off for the same reason. It was felt that such work required an organization ready made and one trained by experience along such pioneering lines and also one that could afford a deficit for several years in getting the plan launched. It was felt that the Fred Harvey system was best adapted to carry on the work and it was then that the petition was sent to Mr. Harvey and it was then that Mr. Clarkson, his assistant, was sent here to go into the matter thoroughly. His final report to the Fred Harvey and Santa Fe railroad officials led to the announcement of the Indian Detour plan Thursday.

The section of New Mexico included in the plan and Albuquerque as its most important city, will get the same advertising as has been given to Southern California as a section by the Santa Fe railroad, and as is given to the Grand Canyon as a special trip. When it is realized that the busses at Grand Canyon handled 50,000 passengers last year, an idea of the magnitude of the present undertaking can be had. It will not only bring tourists directly to New Mexico and Albuquerque — something which has never been done before on a large scale, but it will have the far more important effect of introducing easterners to the resources and beauties of New Mexico which can be seen in only few instances from the railroad car windows. It will, in a sense, be an announcement of the "open door" to New Mexico. It will result in thousands of monied people seeing the possibilities of the state where only a very few see them now.

The new plan will also have the effect of taking the burden from local organizations of trying to advertise the scenic, archaeological and historic features of the entire state with an advertising appropriation only adequate for local uses. It will, for instance, allow all energies of such an organization as Advertising Albuquerque Inc. to be centered in the health and industrial possibilities of the city and vicinity with the certainty that the very most in decisive advertising results can be obtained by the local appropriation.

A somewhat perplexing editorial appeared in the Las Vegas Daily Optic on August 29th. In it, the editor lamented the lack of cooperation between Las Vegas, Santa Fe and Albuquerque, and felt the Detours would iron out the problem, and then concluded with the hope that the entire state would benefit from the promotion of these three cities.

La Fonda in 1925

Records show that local interest in the plans continued through the month starting with an impressive gathering of delegates from areas expecting to benefit from the tours. The Albuquerque Morning Journal of August 30, 1925, carried an item in depth on the dinner which had been held the night before. Immediate promises, plus legal action, guaranteed the improvement of the roads in time for the debut of the tours, and it went on to state:

". . . a tone of optimism, prosperity and good fellowship . . . were the outstanding features of the inter-city dinner and meeting held at La Fonda last night under the auspices of the Santa Fe Chamber of Commerce, with President O. W. Lasater in the chair, and R. H. Clarkson, assistant to Ford Harvey, in charge of plans for the big automobile project as the principal speaker. There were about 115 men present; there were close to 50 prominent citizens there representing Raton, Las Vegas, Taos, Española and Albuquerque, and Mrs. Miller of the Valley ranch had the distinction of being the sole woman delegate.

Speakers were Senator Sam G. Bratton, a tribute to the late Col. R. E. Twitchell; Judge Reed Holloman and Judge Wright, welcoming speeches in behalf of local Kiwanis and Rotary clubs: Clarkson, Dr. Livingston for Española, J. W. Giddings for Taos, "Long John" for Taos; Kenneth Baldridge, president Rotary Club for Albuquerque; L. S. Wilson for Raton; W. F. Nicholas, president of Kiwanis club for Las Vegas; C. W. G. Ward, Las Vegas, Pearce C. Rodey, Albuquerque; C. J. Crandall for the Indian service; Don Stewart of Las Vegas; Mayor Nathan Jaffa of Santa Fe and other scattering remarks by various persons.

The Santa Fe Rotary club turned out a good representation, as did the Kiwanis club and there was a good attendance of members of the Chamber of Commerce.

Mr. Clarkson briefly outlined again the plans for the three-day, 300-mile motor tour to be furnished Santa Fe railroad tourists on an all-expense, bother-eliminated basis, starting from Las Vegas and taking in Santa Fe and the other points of interest between Las Vegas and Albuquerque. Close cooperation between all towns affected and absolute good will from all, he declared, are vital.

Highlights in Clarkson's talk were:

There is more of historic, prehistoric, human and scenic interest in New Mexico than in any other similar area in the world, not excepting India, Egypt, Europe or Asia.

From 10,000 to 12,000 ticket agents will become media of advertising New Mexico.

The influx of tourists will mean more prosperity for everyone in the state.

The big idea is not only to let people know what is in New Mexico, but to tell them what it is when they see it. Raton will be the point of departure for special tours. The first stop out from there will be Taos. Gerson Gusdorf's plan for a big Taos hotel is splendid. Taos undoubtedly will get on the "standard tour" itinerary later.

Puyé is one of the most interesting points on the route and the route from Española to that point should be improved at once, as also the road from Pojuaque to Otowi bridge, on the route to the Frijoles, and the ten miles south out of Las Vegas.

Clarkson wants a small committee representing all communities to confer with and advise him as the project is carried out.

Optional side trips to Santa Fe, Taos, Frijoles, out of Albuquerque to Laguna and Acoma, and from Las Vegas to El Porvenir, etc. will be an important development.

A three-day standard tour is long enough for a starter, and will keep visitors long enough to interest them in the optional side trips. It may be expanded to four days later.

The "personally conducted" feature of the tour will be the secret of its success, and a school of drivers and guides will be conducted by the Santa Fe and Harvey system.

The following day, August 31st, the same paper carried an item concerning one of the Santa Fe officials who had come in for the dinner but had held his tongue at the speaker's table until he could see for himself what the huzza was all about.

Traffic Head For Santa Fe Seeing Detour

A. Morison, Assistant to Mgr. Black, Goes Over Route of Bus Lines to Be Run by His Company

A. Morison, assistant passenger traffic manager for the Santa Fe railway, has arrived with Mrs. Morison from his headquarters in Chicago and will go over the route of the Indian Detour to be established next year by the Santa Fe and Harvey systems. Mr. Morison said that he is among the first victims of the "lure of the opportunity to tour through the scenic section of New Mexico".

"I have been coming to New Mexico often for the past 20 years," said Mr. Morison, "and I have never been off the steel rails, except for one trip to Bishop's Lodge. Now that the opportunity is provided to go into the scenic country on rail schedule, I am making the trip as a pioneer. I imagine there are thousands of people who, like myself, have been going through the state and sticking to the rail route and who will avail themselves of the wonderful detour."

Mr. Morison's trip is largely preparatory to working out the schedules. He said that the railway expects to spend a large amount in advertising New Mexico. This was his first visit to Albuquerque in three years. He said he could see that the city has made substantial growth in that time. Both Mr. Black and Mr. Clarkson of the Santa Fe-Harvey system, who have been working on the Indian Detour project for several months, said they appreciate the support the plan has received from the New Mexico people.

After that item, the papers carried no further word of what was being planned for some time. A terse announcement was made in the October 25th issue of the Journal that the police in Albuquerque had allowed the local traffic policeman to buy a motorcar, since the expected increase in tourist traffic would warrant such expenditure.

The lack of publicity had no effect on the buzzing activity in Harvey headquarters. The contract for the first buses to be used on the Detours was given to the Yellow Coach Company of Chicago. The first two, which were to serve as a test for the balance of the contract, were of different sizes. The larger one, Type Y, had a wheelbase of 230", was 26 feet long and weighed 11,290 pounds. It was designed to carry 25 passengers and stressed comfort. A narrow aisle ran through two compartmented sections. Seats were individual, two on each side of the aisle, and the

*The original
La Bajada Hill*

passengers in the back compartment would not be an-
noyed by men who lit up large cigars, or the flappers who
were taking to cigarettes.

The larger bus was painted cream color with blue trim-
mings and the smaller bus, a Type X model, which would
carry 18 people, was all blue.

The buses were shipped to Las Vegas on the train,
unloaded and put to the test on Tuesday, December 15,
1925. Frederick Harvey, his son Frederick, Jr. and wife from
Kansas City, Clarkson, Governor Hannett and his family,
State Highway Engineer French and J. S. Shirley, transportation manager of the Fred Harvey Company at the Grand
Canyon, were all participants in the test run.

Early Wednesday morning, the 16th, the buses started
out from Las Vegas on their way to Santa Fe. The torture
test would be La Bajada Hill, whose tight curves were difficult to negotiate in a long-wheelbased car. The buses had

TENTATIVE WESTBOUND SCHEDULE, THE INDIAN-DETOUR
Effective May 15, 1926

FIRST DAY

9.00 a.m.   Leave Castañeda Hotel. **LAS VEGAS** (Fred Harvey) by motor.

9.30 a.m.   Kearney's Gap. Named for General Kearney, who captured Santa Fé in 1846.

10.00 a.m. Tecolote. Quaint old Spanish-American settlement.

11.15 a.m. San Jose. Has a picturesque old Spanish mission.

11.30 a.m. Arrive Cicuyé (Pecos Ruins). Important Indian pueblo ruin. Inhabited 2,000 years ago. Excavated and partly restored. Remain one hour.

1:00 p.m.   Arrive Apache Inn, (Valley Ranch.) at entrance to Pecos Canyon, for lunch.

2:00 p.m.   Leave Apache Inn, Valley Ranch.

3:30 p.m.   Arrive **SANTA FÉ**, La Fonda Hotel.

4:00 p.m.   Conducted tour of Indian Museum and Art Gallery.

6:00 p.m.   Dinner.

8:00 p.m.   Lecture by School of American Research on the history, arts, crafts and quaint ceremonials of the Pueblo Indians. St. Francis Auditorium.

SECOND DAY

9.00 a.m.   Leave **SANTA FÉ**, La Fonda Hotel.

9.15 a.m.   Arrive Tesuque Indian Pueblo (inhabited).

9.45 a.m.   Arrive Española, on the Rio Grande. Ten minutes at hotel.

11.00 a.m. Arrive Puyé Ruins. Large cliff pueblo, partly excavated and restored. Remain one hour.

12:40 p.m. Arrive Santa Clara Indian Pueblo (inhabited).

1:00 p.m.   Arrive Española. Lunch at hotel.

2:20 p.m.   Arrive San Juan Indian Pueblo (inhabited).

4:00 p.m.   Arrive **SANTA FÉ**.

5:00 p.m.   Conducted tour of Santa Fé.

6:00 p.m.   Dinner.

8:00 p.m.   Indian play in St. Francis Auditorium.

THIRD DAY

9.00 a.m.   Leave **SANTA FÉ**, La Fonda Hotel.

10.15 a.m. Arrive Santo Domingo Indian Pueblo. Largest inhabited pueblo. Population 800.

12.45 p.m. Arrive **ALBUQUERQUE**, Alvarado Hotel (Fred Harvey).

1:00 p.m.   Lunch.

3:00 p.m.   Leave for Isleta Indian Pueblo and Albuquerque Drive.

5:30 p.m.   Arrive **ALBUQUERQUE**, Alvarado Hotel.

6:30 p.m.   Dinner.

7:00 p.m.   Tour of Indian Building.

TENTATIVE EASTBOUND SCHEDULE, THE INDIAN-DETOUR
Effective May 15, 1926

FIRST DAY

9.00 a.m.	Leave Alvarado Hotel, ALBUQUERQUE (Fred Harvey) by motor.
9.45 a.m.	Arrive Isleta Indian Pueblo (inhabited). Remain half an hour.
11.15 a.m.	Arrive Alvarado Hotel, returning via ALBUQUERQUE Old Town Drive.
11.45 a.m.	Lunch. Alvarado Hotel.
12.45 p.m.	Leave Alvarado Hotel.
2.15 p.m.	Arrive Santo Domingo Indian Pueblo. Largest inhabited pueblo. Population 800.
2.45 p.m.	Leave Santo Domingo.
4.15 p.m.	Arrive SANTA FÉ, La Fonda Hotel.
4.45 p.m.	Conducted tour of Indian Museum and Art Gallery.
6.00 p.m.	Dinner, La Fonda Hotel.
8.00 p.m.	Lecture by School of American Research on the history, arts, crafts and quaint ceremonials of the Pueblo Indians. St. Francis Auditorium.

SECOND DAY

9.00 a.m.	Leave SANTA FÉ, La Fonda Hotel.
9.15 a.m.	Arrive Tesuque Indian Pueblo (inhabited).
9.45 a.m.	Arrive Española, on the Rio Grande. Ten minutes at hotel.
11.00 a.m.	Arrive Puyé Ruins. Large cliff pueblo, partly excavated and restored. Remain one hour.
12.40 p.m.	Arrive Santa Clara Indian Pueblo (inhabited).
1.00 p.m.	Arrive Española. Lunch at hotel.
2.20 p.m.	Arrive San Juan Indian Pueblo (inhabited).
4.00 p.m.	Arrive SANTA FÉ.
5.00 p.m.	Conducted tour of Santa Fé.
6.00 p.m.	Dinner.
8.00 p.m.	Indian play in St. Francis Auditorium.

THIRD DAY

9.30 a.m.	Leave SANTA FÉ, La Fonda Hotel.
11.00 a.m.	Arrive Cicuyé (Pecos Ruins). Important Indian Pueblo ruin. Inhabited 2,000 years ago. Excavated and partly restored. Remain one hour.
12.30 p.m.	Arrive Apache Inn (Valley Ranch).
1.00 p.m.	Lunch Apache Inn.
2.00 p.m.	Leave Apache Inn.
3.15 p.m.	San Jose. Has a picturesque old Spanish Mission.
4.00 p.m.	Tecolote. Quaint old Spanish-American settlement.
4.30 p.m.	Kearney's Gap. Named for General Kearney, who captured Santa Fé in 1846.
5.00 p.m.	Arrive LAS VEGAS, Castañeda Hotel (Fred Harvey).
6.00 p.m.	Dinner.

W. J. BLACK,
Passenger Traffic Manager, Santa Fe System Lines

Chicago, November 14, 1925

to back up in several places to make the curves, and there was immediate agreement that work would be started the following week so the daily trips of the vehicles could be made without the annoying, and to flatlanders, frightening negotiations. The buses were taken in both directions to be sure all the problem curves were noted, and once back in Santa Fe, Shirley and Harvey caught the next train to Albuquerque. The buses were to be driven to Albuquerque the same week, loaded on a train for Arizona, and put to a test on the Grand Canyon roads.

Never one to waste a minute, Ford Harvey put his name to a contract that gave him operational headquarters for the Indian Detour busses. He had been dickering for the garage of the Thomas Motor Company, in Santa Fe, but had waited for results of the road test before closing the deal. The purchase price was around $60,000 (the exact amount was never released) and Harvey had already drawn up plans to enlarge the facility so it would take care of not only the buses he had ordered, but a fleet of 7-passenger cars he intended to add. The garage was bought in the name of the Santa Fe Realty and Investment Company; the money was all Harvey.

Meanwhile, the first brochure on the Indian Detours had been prepared and printed on November 14th. For the first time, the word Harveycars appeared, and the price of the three-day tour was announced, $45 per person. A tentative schedule was set forth so readers could read it, drool over it and plan for it. It would be six months to the day from the date of the brochure to the beginning of the trips.

The Indian Detours had been born.

4

THE HOW OF IT

The next six months were a busy period for Major Clarkson. The responsibility for the entire operation was put in his hands, everything from scheduling tours to blocking out hotels. Being a good organizer, the first thing he did was to surround himself with an expert staff, each with an excellent knowledge of his own particular job and how it fitted into the overall picture.

Ellis L. Bauer, a long time resident of Santa Fe, was chosen as Superintendent of Transportation; his assistant, Frank J. Horne, was a native of New Mexico and knew its Indian attractions from a firsthand experience with them. Roger W. Birdseye, the well-known freelance writer, was selected as publicity and advertising department head.

Roger Birdseye had come to Clarkson's attention through his prolific writings, which had been published in many magazines, on the scenic points of interest all over the United States. Clarkson felt anyone who could write with such glowing enthusiasm would write brochures and news releases that would have the tourists begging to join the Detours.

Roger's brother Clarence (who was invariably called 'Bob') was the founder of the frozen food process. While

R.W. BIRDSEYE
PUBLICITY & ADVERTISING

O. J. JACOBS
MGR. LA FONDA

ELLIS S. BAUER
SUPT. TRAVEL &
TRANSPORTATION

MISS ERNA FERGUSSON
COURIER SERVICE

MAJOR R. HUNTER CLARKSON
IN CHARGE HARVEY COMPANY
AND
SANTA FE TRANS. CO. INTERESTS

FRANK J. HORNE, ASST. SUPT.
CHARGE OF OPERATION

Roger concentrated on the power of the pen, Bob dealt in the exotic, trapping rats, frogs, birds, and insects for zoos and University laboratories. In winter, he trapped timber wolves in Michigan, and finally his wandering foot caused him to sign on the hospital ship of Sir Wilfred Grenfell. He left the ship in Labrador, deciding to try his luck at trapping for fur pelts.

Bob was also a United States government employee for a time, doing an Arctic fish and wildlife survey, and using this experience turned to professional fishing. Living in the frozen vastness of Labrador, he experimented with freezing vegetables which came in infrequently on the ships, and also freezing the excess of his fish catch. By trial and error, he discovered the flash freezing of the sub-zero cold preserved the taste and nutritional value of the food, and he started a small company to process foods. But the public wasn't ready for frozen foods, and his 'Birdseye Seafoods, Inc.' in New York went bankrupt.

Moving to Gloucester, Mass., he opened another company, calling it 'General Seafoods'. In 1929, tired of trying to convince an unbelieving public that frozen foods would be a way of the future, he sold out to General Foods, who foresaw the possibilities, for $22,000,000.

Roger had tried to interest Harvey in serving Bob's frozen seafoods but again, resistance to the thought of frozen versus fresh was too much, and it wasn't until General Foods threw millions of dollars into advertising that Harvey put frozen trout in the kitchen. Meanwhile, Roger put his share of the family sale into a trout farm in Santa Fe in partnership with Ellis Bauer, raising fish for the Harvey diningrooms.

(Bob took his share of the profits and went to Peru to set up an experiment in paper pulp, and the high altitude caused him to have a fatal heart attack less than four months after the sale. A younger brother, who also shared, died of a heart attack in New England a year and a half later, and Roger died of a heart attack in 1933.)

To complete the roster of experts, Clarkson chose O. J. Jacobs, whose long experience in hotel management would see him made manager of La Fonda when the necessary improvements were completed in 1926. Jacobs would be in charge of overseeing all accommodations to be used on the Detours. His homework done, Clarkson turned to his specialty, transportation.

Clarkson and Frederick Harvey studied the results of the bus tests, and made some final changes in the specifications which were forwarded to the Yellow Coach Company. Designated Models X and Y, carrying 16 and 26 passengers respectively, the leather upholstered seats were designed to swivel so passengers could see without a lot of head turning. The coaches were made with huge glass windows for good visibility. Although the Santa Fe offered free baggage checking for 'Detourists', as the vacationers were promptly named, the offering was not feasible for passengers not returning to the disembarking station, so long baggage racks on the roof ran the length of the bus.

Keeping the railroad theme, it was decided to call the buses 'road pullmans'. A second contract went to the White Company of Cleveland. They, too, had swivel seats, large windows and carried 13 including the courier and driver. Dual wheels on the rear helped smooth out the rough roads. The buses also featured a heating system for the tourists' comfort. The initial order was for 19 of these buses, granted mainly because the buses in use at the Grand Canyon were Whites and their record of performance had impressed Clarkson.

The blue coloring of the first test buses had been discarded in favor of desert tones. The 'road pullmans' were tan and brown. It was decided an official coloring should have an official name, and although the White factory designated them as Mecca tan and Biskra brown, it was decided by Clarkson to call the brown 'Tesuque' in honor of one of the pueblos they would visit.

An official insignia was also chosen for the vehicles. Done in brilliant colors, it was a stylized version of the Indian Thunderbird symbol. A description of it appeared in the July 1926 National Motorbus and Taxicab Journal:

> ". . . an enigmatic black fowl upon a vivid orange background. This Thunderbird is a creature of early American mythology whose obsidian feathers clash against each other as he flies, making the thunder of the summer showers, so life giving to the crops. He is considered a harbinger of abundant harvests and is the symbol of good luck."

Model 53 White Bus

The New Logo

Very obviously, Clarkson was taking no chances on angering the Indian gods; the insignia was painted on the vehicles before they left the factories.

Besides the buses, a fleet of 7-passenger cars was also ordered. After comparing the models available that year, it was agreed by all that the Packard straight-8 would be the most reliable vehicle for the purpose. Nine cars were ordered and arrived at the Santa Fe Transportation Garage on April 15, 1926, painted Tesuque brown. A special script on the radiator labeled them 'Packard Harveycars', and the official Thunderbird insignia was on the door.

The cars were open touring models with folding rear-seat windshields which would help protect rear seat passengers, heavy leather upholstery and two jump seats. Luggage carriers on the running boards carried essential baggage and dual spare tires were carried in the fender wells.

It was even decided how to avoid problems that might arise from passengers jockeying for a special seat on the buses. Seats would be assigned by the travel, ticket or train agent when tickets were purchased. The only necessity was to find out if the traveler wanted the smoking or non-smoking section of the bus. Anyone who might decide to extend a trip after arriving in New Mexico, would be assigned from the unoccupied seat choices at the time of changing plans.

A stickler for detail, Clarkson worked out a precise record-keeping system for the vehicles. Each bus or car had its own ledger card, and every vehicle had an assigned number. The ledger card showed the date of purchase and would show every service performed and every shortcoming from the time of acquisition until the time of disposition. Each vehicle also had a printed tablet for the driver to use. This 'trip report' was turned in daily, showing the starting mileage, ending mileage, total miles driven, any changing of tires or oil, any gasoline bought on the road. Included were the driver's name and the tour guide's name. A list had to be checked which covered all parts of the vehicle that might need attention at the garage before going out on the road again.

The mechanics of the transportation having been worked out, there now remained the mechanics of tying in the tentative schedule of the brochure that had been released in November of 1925. The main change was to accommodate people arriving on two different trains, at two different times, all headed for the same Detour. For the East bound tourists coming into Albuquerque early in the afternoon, a shortened version of the tour to Isleta Pueblo was a bonus to entertain the tourist and give an appetizer of what was to come. For the late afternoon arrival, a reliable Harvey meal plus a tour of the Indian Building offered a get-together so people who would be sharing the same vehicle the next day would have a chance to get acquainted.

The schedule was designed to keep the Detourist busy. The only place food was served by a hotel other than a Harvey House was Española, where in true Harvey consideration, the food had to meet the System's taste test.

Meanwhile, Publicity Manager Birdseye was busily writing what he felt would be his most tempting brochure. For the cover, an artist sketched a road pullman with blanketed Indians in squaw boots selling wares through the windows and in the corner placed the Santa Fe Railway insignia interlocked with the Harveycar Thunderbird. In the background, a pueblo rose starkly against a formidable mountain, while a train steamed along the base of the hills.

Driver Ray Andrews at the wheel of Packard Harveycar

The introduction stated:

"It is the purpose of the Indian Detour to take you through the very heart of all this, to make you feel the lure of the Southwest that lies beyond the pinched horizons of your train window. In no other way can you hope to see so much of a vast, fascinating region in so short a time — and with the same economy, the same comfort, the same leisurely intimacy and the same freedom from all trivial distraction . . . It is 3 days and 300 miles of sunshine and relaxation and mountain air, in a land of unique human contrasts and natural grandeur."

The brochure emphasized this was all part of the transcontinental train trip and spelled out what the Detourist could expect:

"Hotel accommodations; meals whether in town or at picturesque ranch houses; the handling of baggage."

Passengers on both the westbound California Limited and Navajo trains detrained at Las Vegas, where the Harvey Hotel Castañeda made them welcome. Passengers on the Navajo rejoined their train at Albuquerque the evening of the third day; passengers from the California Limited would stay the third night at the hotel and board their train the following morning.

A Harveycoach leaving on a trip

Eastbound passengers on the same train had the same schedule, but they detrained at Albuquerque and rejoined their trains at Las Vegas. This constant shuttling of buses and cars made efficient drop-offs and pickups.

For the passengers arriving on the Westbound California Limited in the morning hours, presumably rested from their night's sleep on the train, the day started with a

Trip Report

Fleet Car No. *300*   Date *6/18/26*

Driver or Operators Name *E. Farmer*

Couriers Name *Miss McFie*

TRIPS COMPLETED

From	To
Santa Fe	*Albuquerque*
Albuquerque	*Santa Fe*

Speedometer Reading   Stop *5568*
Start *5436*
Mileage *132*

List Purchases of Gas, Oil and Other Supplies out of Santa Fe

✓			✓	

TIRE CHANGES ON ROAD

TIRE NO.	Speedometer Reading	FROM	TO
18	*5498*	*L. F*	*Spare.*
126	*5498*	*spare*	*L. front.*

CAR DEFECTS

Mark OK of defective against each. State nature of defects below.

Motor	✓	Speedometer	✓
Clutch	✓	Horn	✓
Transmission	✓	Oiling System	✓
Differential	✓	Steering Gear	✓
Brakes	✓	Dash Instruments	✓
Elect. Equip.	✓	Wheels	*check alignment*
Lights	✓	Body	✓
Chains	✓ Tools ✓	Road Equip.	✓
Unusual noises not located	✓		

One of the daily
ledger cards

breakfast at the hotel, then it was off to see the sights. By the time the three days of exploration were over, the exhilarated but exhausted tourist climbed wearily back on the train, head full of dates and memories, pockets full of exposed film, a little poorer in wallet, but a lot richer in experience. And just in case the planned sightseeing missed some places the tourist had read about and wanted to see in this endless land of sights and sounds, all strange to the New Yorker, San Franciscan or Chicagoan, the brochure suggested indulging in private trips in one of the luxurious Packards, branching out into Arizona and Colorado.

It was back in Clarkson's court with the decision as to rates for the Detours. Starting with the basic three-day tour, it was finally decided to price the first tour at $45.00 per person, over and above the rail ticket. With the com-

the Indian-detour schedule

West-bound

FIRST DAY

9.00 a.m. Leave LAS VEGAS, Castañeda Hotel (Fred Harvey), by motor.

9.30 a.m. Kearney's Gap. Named for General Kearney, who captured Santa Fé in 1846.

10.00 a.m. Tecolote. Quaint old Spanish-American settlement.

11.15 a.m. San Jose. Has a picturesque old Spanish mission.

11.30 a.m. Arrive Cicuyé (Pecos Ruins). Important Indian pueblo ruin. Inhabited 2,000 years ago. Excavated and partly restored. Remain one hour. Arrive Apache Inn (Valley Ranch), at entrance to Pecos Canyon, for lunch.

1.00 p.m. Leave Apache Inn (Valley Ranch).

2.00 p.m. Leave Apache Inn (Valley Ranch).

3.30 p.m. Arrive SANTA FÉ, La Fonda Hotel.

4.00 p.m. Conducted tour of Indian Museum and Art Gallery.

6.00 p.m. Dinner.

8.00 p.m. Lecture by School of American Research on the history, arts, crafts and quaint ceremonials of the Pueblo Indians. St. Francis Auditorium.

SECOND DAY

9.00 a.m. Leave SANTA FÉ, La Fonda Hotel.

9.15 a.m. Arrive Tesuque Indian Pueblo (inhabited).

9.45 a.m. Arrive Española, on the Rio Grande. Ten minutes at hotel.

11.00 a.m. Arrive Puyé Ruins. Large cliff pueblo, partly excavated and restored. Remain one hour.

12.40 p.m. Arrive Santa Clara Indian Pueblo (inhabited).

1.00 p.m. Arrive Española. Lunch at hotel.

2.20 p.m. Arrive San Juan Indian Pueblo (inhabited).

4.00 p.m. Arrive SANTA FÉ.

5.00 p.m. Conducted tour of Santa Fé.

6.00 p.m. Dinner.

8.00 p.m. Indian play in St. Francis Auditorium.

THIRD DAY

9.00 a.m. Leave SANTA FE, La Fonda Hotel.

10.15 a.m. Arrive Santo Domingo Indian Pueblo. Largest inhabited pueblo. Population 800.

12.45 p.m. Arrive ALBUQUERQUE, Alvarado Hotel (Fred Harvey).

1.00 p.m. Lunch.

3.00 p.m. Leave for Isleta Indian Pueblo and Albuquerque Drive.

5.30 p.m. Arrive ALBUQUERQUE, Alvarado Hotel.

6.30 p.m. Dinner.

7.00 p.m. Tour of Indian Building.

East-bound

Day of arrival in Albuquerque

2.00 p.m.	Arrive Albuquerque.
2.00 p.m.	Lunch, Alvarado Hotel.
2.30 p.m.	Leave for Isleta Pueblo.
3.15 p.m.	Arrive Isleta.
3.30 p.m.	Leave Isleta.
4.15 p.m.	Arrive Albuquerque.
6.00 p.m.	Tour through Old Town. Dinner, Alvarado Hotel.
7.00 p.m.	Tour of Indian Building.

Passengers from Train No. 4
Day of arrival in Albuquerque

5.10 p.m.	Arrive Albuquerque.
6.00 p.m.	Dinner, Alvarado Hotel.
7.00 p.m.	Tour of Indian Building.

FIRST DAY OF INDIAN-DETOUR
Passengers from Train No. 2

9.00 a.m.	Leave Albuquerque.
10.30 a.m.	Arrive Santo Domingo, Indian Pueblo.
11.15 a.m.	Leave Santo Domingo.
12.30 p.m.	Arrive La Fonda, Santa Fé.
1.00 p.m.	Lunch, La Fonda.
2.30 p.m.	Conducted tour of Indian Museum and Art Gallery, points of interest in town.
6.00 p.m.	Dinner, La Fonda.
8.00 p.m.	Lecture, St. Francis Auditorium.

FIRST DAY OF INDIAN-DETOUR
Passengers from Train No. 4

9.00 a.m.	Leave Alvarado Hotel, ALBUQUERQUE (Fred Harvey) by motor.
9.45 a.m.	Arrive Isleta Indian Pueblo (inhabited). Remain half an hour.
10.15 a.m.	Leave Isleta.
11.15 a.m.	Arrive ALBUQUERQUE via Old Town Drive.
11.45 a.m.	Lunch, Alvarado Hotel.
12.45 p.m.	Leave Albuquerque.
2.15 p.m.	Arrive Santo Domingo Indian Pueblo. Largest inhabited pueblo. Population 800.
4.15 p.m.	Arrive SANTA FÉ, La Fonda Hotel.
4.45 p.m.	Conducted tour of Indian Museum and Art Gallery.
6.00 p.m.	Dinner, La Fonda Hotel.
8.00 p.m.	Lecture, St. Francis Auditorium. Second and third days same for passengers from both trains.

SECOND DAY

9.00 a.m.	Leave SANTA FÉ, La Fonda Hotel.
9.15 a.m.	Arrive Tesuque Indian Pueblo (inhabited).
9.45 a.m.	Arrive Española, on the Rio Grande. Ten minutes at hotel.
11.00 a.m.	Arrive Puyé Ruins. Large cliff pueblo, partly excavated and restored. Remain one hour.
12.40 p.m.	Arrive Santa Clara Indian Pueblo (inhabited).
1.00 p.m.	Arrive Española. Lunch at hotel.
2.20 p.m.	Arrive San Juan Indian Pueblo (inhabited).
4.00 p.m.	Arrive SANTA FÉ.
5.00 p.m.	Conducted tour of Santa Fé.
6.00 p.m.	Dinner.
8.00 p.m.	Indian play in St. Francis Auditorium.

THIRD DAY

9.30 a.m.	Leave SANTA FÉ, La Fonda Hotel.
11.00 a.m.	Arrive Cicuyé (Pecos Ruins). Important Indian Pueblo ruin. Inhabited 2,000 years ago. Excavated and partly restored. Remain one hour.
12.30 p.m.	Arrive Apache Inn (Valley Ranch).
1.00 p.m.	Lunch Apache Inn.
2.00 p.m.	Leave Apache Inn.
3.15 p.m.	Arrive San Jose. Has a picturesque old Spanish Mission.
4.00 p.m.	Arrive Tecolote. Quaint old Spanish-American settlement.
4.30 p.m.	Arrive Kearney's Gap. Named for General Kearney, who captured Santa Fé in 1846.
5.00 p.m.	Arrive LAS VEGAS, Castañeda Hotel (Fred Harvey).
6.00 p.m.	Dinner.

Passenger Traffic Manager, Santa Fe System Lines

Chicago, Ill., April 23, 1926

plete brochure still being put together, a pocket-sized brochure of only four pages was printed, the cover featuring an Indian in full feather headdress, sporting a boy scout neckerchief! The Detourist was promised closed automobiles, and extra Pullman service from Chicago to Las Vegas and Albuquerque to Los Angeles, and reverse. Although the 'closed cars' turned out to be touring models due to non-delivery of the closed models, and although the promised 'plenty of time to see all of the historic enchanted empire' could in no way be done in the three days allotted, the folder tickled the sightseeing appetite of a lot of cross-country travelers.

By the time the full brochure — a 62 page folder liberally illustrated with tempting photographs of Indians doing their thing at the pueblos, luxurious hotels and ranches, and automobiles on well-graded highways — came out a month later, most of the final details had been worked out. Birdseye had released stories to most of the major newspapers, and had written a precise article for the Santa Fe Magazine. He wrote glowingly of the ease, delight and interest of the Indian Detours, and went on to point out what had been done to insure the comfort of the Detourists.

The average traveler needed this reassurance. Those who had ventured into the Southwest in past years to see some of its splendors, had been afoot once they left the train. Although the cities of Santa Fe and Albuquerque had a primitive taxi service within the city limits, few of the drivers would agree to visit the Indian pueblos in the vicinity. If a willing driver could be found, the trip could be a most uncertain undertaking since most of the taxis were not of recent vintage and usually inclined to break down once out of town. Until the middle 1920's, the roads leading to the pueblos were bumpy trails used by burro trains bringing firewood down from the hills, by horseback riders or traders dealing with the pueblo occupants. The expansion of the highway system in New Mexico meant the Indian Detours could promise easy riding and deliver.

There remained now only one more step to be taken before cutting the inaugural tape for the tours; a preview had to be arranged. Using the same schedule that had been released to the public, using the official cars and buses,

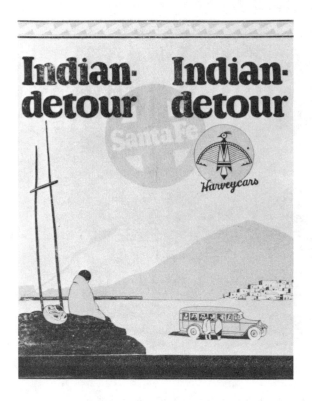

The 62-page
brochure cover

Santa Fe and Harvey representatives followed the timetable to the minute. The cavalcade left Albuquerque Saturday morning, March 27th, 1926, arriving in Las Vegas on time on Monday evening the 29th. With a comfortable 45-day cushion before the official start of the tours, had things not gone well something could have been done about it; but everything did go well, and the only decision of note was to limit the Packards to four passengers, one in front with the driver, and two in the back seat for comfort. The courier would ride in one of the jump seats, turning to answer questions front or back as necessary. The fourth passenger occupied the other jump seat. The only exception would be if any of the passengers had a child; then five would be allowed.

Even the evening schedule had been thoroughly enjoyable to the invited preview audience. An informal talk had been held on the archaeological and ethnographical aspects of the region, and there were complimentary comments after the program. The previewers even had a chance to trade with the stolid Indians sitting motionless for hours on the covered patio floor of the Governor's Palace. They went back to their respective cities, full of en-

Indian Detour Hotels shown in new brochure

El Ortiz Hotel, Lamy, New Mexico, 1925

Top: Alvarado Hotel, Albuquerque, trackside
Bottom: El Navajo Hotel, Gallup, trackside

The Castañeda Hotel, Las Vegas, N.M.

Even today, the Indians sell their wares at The Governors Palace

thusiasm and ready to sell the Detours from a first-hand knowledge of its delights. They could speak with authority about the comforts offered the traveler to the unspoiled regions of the Southwest.

The comfort of the travelers had been assured by the fact the best hotels had been selected, the most comfortable cars and buses had been ordered, the most interesting Indian pueblos had been chosen. Now the comfort of the travelers would be guaranteed by adding one more ingredient and the announcement would be made in the press.

The Indian Detour Couriers were ready for their debut.

5

THE WHO OF IT: THE COURIERS

A native New Mexican had been touting the beauties of her home state long before the Indian Detours began. Erna Fergusson had formed the Koshare Tours in partnership with Ethel Hickey early in 1921, acting as personal guide to the many people who came to Santa Fe with a desire to explore beyond the city limits. Her 7-passenger air-cooled Franklin sedan, whose driver was never without his trusty shovel, was a familiar sight in the pueblos. She had many friends among the Indians, a friendship which allowed her unusual freedom of the pueblos and a chance to get 'close' to the occupants. She was equally at home in the gracious houses of the Hispanic Santa Feans.

She had named her tours after the Koshare Indian dancers, who represent the spirit of the dead. They are supposed to be invisible to the other dancers and having absolute license, are often very funny, clownishly disrespectful and frequently obscene. Miss Fergusson's tours were the ultimate in decorum.

She was extremely well educated, having received a BA degree at the University of New Mexico and an MA in history from Columbia University. Travel in Europe had broadened her interests and given her a fluency in

Erna Fergusson

languages, but her familiarity with her own state came about because she was field director for the Red Cross in New Mexico during the war, bringing her into contact with all its cultures.

Miss Fergusson had used women guides in her Koshare Tours, a departure from the usual male guides employed by resorts in the West. Instead of rough sweaty cowboys, more often taciturn than talkative, the Koshare guides were expected to talk, long and knowledgeably, about the area.

Erna Fergusson's talents were best exhibited in the number of repeat customers she had, and the success of her tours was no secret to the Clarkson/Harvey/Birdseye triumvirate. She was immediately contacted and an offer made to buy not only her tour business, but her talents. She was made head of the girl guides, who, after a short discussion, were named 'couriers'.

Determined that the couriers would be in every way as well prepared for their job as the Harvey Girls were for theirs, Clarkson gave Miss Fergusson free rein in the hiring and training. Uniformed guides were usual sights in Europe and Clarkson suggested the women be costumed appropriately so they would be easily recognizable. Other than that, no directives were considered necessary for such a capable executive as Erna Fergusson.

When asked by the press to describe the type of person Miss Fergusson was seeking, she said:

"Couriers are expected to be young women of education and some social grace, able to meet easily and well all kinds of people. They are expected to be intelligent enough to learn many facts about this country and to impart them in a way to interest intelligent travelers. They are selected also with an eye to their knowledge of this country, their knowledge of Spanish, and any special knowledge or ability that will assist them in presenting this country properly."

Very obviously, the press got the message: The Indian Detours had been designed to 'sell' the Southwest.

The choosing of the girls was done in a systematic process of elimination. First, the top candidates were college graduates. They had to understand the Southwest, which was the same thing as saying they probably should be natives of the area. They had to be at least 25 years old to be a regular courier although a younger girl could work as a substitute if she was 23 or 24. Other qualifications would receive less important consideration.

A starting number of twenty was suggested because some, very naturally, would fall by the wayside, like Harvey Girls, when romance moved them away from the tour region; however, there was no rule that they must remain unmarried in order to continue working. Of the twenty, it was estimated eighteen would stay with the Tours. Ten of the eighteen would be assigned to regular Tours, eight would substitute as needed.

Some of the first applicants were daughters of prominent New Mexicans — judges, senators, ambassadors. Amelia McFie was the daughter of a Federal Judge in Santa Fe. Claire Bursum was a New Mexico Senator's daughter. Maria Baca's mother was Secretary of State; her sister married Oliver La Farge. Margaret Hubbell was the niece of Lorenzo Hubbell whose outstanding Arizona trading post has recently been designated a National Historic Site.

All of them had to have one common quality; they had to be willing to learn and the learning was equivalent to a crash course in history, politics, sociology, anthropology, geology and arts. Test questions might include, "How do Indian women bake bread in outdoor ovens?", "When did

Winifred Shuler

Mary Tucker

Dorothy Raper in the first Courier uniform

the cliff dwellers inhabit Puyé?", "When was Santa Fe founded?", "How many crops of alfalfa can be raised in a season?", "How much is an acre of land in New Mexico?", "What language do the Indians speak?".

The Indians spoke not only their own tribal dialect, but also in many cases Spanish, and the couriers were expected to learn enough Spanish to be able to carry on at least a basic conversation at the pueblos. For linguists like Maria Baca and Erna Fergusson, this was no problem, and for couriers like Dorothy Raper, they got by on such basics as — "Donde esta la llave de la iglesia?".

The couriers had to be able to rattle off statistics such as the heights of the mountains, the number of Indians in a pueblo, the names of the Taos painters and explain why the desert wasn't one big sand dune.

Plans for the concentrated training course were completed in March of 1926 and on April 15th, school began for the first twenty girls. Others would be trained as they were chosen, but the core of the women who would give tender loving attention to the Detourists was a reality.

To educate the couriers in the shortest time possible, a veritable battery of instructors was hustled into New Mexico. The final teaching staff included Dr. Edgar L. Hewett, director of the School of American Research; Dr. A. V. Kidder, department of archaeology at Andover Academy; Dr. S. G. Morley, associate of the Carnegie Institute; F. W. Hodge, staff member of the American Museum of the American Indian in New York; Charles F. Lummis, author of Indian articles, and Paul F. Walter, president of the New Mexican Historical Society.

The couriers brought varied professional backgrounds into the group. Two, Marcella Matson and Hazel Miller, had been with the Koshare Tours and would serve as helpers in training the newcomers the way Miss Fergusson expected things to be done. Some had been newspaper women; one was a writer and another a member of an interior decorating firm. There were teachers; one had taught at the U. S. Indian School at the Tesuque Pueblo, and another at the New Mexico School for the Deaf. The widow of a prominent Wichita, Kansas, man joined the group because she had always been interested in the archaeological aspect of the Southwest and had done some studying on the origins

The first group of Couriers

of the tribes. One girl, Anita Rose, had studied at the Chicago Art Institute for two years.

Since at this time the treatment for tuberculosis was to send patients to desert areas, many sufferers were sent to New Mexico. One courier, Anna Kardell, had ridden the train from Chicago to see a close friend taking the cure and liked the country enough to sign up for training.

Dorothy Raper, another transplant, had teamed up with Emily Hahn, now a well-known writer, and bought a Model T Ford sedan in 1924. Dorothy's uncle was recuperating from tuberculosis in Santa Fe, and was lonely for kinfolk. The two girls had the backs of the front seats cut so they would recline, stacked their luggage behind the seats to make a level foundation, and crossed the country camping out along the way. They returned to finish their education at the University of Wisconsin, then both returned to work as couriers. With a degree in geology, Dorothy was usually assigned to the Carlsbad Caverns tours.

One courier who would join in 1927, Hester Jones, was herself a tuberculosis patient. One of the new breed of post World War I working ladies, she had parlayed a Vassar education into a job as a commercial researcher, but, as she puts it — "running for street cars and trains through the cold slush of New York" had affected her lungs. Cured by the New Mexico climate, she stayed with the Indian Detours for six years.

Dorothy Pond, of the cosmetic company family, was one of the local girls chosen. Her father was the Santa Fe fire chief, and she was the life of weekend parties when her invited guests were allowed to slide down the brass pole in his bedroom.

The one major qualification for every courier was their inter-relationship with people. Not only were they a walking information desk, they had to arrange reservations, pay hotel bills, settle meal chits, gather up the usual items travelers always leave behind as they go — umbrellas, gloves, purses, glasses — and they had to be listeners as well as teachers. They had to have tact that would be required when one tourist rattled on about the beauties of his or her hometown, annoying other tourists who wanted to hear about the cave dwellers. They had to reassure frightened Detourists that the bus would not back off the cliffside, the woods were not full of wild Indians, the brakes would not fail coming down La Bajada Hill, and it was safe to climb up the fragile looking ladders of Puyé.

It has been claimed by some of the couriers that the airlines got the idea of stewardesses from the couriers, and indeed they may well have, for the early airline hostesses were cut from the same cloth as these charming, informed and trained couriers. Even the fact Western Airlines put the first airline stewardesses in uniform might have come from the couriers, for Clarkson's suggestion was carried out.

The uniforms were selected with thought to the duties of the girls (they had to be hard wearing), the attractiveness (they had to be colorful), the theme of the tours (they must show Indian influence) and they had to be comfortable. Erna Fergusson had paid little attention to costume in her Koshare Tour stint. She usually wore a Smokey the Bear hat, a khaki man's shirt, a pair of ballooning riding britches and high laced boots. With all her other attributes, she lacked a sense of style. The first clothes she chose for the couriers consisted of a pair of britches over which a utilitarian skirt buttoned to 'formalize' the outfit. The shirt was a man's ordinary cotton shirt, in varied colors, to be worn with the tail hanging over the pants or skirt. A braided belt could be added if desired, and high laced boots completed the costume.

Certainly Major Clarkson had better taste, but he was

apparently too busy with other details to comment on the courier costume, and so the first few tours went out on schedule with the girls dressed in this somewhat hippie combination. One of the couriers, Rainey Bartley, whose mother owned a tasteful dress shop in Santa Fe, took one look at her daughter as she came to visit one day wearing her uniform, turned pale and delivered an ultimatum; "If you must wear that type of clothing, don't come into my shop. You'll ruin my business."

Shortly afterward, one of the couriers, Winifred Shuler, whose taste in clothes was the envy of her friends, had a heart-to-heart with Erna about the uniforms. Up to her hat-brim in training schedules, she turned the redesigning of the clothes over to Winifred, and a new look was promised. Orders were placed with an Albuquerque tailor to make a skirt with a walking pleat and velveteen shirts in jewel colors patterned after the Navajo blouses. The hat was changed from a stiff-brimmed model to a soft-brimmed cloche. Tan stockings were to be worn with comfortable walking shoes, although for more strenuous hiking, boots were suggested.

Many of the couriers substituted the britches they owned when climbing the ladders of Puyé. Soon after the tours started, Clarkson's wife Louise went on one of the tours to Puyé, gave a gasp of dismay as she looked at the couriers stepping out of the cars and ordered them to put on skirts and behave like ladies. For a brief period, they did, but the vivid description of couriers climbing steep ladders ahead of male tourists was brought to her attention, and the girls went back into britches, although they were instructed to put their skirts on over them, before climbing back in the car.

Each courier was assigned a silver Thunderbird emblem that was 'to be worn fastened to the exact center of the felt hat.' Courier Ruth Champion took one look at herself in the mirror and promptly fastened it on the side, and no amount of regularly issued orders resulted in her moving it. "With it in the center, I looked just like a boy scout going off to win a merit badge." Henrietta Gloff always wore hers pinned to the low point of her blouse neckline since she refused to wear the hat at all.

The company paid part of the uniform cost, the tailor

The Harveycar
Emblem

giving a wholesale discount to the couriers. A leather top-coat was used in the cooler weather, but it was optional, not required. A second blouse was usually corduroy which could be easily washed and would brush up like new.

The couriers frequently added a silken handkerchief, more for use than decoration, since dusty roads were an everyday affair and the handkerchief could be tied around the nose and mouth. Each courier was requested to wear a silver concho belt and either a squash blossom necklace or other Indian jewelry. These examples of the Indian silversmithing art not only intrigued the Eastern tourists and gave the couriers a conversational spring board, but tempted the Detourists to buy from the Indians when touring through their pueblos.

One Detourist wrote a report for the New York Times Magazine, saying "our guide tells the tale, a pretty young college girl in high boots and a 10-gallon hat, with enough Indian jewelry to open a curio shop". He might have been slightly wrong in the capacity of the hat, but he was right about the rest of the costume.

A courier was assigned to each Packard, and very quickly the couriers acquired a following. Quick to realize this could mean 'holdovers' on tours, Clarkson instructed Miss Fergusson to keep her assignment list flexible. Thus, if a certain courier aroused interest in any trip to the extent of signing up enough passengers to fill a car, that courier was scheduled to make the side trip with the passengers while another courier filled in for her on her usual Coach assignment.

There are many letters in the files that attest to the popularity of these couriers. A doctor from New Jersey wrote, "Your courier, Miss Claire Bursum, was a marvel. She was the wonder of everybody on board. Her attention to detail and her kindness in telling everything that we wanted to know and lots of things that we didn't think of and her kind way of telling and attention to detail was something wonderful."

A woman from New York wrote, "Miss Hubbell's interest in her work did much to enhance our pleasure." And a letter without a return address said, "Miss Rita Brady, Miss Mary Heller and Miss Margaret Wennips made us feel at home at once. Their quiet, interesting way of imparting information and in describing points of interest certainly added much to the pleasure of the trip." Other letters were more general, not naming names, but saying simply, "The couriers were exceptionally intelligent and courteous and did everything possible to please the tourists." A few letters were content with saying, "Please say thanks to Mrs. Parsons and Mrs. Cooper", or "Your couriers are both intelligent and courteous."

In the beginning, the couriers did not end their day when the tour cars were stabled for the night. The word 'overtime' wasn't mentioned, but the girls were expected to be on duty until the last Detourist had retired. In a way, her life was a lot easier than male cowboy guides because she could leave the cooking and serving of meals to the Harvey hotels; but she was instructed to change from her sturdy and certainly dusty clothing of the day's trip to something more feminine — a dress, or a skirt and silk blouse and more attractive shoes replaced her walking shoes or boots. She was expected to be a charming dinner companion, still answering questions both about the day just past and the days to come, and when the weary travelers made their way to their deluxe rooms, the courier retired to brush up her clothes and set the alarm in plenty of time to appear fresh and eager the next morning. Before long, this rule was relaxed and the girls were allowed to say goodnight on returning to the hotel.

In 1927 classes began at 8:30 in the morning and went on until 5:40 in the afternoon, with a lunch break, and were held in the New Museum in Santa Fe. After three days of

The second corps of Couriers

this schedule, two evening classes were held, and this was followed by four days spent along the trail riding with a working courier, and with special instructors. On-the-spot classes at Puyé were conducted by Dorothy Raper who was an expert in geology. Hugh Cassidy of the U. S. Forestry Service took over when the training tour stopped at Valley Ranch, talking on the trees, brush and flowers of the region. By that time, the Taos tour was on the agenda and an on-the-spot course in New Mexico artists took the couriers to many artists' homes.

Coming months would show the couriers would need to be augmented, both because of the increasing numbers of tours, and the natural attrition in such a group. A tentative schedule of training new recruits every six months was decided upon, and by the time the third training session was offered in January of 1928, there were 16 qualified new applicants willing to take on the rigorous learning sessions.

By 1929 new couriers were trained in part by ones who had taken the first intensive courses and by printed bulletins written by courier Elizabeth DeHuff, issued at regular intervals and frequently updated.

Although the tickets for the Indian Detours were sold on trains, by travel agents and by station agents, there were always people who decided to take the tour after arriving in New Mexico. For this reason, and to answer questions that those on the Tours might ask, a courier office was established in both the Alvarado and La Fonda hotels. At La Fonda, a little-used checkroom was turned into an office at first, then when the hotel was enlarged in 1929, a special lounge was remodeled for their use. A large wooden sign, hand-carved by one of the drivers, hung in the entrance hall of the lobby, directing tourists to the office.

Sometimes the tourists would come seeking information about the following day's tour, what they would see, where they would eat, what could they buy. Ann Cooper found herself explaining why the smoke around the Mexican village they had visited that day had an unusual odor,

Carved wooden sign at La Fonda

Couriers on a publicity photographing trip

telling the tourists it was Palo Verde, which being green had a rather pungent odor. The next day, showing off her newfound knowledge to her seat companion, the woman asked her if she had smelled the pee-on smoke yet.

The office help required the same basic training as the couriers and often the couriers would fill in on the desk. Anna Kardell had applied for the office job before being selected for courier, but part of the job was balancing the daily books and "I couldn't ever balance books. In fact, my personal budget book always had a column labelled SPG in it. That was for money spent that I couldn't account for, and it stood for Something — Probably Gum."

The couriers were paid a monthly salary of $150 to start. If they were really fluent in a language, such as Maria Baca in Spanish, or Margaret Wennips in German, they were given an extra $10 a month. All expenses away from home base were paid — meals, accommodations, entrance fees — and the girls were able to save enough to buy fine Indian jewelry and fatten a bank account. They were not allowed to take tips, but many of them received valuable presents when the Detourists returned home. The hours were long, the work could be physically hard when they were called upon to man the pry poles used to free cars from sand and mud, but there was a charisma in being able to say they were a Harveycar courier.

For the couriers who had come from other places and did not live in the vicinity, various living arrangements were made. Some rented rooms near the Alvarado or La Fonda. Some stayed with friends, some even bought small homes. Dorothy Raper and Emily Hahn shared a house they had rented, but because it was some distance from La Fonda, they bought roller skates to hasten their morning roll call arrival. Shortly after finishing her training, Dorothy came racing around the corner of La Fonda, knocking Clarkson to his knees. The Major drew himself up stiffly but never said a word. That afternoon, a bulletin was given to the couriers stating there would be no roller skating to work. It didn't stop Dorothy and Emily from using their own method of transportation, but from then on both girls unhitched their skates while still a block away from La Fonda.

It had been planned in the early projections of the Detours to have couriers ride the Santa Fe trains to hand out brochures, answer questions and lure the travelers into signing up for one of the Indian Detours. It was not a voluntary assignment, and many of the girls placed on the trains hated it; some liked it. Some of them still remember they walked through the train several times to get up enough courage to accost strangers. The couriers would get on the train at Lamy or Albuquerque, riding to Gallup or Winslow, pick up the tickets from the conductor, and go through the trains knocking on doors or checking into the club car to see if they would whip up interest. Many of them had doors slammed in their faces.

The couriers who rode the trains were paid $195 a month, but received no commission on the tickets they sold. One of their complaints was they would sell say 20 tickets, tell the buyers to all meet in the club car in 30 minutes, and then go back to the club car to wait for the train to arrive at the station. Inevitably a couple of buyers would be missing and the girls had to run through the train, pulling open the heavy doors, trying to locate the missing Detourists.

Group of Couriers at Santa Fe reporting for assignment

An advertising bro-chure featuring a draw-ing of Winifred Shuler

On the Lamy train, they hawked the Isleta tour. On arrival at Albuquerque, the Detourists would be hustled into a bus, driven as fast as roads would allow to Isleta, be pulled through the Pueblo, shoved back into the bus and hustled back to the train. Meanwhile, the train passengers would be enjoying a leisurely lunch at the Alvarado Hotel. If the bus was delayed, irate train travelers would be waiting to complain to the couriers.

On the Petrified Forest Tour, the Westbound passengers would be taken from the train at Adamana, Arizona, taken by bus to the Forest, then on to rejoin the train which had deliberately dawdled along the tracks until reaching Holbrook. Not only were the train travelers irate at the delay, many of the Detourists would abuse the couriers because they had expected to see a lovely standing forest of trees and instead had seen nothing but a bunch of rocky kindling.

   Margaret Wennips, who usually held her temper under all trying circumstances as couriers were trained to do, lost her cool only once in public. A light snowfall had made the Painted Desert a photographer's dream. Using her scarf, she swept the snow from one of the logs, showing how the moisture gave a gemlike finish to the petrified wood. One of her dudes vocally expressed his disappointment in the 'Forest', whereupon Margaret tartly announced, "anyone of average intelligence would appreciate this", and marched off to the Harveycoach.

Couriers at the Petrified Forest

   There was a second reason to put the girls on the trains. They were to hand out folders about the regular Indian Detours in an effort to get the travelers to come back and take the trips. It was not unusual for their train appearance to so impress the travelers that they would agree to take it 'if that young lady can go along with us.' And such a request was always honored, for the Harvey customer was always right.

The train trips have stayed in the memory of the couriers more vividly than any other part of the Detours, especially when the trains were hauling summer tourists. Then the couriers would make dashes to the ice-water coolers at the end of each train and run the refreshing water over their wrists. For their train costume was the same as their touring costume — despite the thermometer, velveteen blouse, khaki skirt, jewelry, hat, cotton hose were a must.

By 1928, Erna Fergusson had chosen as her assistant a Mrs. Victor Miller and had placed Winifred Shuler in charge of the couriers. One of these capable women, it is not certain which one, advanced the suggestion one of the couriers be sent into places other than the trains to tout the wonders of the Indian Detours. Miss Fergusson was enthusiastic. Their unanimous choice for ambassador was

Group of Couriers outside La Fonda office. Left to right: Marcella Matson, Kay Angle, Margaret Wennips, Hazel Connor, Henrietta Gloff, Zoe McGonagle.

Anita Rose, daughter of U. S. District Clerk and Mrs. William Rose of Santa Fe. She had been one of the first couriers to be selected for training and had a large following of 'repeats'. So right after the Christmas holidays, Anita Rose packed up her courier uniform and took off on a goodwill mission that included three weeks in Chicago, a week in Cleveland, a month in Boston, and over a month in New York. On one of her many trips to the East, she met her future husband, the brother of Fred Waring.

Interviewed by the newspaper and on radio, Anita Rose was a visiting celebrity everywhere. The Cleveland Plain Dealer, in its article, called this "pioneer hostess among cliff dwellings" an example of the new college woman.

Personal appearances included handing out folders and information in department stores, lecturing to luncheon groups and being a dinner guest at prominent peoples' homes. Papers cooperated in tickling the reading public's interest with such items as this one from the Cleveland Plain Dealer:

"Miss Rose will be at the Foster Service Bureau at the Higbee Co. today, dressed in the brilliant Navajo skirt and silver jewelry which forms the courier costume."

The photograph showed Miss Rose in her regulation whipcord skirt, but newspapers are not known for their attention to minute reporting details. They did better on listing her duties, which must have impressed every reader:

"The duties of an Indian Detour courier are various. She must know every interesting spot in her territory; every pueblo, whether ancient or prehistoric; every Mexican village; every natural wonder; every trail, with its historical significance, its traditions or its archaeological facts. She must answer more questions than an information bureau in a union station. She must know all the places to eat and drink and rest which make so much for the perfect tour. She must be able to handle any situation or to cope with any emergency which may arise, and at the same time be always the perfect hostess. Above all, she must love this vast, strange country she is interpreting to visitors. She must have in her makeup the fundamental lights, shadows and intensity of the Southwest."

Anita Rose in Cleveland

It's no wonder the people who signed up for the tours out of Chicago believed every courier was a paragon of guides. And thanks to Erna Fergusson and her assistant directors, no one would ever doubt it.

But the couriers needed another paragon of virtue on the Indian Detours.

6

THE WHO OF IT: THE DRIVERS

Not only were the couriers hand picked, so were the drivers. Clarkson's exposure to good railroading management had left him with a blueprint for administrative practice he could apply to such distant ideas as chauffeur training.

Before the driver applicant was accepted, he had to pass a rigorous health examination, and answer a long and probing questionnaire. Not only was it a classroom situation, the man was also tested on the road, where his reactions were noted and his ability minutely criticized. At least the first set of drivers were subjected to this routine; many of the later drivers remember the health examination consisted of whether the man looked and acted healthy, and the road testing was whether he could double clutch.

Once he passed and was accepted, he was impressed with the fact he was a member of a very elite group. His uniform had been designed to make the Detourist realize this was a bit of the Wild West, for a large Stetson hat was worn high crowned Tim McCoy style. The silver Thunderbird Harveycar emblem was fastened front and center on the hatband. From the head up, the driver looked like a cowboy; from the neck down, he looked like a Scout

Master. Leather puttees ended in widely flaring khaki jodhpurs. Blousy gay plaid shirts were made even more colorful by a huge silk neckerchief, knotted sailor style, the ends reaching to his beltline. His belt buckle was more than likely to be a heavy silver one, set with turquoise.

At a time when most right hip pockets were slightly larger than left ones due to being stretched by a form-fitting flask, the drivers were forbidden to touch liquor, even on their own time, although after hour activity was sometimes hard to prove. A man reporting for work with the slightest hint of Sen-Sen on his breath was immediately discharged.

The men were forbidden to date the couriers for the first four years, then one of the drivers, Kaye Montgomery, went to Clarkson and had a long talk, pointing out there was a lack of singles of both sexes in many of the overnight stops, and suggested the rules be relaxed. They were, and many of the couriers married drivers, gaining a good looking and personable husband in exchange for being a capable and educated wife.

While linguistic accomplishments were not part of the package of driver requirements, many of the men had at least a working knowledge of Spanish, and a few could say a few sentences in one or more of the Indian dialects. Only one of the drivers, Tom Dozier, was an Indian, a Tewa and he spoke both Tewa and Hopi fluently.

Unless large groups required calling everyone in to work, the men who drove the buses did not drive the cars, and the car drivers never substituted for bus drivers. The handling of the larger vehicles required some special training, and some special rules.

Drivers were not allowed to smoke while driving. Cigarette lighters were still to be made part of every luxury car dashboard and it was felt many private accidents happened because the driver took one or both hands off the wheel to light a cigar, cigarette or pipe, (although no statistics ever backed up this claim). If drivers wished to smoke while the dudes were sightseeing, they were required to 'hide' out of sight of the dudes and couriers.

The bus drivers were required to stop at all railroad crossings, a bit of common sense that was not required by law for public buses for several more years. The car and

The first drivers at parade rest

bus drivers were not allowed to converse with the passengers, as it was felt any questions could be answered by the couriers, including "what's that funny noise?" A talkative driver was considered an inattentive driver. And there were no exceptions on signalling; every turn, every stop had to be indicated to following drivers.

Since most roads were not paved, a Harvey driver was required to keep enough distance between his vehicle and the one ahead to be able to see clearly. If necessary, he must either slow down or totally stop until the dust settled.

In an area of no signs (the Highway Department did put up signs, but being of wood, they were usually torn down and used by the Indians for firewood) it was customary for the drivers to follow those puffs of unsettled dust, even at a distance, when the lead car was driven by someone familiar with the route. One of the drivers always tried to be first at the Hopi villages for festivals; he was fascinated by standing on the mesa and watching the little puffs of dust coming from all compass points as the Harveycars grouped for the celebrations.

Sometimes following the puffs of dust could be less than a success. Charles Seery was deadheading on a trip to Winslow one night, following Forrest Good, who knew the country well. They both stopped for gas in the Arizona boonies near Holbrook. Good filled up and drove off, his taillight flickering in the dust; Seery paid the bill and dug out trying to catch up. For hours he followed the now-you-see-it-now-you-don't light until the car pulled into a ranch along the road and stopped. Realizing he had been following the wrong car, Seery stayed on the road to the next small town. Knowing they were to stay at La Posada in Winslow, he turned his lights onto the town sign to read 'Snowflake'. Knocking on the door of a house that still showed lights along the road, he asked where the nearest Harvey House was. The man scratched his head and drawled, "Well, the nearest one is about 60 miles, kinda back in the direction you come, and then turn West."

Getting lost was part of the game for the drivers. They were sent on trips with other drivers who knew the area when possible, but one road looked a lot like another in the desert. The one thing they dreaded was running out of gas, first because it was hard to find, and second because they were fined $5 by the company for running out, plus having to pay for the gas themselves. The cars had been ordered from the factory with extra large gas tanks on them but the drivers who drove the Reservation tours usually had a spare can of gas as insurance, for the Indians would sell only five gallons of gas at a time no matter how much money was offered.

A few of the drivers used a compass when driving, but as any accomplished boy scout will tell you, it's necessary to know how to use one or you might as well leave it at home. And asking directions of people along the way wasn't reliable, as many of them had never driven further than out to the south forty. In Navajo country, it was especially unreliable, for the Indians would obligingly answer "yes" to any question of direction. Not believing this, Charles Seery asked a man the way to Kayenta — was it that way (pointing) and was told yes. In turn he pointed in each of the four directions and asked again, and each time was told "yes".

Drivers were required to carry an inner tube, fan belt, spark plugs, a distributor, plus a tarp for tire traction and a shovel, and were supposed to know how to make minor repairs using the spare parts. If a car broke down on tour and couldn't be fixed, he had to hike to the nearest phone, which could be a good three hours away, and send for the company wrecker. Most of the problems could be summed

A winter trip

up in a word — flats. Tires were 'iffy' and roads were primitive; the combination usually meant a tour without a tire change was an exception.

On tours into the Indian country, flats occurred so frequently the drivers spoke of having them in pairs. In this case it wasn't the roads that caused all the tire trouble, but the nails that shook loose from the Indian wagons.

Most of the drivers became real experts at unloading the passengers, sending them off with the courier to study the wildflowers so they could speak freely as they changed tires. Only one driver lacked the proper attitude — instead of changing the flats, he called the nearest garage and said "I have a tire that is going psssss. What should I do?" What he did was have the shortest employment record with the Detours.

The drivers were given a list of road regulations covering such things as the proper speed on curves, how to negotiate a sandy stretch, what to do when crossing a riverbed — with or without water in it, how to pass horse-drawn vehicles, how to pass other automobiles, how to cope with dirt roads. He signed his name to the ledger card that was his daily log. If he changed a tire, the number of the removed tire and the number of the replacement had to be logged in the proper space, and if the tire was complete-

The gas station at Medicine Hat, Utah. Here the Harveycars filled up for Arizona tours

ly ruined, it had to be returned to the garage that night. If the rough roads caused strange noises to appear, the noise had to be described in detail, so the garage mechanics could track it down before the car went out again.

Because of the possibility of trouble, the cars were equipped with lap robes for every two passengers, a first-aid kit, water and coffee thermos bottles and some snacks as a survival kit. This came in handy when flooded arroyos called a halt to the tour. With very few bridges, most of the rivers had to be forded. In the desert regions, this was a minor concern except during the rainy season. Then it was not unusual for cars to get caught between arroyos, unable to return home or proceed ahead until the thirsty desert had absorbed the water. Fortunately, the drivers were experienced enough to realize a fact of the desert that the Detourists didn't; that is, a storm in the mountains miles away could mean a rushing wall of water that would flood the washes moments later. Only once did a car get caught in the water due to the driver misjudging the roadpath and going into a hole. Unable to dig the car out and knowing the rain would present problems, he abandoned the car, helping the passengers to the banks of the dry river. Just as the last detourist climbed up the bank, the water swept the car over on its side.

Another flooded arroyo had more hilarious results. Driving one of the closed Cadillacs the company added in

1930, Seery was taking three passengers to Carlsbad on a private Harvey Land Cruise. Leaving Roswell he ran into a bad storm that left many angry rivers where dry beds had been. They made it through two arroyos, but the third was running four feet deep, so there was nothing to do but wait until it went down. While waiting, Seery got out to stretch his legs and noticed something bobbing against the water-depth post. Cutting a stick from a roadside bush, he fished out a jackrabbit, half frozen from the cold water and about drowned. Wrapping it up in a dustcloth, he laid it at the feet of the women in the backseat where the heater warmth would dry it out.

Waiting for a flooded arroyo to go down

"The water went down and we started off again. The heater was working fine, and suddenly that jack came to life. He hit the window, bounced off into one lady's lap, hit the other window and that knocked him over into the front seat against the windshield. I was trying to get the car stopped, the jack was hitting every window in turn, the women were screaming. I finally got the car steered to the side of the road and got the door opened. You never saw a jack run so fast."

It was accepted procedure for the drivers to carry dudes bodily across the washes after they had gunned the empty car across the drying-up streams. Usually their couriers went with them, drying off the car while the driver went back for the passengers. Once Russell Nelson had an overly-endowed matron in the car when he approached a recently flooded arroyo. Taking one look at his courier, who weighed slightly over 100 pounds, and the dude who weighed well over 200, he left his courier on the bank, gunned the car across the wash and returned to carry the courier across.

Coming out of the Canyon de Chelly on one trip, Norbert (Chick) Berchtold stopped at the edge of water flowing down a wash, when suddenly the water changed course and by the time it had subsided, the car was hung up on two banks with enough room underneath for Berchtold to stand upright. Out came the shovels and courier and while dudes enjoyed a snack from the picnic kit, they rebuilt the road. The group arrived at Kayenta at 4 the next morning.

There was only one fatal accident in all the years of the Indian Detours. Norbert Staab was making extra money by driving a day trip, arriving back at the garage at 5:00 P.M. Then he would work as a night dispatcher until 1:15 A.M. when the last truck came in from Lamy. The men worked under a 'rest registry' required by the Corporation Commission that kept track of the total hours put in along with records of the vehicle, destinations, and other facts.

One night in the middle 1930's, Staab checked the board to find he had been assigned a trip from Santa Fe to the Puyé ruins, to Taos, and back to Santa Fe, a long day's outing. Driver Hank Paxton was to take the shorter Santa Fe to Taos and return trip. Trouble on the road had made a late arrival at the garage for Staab and this plus his work as dispatcher meant he would be working longer than the Commission rules allowed. So he was told to change trips with Paxton.

Harvey drivers had a 'break' rule to follow —

Tom Dozier

Norbert Staab

something drivers of private cars took another 40 years to believe in; they were required to take regular rest periods when driving, to get out, walk around and relax before continuing on the way. Staab stopped at Sagebrush Inn to get coffee and stretch his legs and the owner asked if he passed Paxton on the return trip to tell him she would hold lunch for him and his passengers, the Cushmans. It was then 4:00 P.M. Staab felt Paxton had had car trouble and decided to go down Pilar Hill, a slightly longer trip back to Santa Fe, to see if the car had broken down. At the bottom of Pilar Hill the car was found overturned, Paxton dead, the courier and passengers badly injured. The highway department had dumped 10" of gravel on the road the day before and it was believed the car went out of control in the heavy gravel.

For a while, after the word was flashed to Santa Fe that a driver had been killed, it was thought Staab was the fatality as his name was still on the board as driver of the Puyé tour.

Considering the miles driven, the safety record was outstanding. To encourage the drivers to live up to their safety rules, the Santa Fe Transportation Company awarded a bronze safety badge for driving 50,000 miles without an accident; 100,000 safe miles got them a silver badge, and although no one had driven enough miles for the 150,000 mile gold badge by the time the garage and its records burned in early 1929, one driver was within pinning distance of it. Kaye Montgomery and Charles Seery won silver badges before the practice of giving them stopped and two men, Tom Madden and Forrest Good each drove 1,000,000 accident-free miles before retiring.

Like the couriers, the drivers came from a variety of backgrounds; unlike the couriers, they were all natives of the region. At the start, Clarkson brought over two of the best drivers at the Grand Canyon, O. H. Goode and Jim English, to teach the new drivers the fine points of double clutching and tourist handling. With them, they brought the term 'dudes' and the drivers never referred to the Detourists in any other way. Most of the tourists didn't mind; dude ranches were synonomous with a wealthy way of vacation life.

The word was put out late in 1925 that a select number of drivers would be employed at good wages and for a prestigious job. The majority of the men chosen came from within 100 miles. Some got their jobs through friends, and since New Mexico was and still is a politically oriented state, many got them by knowing the right official. A few came in through the back door like Seery, who was on the basketball team at the Agricultural College. The drivers had formed an athletic group and could use a few good ball players. Montgomery was a law student, working part time as a driver; Staab had a wintertime job and drove only in the summer at first.

The wages were good, $125 a month, and since all expenses were paid when on the road, many of the drivers were able to bank most of their salary. Tips were generous and there was no rule against drivers accepting them. Hours were long, many of the drivers remembering that they worked with only one day off a month, but like the couriers, they felt the fact to be chosen for the job was an honor. Once they were free to date and marry the couriers, they had a permanency to their life, and much like the truck driving teams of today, their home life was stable since they took their wives with them.

While couriers stayed at the hotels with the dudes, the drivers were usually assigned rooms in less expensive hotels or rooming houses, many of them without the niceties of the Harvey Houses. It was not unusual for drivers to have to go to the rivers to bathe and when the Arizona tours became popular, it was customary to pull rank and volunteer for the Canyon de Chelly trips because there were bathing houses with warm showers provided for both men and women. Once Bruce Cooper, who spent his hours away from the wheel in designing and making much of the beautiful carved furniture for La Fonda, and his courier wife Ann were deadheading from the Navajo trip when they saw a stock watering tank in the middle of nowhere. With no one around and the temperature well over one hundred degrees, Bruce jumped in. Just as his wife shed her clothes to climb in, a Navajo and his squaw rode up, took one look, grunted and rode off, the brave shaking his head, the squaw giggling.

There were times when the drivers preferred dust. When the rains came, the roads were churned into quagmires. If the arroyos flooded, it was usually necessary for the driver to rebuild the banks after the water receded before the car could make it down, across and up. John Dunn, who drove only buses between Santa Fe and Taos, came into the Don Fernando Hotel in Taos one night two hours after he was due and made straight for the bar. As he downed a neat whiskey contrary to company rules, he told the bartender he had been driving the same trip for four years and had finally found a new road. The bartender asked him in surprise where, and John replied, "two feet under the regular one."

One of the ingredients that made a good driver was a sense of humor, often needed when coping with cars, roads and dudes. Dunn was known for his wit. Once he was called upon in an emergency to drive two ladies from the East on the Santa Fe to Taos run. At that time, the road was so narrow one car would have to pull into the mountainside and stop to let another car go by. It was 1,000 ft. down and there were no guard rails. Dunn had pulled in to let an oncoming car pass. Looking back to check on his passengers, he found them bolt upright, frozen in fear, clutching the seat. One lady finally gasped, "Mr. Dunn, do people go over here often?" "Only once, lady," he drawled.

Dunn sold firewood on the side to supplement his driver's wages, and because he was often away overnight on tours, his firewood had a habit of disappearing in small quantities. Determined to put an end to that, he carefully drilled a hole in a few of the logs and filled them with dynamite. He forgot to mention it to his wife before leaving on a tour and when he came back he had to rebuild the roof on his house. Stoves were apparently inimical to him for once when he was adding to his income by making a little bootleg whiskey in his spare time, a friend told him it would age faster if he would put it in a warm oven. Returning from a trip one December night, he lit a roaring fire, forgetting to remove the whiskey, and again he repaired his roof.

Whiskey might have been a no-no during working hours, but there were times when circumstances seemed to justify it. Staab was driving a party of twelve people from the Reader's Digest staff on a tour of the Navajo/Hopi country when they one and all came down with a virus. For a week the party was bedded down in the Presbyterian Mission in Ganado, Arizona, not exactly the fun spot of the

Norbert Staab (center) with dudes at Frijoles

West. Staab went out for a walk and came back with a bottle under his coat. He asked one of the nurses where to get ice and she sent him down the road to the icehouse where the smallest piece they would sell was 50 lbs. Lugging the ice back to the Mission, he dumped it in the one and only bathtub. There were two cars on the trip, the other one being driven by Andy Rich, who had some compunction about drinking in the Mission. Rich walked by the bathroom a few times, and finally agreed he could stand a little 'Taos Lightning' as the drivers had named bootleg whiskey. Staab found out Rich was unused to drinking when he spent the night hollering as he chased the Navajo nurses through the halls. The next day Staab explained to the dudes Rich had been delirious with fever the night before!

The drivers and couriers made a social enclave in New Mexico, with friendships that lasted long after they left the Detours. Few of the drivers worked less than two years, and many worked more than five. Very few were fired, one driver being released because he was 'too arrogant with the dudes'. Another driver was fired because he made the mistake of saying "Good morning, Hunter," instead of "Mr. Clarkson." When Kay Sayre, wife of driver Frank Sayre asked him what happened, he said the same thing that happened to Hess when he called Hitler "Adolph".

Many letters were received by the company complimenting them on their choice of men and saying they were "very gentlemanly and accommodating"; "Charlie's careful driving did much to enhance our pleasure"; "special commendation should be mentioned for the particular ability of Davis, the driver". Only occasionally would a letter be received saying "the drivers of your cars sometimes maintain a very high rate of speed on the highways, which, I think, caused a feeling of nervousness among some of your tourists." Considering the highways of the day, the high rate of speed was probably somewhere around 35 MPH and the complaint was offset by another letter of the same month which said — ". . . men who managed their cars so well that the riders had perfect confidence over the steep grades and sharp turns."

Not all of the men were regular drivers. Like the courier staff, there were extras who were available on call, and the system of checking each day to see how many men would be needed was called 'bucking the board.' Those with seniority were first to be used; the low men on the board usually had part time work to help pay their bills.

In charge at the Santa Fe Transportation Garage was the dispatcher. And his duties were much the same as a train dispatcher. He was expected to know at any moment where one of the vehicles would be. When the bus or car left the garage in the morning, he worked his dispatcher's board. The board was marked off in squares with the names of the tour routes across the top. Each vehicle had a brass identifying tag with the company number on it. Buses had one series of numbers, in the 300's; Harveycars had a 500 series. Other vehicles in the company had other serial numbers.

When the vehicle moved out of Santa Fe or Albuquerque, or any headquarter point, the tag was moved to the appropriate box showing which route that particular vehicle was taking. At night, the tags went back to the central board and if one was missing, the search went out for a stranded car or bus.

The dispatcher's job was like a mother hen with chicks. He had to be in the office until the last car came in, and with stranded cars, breakdowns, flooded arroyos and other problems, this sometimes meant all night. Exact scheduling was impossible in some cases. The dispatcher had to avoid as much deadheading as possible; this was accomplished partly by holding drivers over until a return paying trip could be arranged, a practice that was unpopular with the drivers because they paid their own expenses when not actually working.

The dispatcher seldom drove, but at times when large tours necessitated using every vehicle in town, including privately owned ones, the dispatcher would close up shop and don a Stetson. The dispatcher was paid the same as the drivers, $125 a month, but were allowed commissions on the tickets they sold. When Clarence Muralter worked as dispatcher, he concentrated on selling tickets to the point the commissions were equalling his salary, and Clarkson overhauled the bonus system, so later dispatchers found selling tickets not that remunerative.

Clarkson's precision principles of management carried over into the maintenance of the cars, trucks and buses. When the day's run was over, the vehicle was driven to the garage where the mechanics went to work to correct any problems. At the height of the Detours, there were nine mechanics at the garage. If the problem was nothing more than a day's driving, the vehicle was completely cleaned out. The supervisor was expected to look for any missed dust, any candy wrapper, any burned match that had escaped the cleanup crew. Just to make sure everything was checked on the trouble sheet, if the driver forgot to make out the slip or failed to turn it in with the vehicle, he was not given his daily pay release slip. Head bookkeeper and emergency driver Wolcott Russel recalls:

"Once cleaned and ready to go again, the vehicles had to be perfectly lined up every night, so you could shoot down the front of them. Clarkson made a personal inspection to see they were properly placed every morning before the first vehicle was sent out. For a long time a young black boy was hired to wash the vehicles and he had a cardboard sign above his wash rack on which he had painted with shoe polish — 'don't slump or liable slap'."

A minute depreciation record was kept for each vehicle showing when it was purchased. Every 500 miles, the vehicle was completely inspected and a detailed record made of its condition. Necessary repairs were made, and the cost entered and once a month all figures were forwarded to the executive office where it was entered in a ledger which was updated as to value only when necessary. The last thing the company wanted was to have a Detourist stranded because of a breakdown, and records show very little occurred that caused more than a minor delay for adjustment or tire changing.

At 1,000 miles, certain parts were removed and tested for wear. If there was the slightest question raised about the condition of any part, a new part was put in the engine. The highway department of Arizona came out in print to say if "private car owners had made inspections approximating the rigidity of those of the Santa Fe Transportation Company, 18% of the accidents attributable to defective vehicles could have been eliminated." And so enviable was the safety record of the Harvey drivers that the New Mexico Highway Department publicized articles to make the driving public aware of what could be accomplished by a few safety rules. In later years, during WW II, when a motor pool was formed at Bruns Hospital in New Mexico, the Army followed the same safety procedures.

The vehicles had more inspections than an Army platoon and every time a bus was scheduled to leave, it was

Indian Detour bus in front of Santa Fe museum

completely gone over with a guiding checklist in hand. If there was the slightest defect on a tire, it wasn't just noted, and the spare checked for air; the tire was removed and a new one installed. And this was a time in motoring history when flats were as common as colds. One motorist was most grateful for their care, as he explained in a letter to the Harvey headquarters:

August 31, 1927

Mr. Ford Harvey,
% Fred Harvey Company,
Union Station,
Kansas City, Mo.

Dear Mr. Harvey:

I am not informed as to your connection with the Santa Fe Transportation Company, or the Harvey Car System, in and about the environs of Santa Fe, New Mexico, but I assume that you are identified with it, and are interested in knowing of my experience with your employees, which occurred at the Hopi Snake Dance, out on the Mesa, North of Winslow, whither I had gone with my family from Santa Fe, where we were spending the Summer, to see the Hopi Snake Dance.

We had bad luck and blew out all of our surplus tires and casing, and landed on the Mesa minus one tire and in a helpless condition. I applied to the Inspector in charge of the Harvey party — a Mr. O. H. Goode — to sell me an extra tire, but he informed me he couldn't do it, but he kindly offered to loan me a tire and casing, and gave me a letter to Mr. F. J. Horne, the Assistant Supt., at Santa Fe, with whom I could settle. He instructed his mechanics to put the tire on my car and extended every courtesy and favor within his power, and would not even allow me to pay the mechanics for their time in adjusting the tires on my car.

When I got back to Santa Fe I called on Mr. Horne. I presented my letter to him, but he informed me he couldn't take any pay for the tire or sell it to me, under a contract with the Company, nor could he charge me any rental for same, so that the only thing I could do was just return the tire, he expressing his pleasure in having been of assistance to me and extending me every courtesy and consideration possible. I am mentioning this to you because as an executive of this Company, you are interested in the attitude of your employees and their conduct in meeting with the public. I have never received such consideration and courtesy any place or under any circumstances, and I am very grateful and appreciative.

I talked with several of the guests of your Company who were at the Dance and all expressed their entire satisfaction and pleasure with the accommodation and treatment accorded them on this detour.

With kindest personal regards and hoping I may have the pleasure of seeing you some time soon, I am

Sincerely yours,

(Sgd.) R. J. Edwards

This was not an isolated case; in fact the drivers often interrupted their tours to help stranded motorists. It was a way of motoring life in those days. Staab remembers one shimmering hot day about 15 miles from Keams Canyon, Arizona, when he was driving some dudes on the Navajo/Hopi tour. They came upon a car with four people in it and a flat tire on the front wheel. For hours they had been trying to get the jack under the axle to raise the car, but there was not enough clearance under the car to put it in place. The people were dehydrated and in real danger of heat exhaustion. Asking the dudes to give them water from the thermos jug, Staab found a large flat rock, drove the wheel that was flat up on it, and put the jack under the axle, then changed the tire for them. Small wonder the drivers were considered heroes by the dudes.

The drivers were not trained in first aid, yet many of them knew some basic treatments, and Montgomery often brought in injured people who had misjudged the steep fall of La Bajada Hill.

More than 50 drivers would serve as the steady hands on the wheel for the Harveycars in the heyday of the Detours, most of them remaining in the vicinity to build homes and raise families.

The cast was complete in May of 1926. The show was about to begin.

7

THE WHERE OF IT — 1926

The Indian Detours were like a circular jigsaw puzzle, composed of many pieces to make a complete picture. Each piece had its own importance — the roads, the buses and cars, the brains behind the plans, the couriers, the drivers, the cooperation of all concerned — but the one piece at the center that the whole idea hinged on was the hotels.

Without the assurance that the tourist would be well fed and have a good night's rest, many Detourists would never have bought a ticket. The very coining of the name 'road pullmans' for the buses was a well-thought out use of words. The Detourist must be made to think of the tours as an extension of his comfortable if somewhat boring trip on the train. The brochures all emphasized the attractions of the hotels.

An article in 'The Santa Fe Magazine' for May of 1926, published by the railroad included this paragraph:

"While the regular hotel facilities in Santa Fe are excellent, Fred Harvey has acquired La Fonda Hotel on the old plaza in order to assure adequate accommodations for Indian Detour visitors. La Fonda will be enlarged and remodelled and operated according to Fred Harvey standards."

The Detourist arriving in Las Vegas on the Navajo train spent the night at the Castañeda Hotel. It was a large mission style building built around a courtyard, with covered patio walks. It had been named for Pedro de Castañeda who wrote of Coronado's expedition into the Southwest in 1540. It was one of the first of Harvey's station-hotels, opened in 1883 when he expanded his food service at train stops into a room for the night. And it never attained the rating of many other Harvey Hotels.

Even the lunch stops on the detours had to live up to Harvey standards, and the first day many Easterners had their initial visit to a working ranch-resort. The Valley Ranch Resort was situated on the Pecos River and its dining room, The Apache Inn, served fresh trout from the stream, or a fortunate fisherman could have his own catch cooked to order.

That evening, the Detourists were treated to one of the most up-to-date hotels in New Mexico, La Fonda. Built originally in 1919, before the Indian Detours were talked about, the Harvey system immediately set to work to 'modernize' the inadequate grande dame of hotels. The expansion would not be finished until 1929, but by 1926 it had a fresh new look to its old Indian and Spanish elements.

In Albuquerque, the Alvarado Hotel was another in the chain of 20 station-hotels planned by Fred Harvey and Santa Fe President E. P. Ripley in 1900. It had been built in 1883 and was renovated in 1922 after a two year tussle with the City Council over who would pay for the needed viaduct to move traffic over the railroad tracks and to the hotel.

Traffic had always been a problem around the Alvarado. The California Limited came through every day at 11:00 A.M. The movie greats would get off the train and walk up and down the platform to stretch their legs. Since movies were a glamorous mystery to most of the country, everyone in Albuquerque who didn't hold down a regular job would arrange to be down at the station, gawking at the stars. It was as close as most of them ever got to seeing Norma Talmadge or Francis X. Bushman in the flesh. Then the Isleta Indians knowing a ready market was theirs for the using, would bring their wares to the station, sitting around in silent groups, and that meant a lot of horses and wagons needed a way to circumvent the tracks.

Santa Fe train at Castañeda Hotel, Las Vegas, N.M.

When there was no Harvey House in sight on the tours and lunchtime rolled around, Harvey food still appeared on the table. The table was usually a flat rock, or perhaps a lap of a tourist seated on the running board of a car, but the food was delicious. This was a function of the couriers, who got up early to check the food prepared by the hotel kitchen at Las Vegas or Albuquerque. The food was packed in leather chests, thermos bottles in leather cases held tea, coffee and water. And there was even the nicety of ice, carried in zinc-lined boxes.

The first trip was a piece of cake for everyone involved. The preview trip had proven it could be done, and the

Margaret Wennips serves a picnic lunch

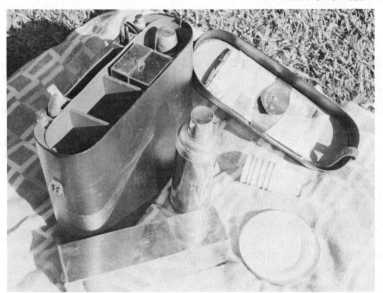

One type of Detour picnic kit

waiting period of 45 days before the advertised start of the Detours became almost a bore; there was nothing to worry about!

The original Santa Fe folder of March, 1926 was printed in 35,000 copies. The company thought this would be sufficient to supply their agents, but within four months the supply was gone and this time 100,000 folders were printed. The Indian Detours were attracting far more attention than anticipated.

The first Indian Detour to carry tourists met the California Limited, Train #3, at 6:50 A.M., Saturday, May 15, at Las Vegas. Detraining passengers were whisked away in one of the luxurious Harveycars to enjoy a hot breakfast at the Casteñeda Hotel. They were joined in the dining room by passengers who had arrived at 10:10 P.M. the night before on The Navajo, Train #9, and had overnighted at the Hotel. The dudes were each given a Detour map, printed in color on rice paper, showing the routes they would travel.

At 9:00 A.M., both parties were escorted to their Harveycars and the tour left for Kearney's Gap. It was a beginning of a trip back into history, for at the gap the tourists were informed it had been named for General Stephen W. Kearney. A little farther on, at San José, they inspected the area where his Army of the West prepared for battle with Governor Armijo's Mexicans in 1846. Starvation Peak, south of the trail, was pointed out and the name explained. Spaniards had been starved by a band of besieging Indians.

The next stop was Cicuyé near the Pecos River. Abandoned in 1838, the pueblo had been continuously inhabited for 1200 years, said the couriers, and in 1539 there were 2,000 Indians living there. The ruins of the Spanish Church built in the early 1600's, damaged by the Pueblo Rebellion in 1680 and rebuilt in the early 1700's only to be abandoned in 1798 was shown to the interested Detourists. And before they could show signs of fatigue, they were helped back into the Packards by the romantic-looking drivers and taken to the Apache Inn for lunch.

While they dined on fresh fish from the river, the couriers explained the Inn was part of the old Valle Grant, won and lost twice in poker games. Lunch over, the drivers guided the cars up 7500 foot Glorieta Pass. Ambush canyons were pointed out and as the cars drove sedately on to the final destination for the day, La Fonda at Santa Fe, the Detourists were filled in on the history of the Santa Fe Trail as they covered the last 70 miles of it.

To orient the tourists to the Indian arts and crafts, a guided tour of the art gallery and the Governor's Palace preceded dinner and after dinner a short talk was given on what would be seen the next day.

The next morning after breakfast it was off again, this time for a very short 15 minute drive to Tesuque Pueblo, eight miles out of Santa Fe, where Detourists could get their first view of an inhabited pueblo. After a short stay, a rest break was made at Española before going on to the Puyé Ruins, where it was explained Puyé is a Tewa word meaning 'gathering place of cottontail rabbits.' The rock cliff was honeycombed with rooms and granaries built by a long vanished tribe. On top of the cliff, a communal dwelling of 1200 rooms was pointed out. The tour stayed an hour here, allowing those who wished to explore, time to stumble over the rocks and through the desert brush to view the ruins more closely. Those afraid to climb ladders, stayed with the cars. Before lunch, a very brief visit was made to Santa Clara Pueblo where the Indians in their boots and blankets offered their shiny black pottery to the tourists. The couriers, informed the Detourists Santa Clara is a Tewa word meaning 'where the wild rose bushes grow near

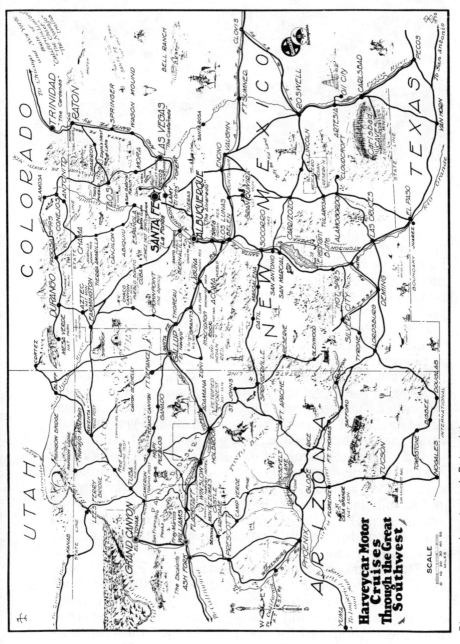

Rice paper map given to each Detourist

Puyé Ruins

the water,' and the inhabitants are believed to be descendants of the Pajarito Plateau people who were forced from their village by drought 800 to 1,000 years before. And then they urged them back to the cars to be on time for lunch at the hotel in Española where they had stopped earlier that day.

The afternoon was spent visiting another Indian Pueblo, San Juan, the largest of the three inhabited ones on the schedule. Again the couriers utilized their training by informing the dudes that the mission, San Juan de los Caballeros, was erected by Onate's colonists in the pueblo then called Yunque, where the Spaniards first settled. Completed in 1598, it is probably the first place of worship built within the United States after the chapel at St. Augustine, Florida. Damaged and rebuilt in the 17th Century, the church was dismantled in 1890 and they were told the building they were looking at was built as a parish church on the mission grounds. Early afternoon saw the group back in Santa Fe with time to explore the more noted spots of the city and freshen up before dinner. After dinner they would watch Indian dances.

The last day of the tour started again at 9:00 A.M. after breakfast. The route turned Southwest with vast open stretches reaching across the desert to the distant mountain ranges still wearing a wooly white cap of snow. Then came the highlight of the tour, the chance for men to be stalwart and strong and for women to turn pale and gasp.

The improved La Bajada Hill road

La Bajada Hill had to be conquered before the tour could visit Santo Domingo. Thanks to the work done on the 23 switchbacks after the initial bus run the previous December, the long cars could make the curves without backing, but for many tourists who had never been on mountain roads the experience was literally hair raising.

The size of Santo Domingo astounded many of the tourists who stared at the homes of 800 Indians; the Indians stared back at the sight of so many visitors being led by girls dressed in men's shirts. Midsummer dudes would have an extra treat for each August 4th the Green Corn Dance Festival was held, when all couples wed by Indian ritual were married in the church. The religious rites were held in the Church of the Pueblo of Santo Domingo, a recent building dating back only to 1886. It replaced an earlier mission destroyed by repeated floodings of the Rio Grande River.

At Isleta Pueblo, time was allowed to look at the Mission of San Augustin de Isleta, built from 1621-1630 by Fray Juan de Salas. Burned and desecrated during the Pueblo rebellion, the church had been completely rebuilt and was in regular use. A late lunch followed at the Alvarado, and then a brief tour of Old Town was taken before giving the dudes time to rest and freshen up for dinner. After an early dinner, they were shown the Indian Building on the hotel premises, and it was bedtime.

There were eight tourists on the first trip, and they

came from widely space global points. One was from Australia, a Miss Agnes B. Nelson, who said "such accommodations, and such service — why I think America must be a lovely country. I think it is most charming this idea of couriers who can point out the interesting places without using a huge megaphone and screaming their lungs out. And the food at the hotels, it is beautiful."

A Mr. and Mrs. F. D. Stone and Mrs. Stone's two sisters, Mrs. Helen D. Judson and Mrs. Cornelia Merritt, all from Vernon, N.Y., let Mrs. Judson do the talking. "We've never been through here before but now I'm sure that we're

Schedule · The Indian-detour · Schedule

Westbound
EFFECTIVE NOVEMBER 14, 1926

PASSENGERS FROM TRAIN NO. 9 THE NAVAJO	PASSENGERS FROM TRAIN NO. 3 THE CALIFORNIA LIMITED
Day of Arrival Las Vegas	
10:10 p.m. Arrive Las Vegas Overnight, Castañeda Hotel	6:50 a.m. Arrive Las Vegas

First Day of Indian-detour
Passengers from Both Trains

8:00 a.m. Breakfast at Castañeda Hotel
9:00 a.m. Leave Castañeda Hotel by Harveycar
9:20 a.m. Kearney's Gap
9:35 a.m. Tecolote
10:20 a.m. San José
11:15 a.m. Arrive Cicuyé (Pecos Ruins)
12:30 p.m. Arrive Apache Inn (Valley Ranch) for lunch
1:30 p.m. Leave Apache Inn
3:30 p.m. Arrive Santa Fé, La Fonda Hotel
4:00 p.m. Conducted tour of old Santa Fé, including old Museum and Art Gallery
6:00 p.m. Dinner, La Fonda
7:45 p.m. Lecture, St. Francis Auditorium

Second Day of Indian-detour
Schedule Same for All Indian-detour Passengers Both Eastbound and Westbound

8:00 a.m. Breakfast, La Fonda
9:00 a.m. Leave La Fonda by Harveycar
11:00 a.m. Arrive Puyé Cliff Ruins
12:30 p.m. Leave Puyé
1:00 p.m. Basket lunch, Santa Clara Indian Pueblo
2:30 p.m. Leave Santa Clara
3:15 p.m. Arrive Tesuque Indian Pueblo
3:45 p.m. Leave Tesuque
4:10 p.m. Arrive Santa Fé
6:00 p.m. Dinner, La Fonda

Third Day of Indian-detour
Passengers from Trains No. 3 and 9, Westbound

8:00 a.m. Breakfast, La Fonda
9:00 a.m. Leave La Fonda by Harveycar
10:15 a.m. Arrive Santo Domingo Indian Pueblo
11:15 a.m. Leave Santo Domingo
12:45 p.m. Arrive Alvarado Hotel, Albuquerque
1:00 p.m. Lunch, Alvarado Hotel
2:30 p.m. Leave Alvarado Hotel for Isleta Indian Pueblo
6:30 p.m. Dinner, Alvarado Hotel
7:30 p.m. Tour of Indian Building
3:15 a.m. Train No. 9 leaves, westbound (Pullmans ready for occupancy early in evening)
12:15 p.m. (following day) Train No. 3 leaves, westbound. Passengers remain overnight at Alvarado Hotel, Albuquerque

Eastbound
EFFECTIVE NOVEMBER 14, 1926

PASSENGERS FROM TRAIN NO. 2 THE NAVAJO	PASSENGERS FROM TRAIN NO. 4 THE CALIFORNIA LIMITED
Day of Arrival in Albuquerque	Day of Arrival in Albuquerque
2:10 p.m. Arrive Albuquerque Lunch, Alvarado Hotel Afternoon motor drives about Albuquerque, including Mexican villages, Volcanoes, etc., available at reasonable rates	5:20 p.m. Arrive Albuquerque
6:30 p.m. Dinner, Alvarado Hotel	6:30 p.m. Dinner, Alvarado
7:30 p.m. Tour of Indian Building Overnight, Alvarado Hotel	7:30 p.m. Tour of Indian Building Overnight, Alvarado

First day of Indian-detour
Passengers from Both Trains

8:00 a.m. Breakfast, Alvarado
9:00 a.m. Leave Albuquerque for Isleta Drive
11:30 a.m. Return to Alvarado
12:00 m. Lunch, Alvarado
1:00 p.m. Leave Alvarado by Harveycar
2:30 p.m. Arrive Santo Domingo Indian Pueblo
3:30 p.m. Leave Santo Domingo
5:00 p.m. Arrive La Fonda Hotel, Santa Fé
6:00 p.m. Dinner, La Fonda
7:45 p.m. Lecture, St. Francis Auditorium

Second Day of Indian-detour

The second day of the Indian-detour is identical for both eastbound and westbound passengers. For complete schedule consult Second Day of Westbound Schedule.

Third Day of Indian-detour
Passengers from Trains No. 2 and 4, Eastbound

8:00 a.m. Breakfast, La Fonda, Santa Fé
9:30 a.m. Leave La Fonda for conducted tour of Old Santa Fé, including old Museum and Art Gallery
11:00 a.m. Leave La Fonda by Harveycar
12:30 p.m. Arrive Apache Inn (Valley Ranch) for lunch
1:30 p.m. Leave Apache Inn
1:45 p.m. Arrive Cicuyé (Pecos Ruins)
2:45 p.m. Leave Cicuyé
3:30 p.m. San José (brief stop)
5:10 p.m. Arrive Las Vegas (Castañeda Hotel)
6:00 p.m. Dinner, Castañeda
7:45 p.m. Train No. 2 leaves, eastbound
10:30 p.m. Train No. 4 leaves, eastbound

Indian-detour Passengers Via Train No. 14, Eastbound

Indian-detour passengers from the South will reach Albuquerque at 7:00 a.m. via local eastbound Train No. 14. Such passengers will purchase their own breakfast upon arrival at Albuquerque. Luncheon, however, is included in their Indian-detour tickets and thereafter they will follow the complete schedule outlined for passengers from Train No. 2, The Navajo, eastbound

The revised 1926 schedule

coming up to Santa Fe for a long visit some day. I never thought there was anything to see here before."

Miss Gertrude Rubenstein and her sister Ethel, of Chicago, expressed their reactions by saying, "I think the La Fonda is a beautiful hotel — it's so rough and primitive looking with all the necessary comforts. We were going home by way of New Orleans, but I'm glad we heard about this trip."

A Miss Marion Seelye from Kansas said, "I don't know what I've enjoyed as well. Such a congenial group of traveling companions and such courtesy and accommodations as are provided. I don't believe there is a thing that could be done to improve the trip."

Mrs. Bertram Murray from Nova Scotia apparently had nothing new to say and wasn't quoted.

Fortunately for the records of that first trip, a writer for the Albuquerque Morning Journal was invited along, and her account was published in the May 18th edition. The language was flowery and her enthusiasm genuine.

Every bend of the road, every turn of the mountainous sky line, every change in the shifting sunlight effects were eagerly anticipated by the group. There were many bends in the road, many striking light and shadow effects, many inundations in the skyline — many delightful surprises — for the tourists in their three days of life in the "Land of Yesterday".

From the time the tourists left Albuquerque for Isleta Saturday morning, they did nothing but perk up to see all there was to be seen, hear all that they could of the state's history, pick up a few Indian terms and Spanish words, romanticise in the days of the past and, matter of fact, though it may be, heartily partake of all the meals, "beautiful ones" as the Australian member of the party called them, provided each day of the tour at one or other of the Harvey houses.

And now that the tour is done and the tourists all bound for new adventures and sights in other states, this writer has gone back to her typewriter, dreamy eyed and sorry that the lovely trip is done. However, as much as possible, she will relive the three-day tour in writing the details of the trip, which will be the first personal account of what the Indian detour is like.

Fascinating though the trip is, any of the nice things which I may write in the next paragraphs, will be but a feeble description of the delights entailed in making the tour. In the first place the Indian detour is a very easy one to make, there are no real hazards on the trip — most of the time one sits comfortably in the car — and when one does get out to walk, one can do so very leisurely. Only one part of the trip is at all strenuous and that is the climb at Puye. The historic wonders seen, however, when the climb is finished, more than make up for the effort expended in climbing up ladders and moccasin footpaths.

The Indian detour, which Major Clarkson originated, is as intriguing and fascinating as it sounds. Think of three days with nothing to do but see things under the guidance of a courier, who is more a hostess than the usual megaphone announcer with a sing song catalogue of facts and data. With such a guide one absorbs the country, its history and lore without the least effort. The couriers do not give formal lectures, but in an arm chair chatty fashion tell of this and that, answer all questions and point out things that may happen to interest them at that particular moment.

When this party under the couriership of Miss Marcella Matson left the Alvarado Saturday morning a few minutes past 9, with many people lining the sidewalk for a look at the tourists and the Indian detour car — an elegant and comfortable affair — it headed toward Isleta. Here the party made its first stop, visited the church, heard the legend of the martyred priest, whose body is said to rise to the surface of the earth every 20 years, and visited some of the homes in the pueblo.

"How clean and what sunlight!" was exclaimed at one time or other by each member of the party.

No wonder the tourists were fascinated. Their first introduction to the history of the region was a story still being told.

About the time the Spanish soldiers were getting a toehold in the Southwest, somewhere along in 1735, a Franciscan friar made his way to the Pueblo contry through hostile Indians to the east of New Mexico. By the time he reached Laguna Pueblo, west of Sante Fe, he was footsore, feverish and on the verge of starvation. The friendly Pueblo Indians gave him shelter, food and the services of their medicine man.

Brother Juan Padilla was halfway a prisoner, but his understanding of the Indian beliefs enabled him to gain the respect of the Pueblos. He had had training in basic medicine in his priory and in the following years, he administered to the physical as well as spiritual needs of his rescuers. He was a gentle friar, teaching his religion by example, blending it with Indian lore, always careful not to offend the Pueblos by trying to force them to his way of thinking. His simple humane contact with the Pueblos made a deep impression on them, and over the years, he was admitted to even the most sacred rites in the underground kivas. He had truly become their brother.

The Pueblos added their knowledge to his, and Friar Juan learned all he could about their language, their symbols, their rituals, their medical skills. The Indians no longer thought of him as their white brother, but considered him one of their own tribe. And the gentle friar was content to remain at Laguna Pueblo.

Friar Juan had lived among the Pueblos for 20 years when a runner brought news that a Spanish army was forming in Mexico, set on invading the Southwest in a last-ditch effort to find hidden gold. Whether there was ever a fabulous gold horde in New Mexico has not been determined, but perhaps the Spaniards believed the Indians were guarding such a cache.

While the tribal chieftain had never had any doubts as to Friar Juan's loyalty, a few members of the sprawling Pueblo tribe felt he had learned too much of the Indian ways and secrets, and they wanted to be sure none of their private knowledge would be passed on to members of a race hostile to all Indians.

One Pueblo brave, more fanatic and suspicious than his more deliberate brothers, decided not to wait until Friar Juan's loyalty to his adopted race was proven. One dusky evening, he planted his hunting knife neatly between the friar's shoulder blades.

The non-violent Pueblos were horrified by this act of treachery. First, it was a violation of their sacred laws of hospitality, for a person invited to stay in your tepee was considered physically immune from danger. Also, the many seemingly miraculous cures the friar had effected on their sick members gave him the status of a medicine man whose knowledge came from a powerful god. Since the invading Spaniards were of the friar's race, who knew what horrible punishment they would inflict on the Pueblos when they learned of the crime against one of their kind. The tortures the Spanish thought up for their prisoners were only too well known.

That night, the chiefs of the village wrapped the friar's body in a sheet and placed it on a litter. Four of their swiftest runners were summoned. They were instructed to see the body reached Isleta, 70 miles to the east, and to bury it there.

The runners took less than two days to reach Isleta. The church at that time had a dirt floor and there, in great haste, they dug a grave six feet deep before the altar. Although the friar had taught them the rites for the dead, their only thought was to return to their village as quickly as possible, so they upended the litter, slid the body into the hole and pressed down the dirt, smoothing it carefully to erase their marks. This was in 1756.

The Spanish army came and left, on their way back to Mexico with no success in their quest for gold. No Indian spoke of the murder of the friar.

Fifteen years passed, and one day in Isleta, an old man, whose job it was to care for the church and sweep out the dirt floor before Sunday services, went inside to do his work. He stopped short at a peculiar bulge in front of the altar. It was the size of a man's body, but only a few inches high. He said nothing, and apparently the local padre noticed nothing in the dim interior.

A year went by, and the bulge had grown higher until a crack appeared in the earthern floor. Still no one questioned it, thinking it was just a natural thing — perhaps caused by water beneath the surface. In two years more, the crack had widened, and dirt had to be added to it and tamped down. Three years, and the same remedy was attempted as the crack grew wider. No use, the crack kept growing and soon had to be walked around.

Exactly 20 years from the death of the padre, the Isletans came into the church one Sunday morning, and there on the floor, face up, lay Friar Juan. The crack in the earth was gone; the friar lay as though sleeping. His flesh was soft to the touch, as though he had just died. The frightened Isletans rolled him over and stared at the knife wound in his back, which had fresh red clotting blood around it. They ran to call the elders.

Knowing nothing of the story of the murder, the superstitious Isletans thought the figure was Heaven-sent, and reburied him by redigging the grave. It was a useless gesture. At the end of 20 years, the bulge, the cracks, the reappearance of the body was repeated. The Isletans buried him again.

The next time the padre reappeared, the elapsed years had shortened. The current Reverend Father of the Mission wrote the Military Chaplain in Santa Fe that the box containing Friar Juan's body was surfacing in 1819 and requested an examination be made. The Chaplain

Above: San Augustin Church at Isleta before remodeling
Below: After the 1960 remodeling (as it looks today)

obliged and made a written report, a copy of which is in the archives in New Mexico. The document was witnessed by several friars of the Pueblo. In it, he confirmed the lifelike appearance of the dead padre saying they placed a new robe on the form since the old one had disintegrated, and that the body was supple enough to dress easily and cross the arms afterwards. The body and been put into a cottonwood box when reburied in 1776, with the old blue habit untouched. The Chaplain also made mention of the decomposed bodies of people buried after the 1776 reburial, with bones remaining although the padre was intact.

When Friar Juan turned up again in 1895, the Isletans sent for a priest, the Governor and the Archbishop of Santa Fe. The Archbishop had a distinguished house guest — a Cardinal visiting from Rome, and he came along to take a look at the padre who wouldn't stay buried. The two churchmen testified they saw a body appearing freshly dead.

This time the burial ceremony was a bit more complete. The body was placed in a heavy oak coffin, along with a copy of the document. The lid was nailed down firmly, and prayers for the dead were said. The coffin was then reburied in front of the altar and the entire floor covered with two-inch planks.

Apparently this satisfied the restless padre for, according to the present Governor of Isleta Pueblo, Alvino Lucero, the friar has remained sleeping this century. But no one knows whether he will show up again or not.

Is it fact or legend? The story of the restless friar is well-known to New Mexicans. Some claim the recurring floods brought the body up. But every 20 years or so? Some claim the condition of the soil under the church is such that a form of mummification took place. But leaving him flexible? And where is the original document, copy of which was found in the coffin in 1895?

(from an article written by the author for Desert Magazine)

No doubt the fact the desert produced a colorful carpet of flowers for the dudes came as a surprise to many who associated the word 'desert' with endless stretches of blowing sand, with everyone from Rudolph Valentino to Tom Mix riding into the heat haze. Reporter Halback continued her report in the May 18th Albuquerque Journal by noting the blooming desert.

From Isleta, the first Indian detourists were taken back to the Alvarado for dinner and then at 1 o'clock started out for Santa Fe. The trip to that historic city was replete with many interesting sights. Outside of the historical features, the mesa along the way was covered with millions of flowers, great patches of primroses, purple sweet peas and other blossoms, which Miss Matson said were a special treat this year, coming out of the ground in response to the pleasant rains of this spring. The sage plant, grease wood and rabbits brush were also pointed out.

At Santa Domingo the party stopped for a look at the Pueblo. An old Indian was working on turquoise here and was gracious enough to permit the tourists to watch him at his work. He was making a long string of turquoise, rounding them off by means of rubbing them up and down on a wet sand stone. One of the party presented him with a cigarette, which he hugely enjoyed as did also the women of his family, judging their chuckles.

"It is good, my!" he told his women folk standing in the doorway as he stopped to puff the cigarette delaying the polishing of his string of beads.

Later on one of the party confided to this writer that she believed the Indian didn't like being watched and that she had seen him draw out a knife. No amount of argument could convince her otherwise.

The church, the governor and several Indian homes were visited at Santa Domingo, a few of the party picking up curios.

So interested in the activities of this pueblo did the party become that they were a half hour late in their schedule and when the detour car came within a few miles of Santa Fe, they were met by Major Clarkson, promoter of the tours, who was worried about their tardiness.

Yet, even though the party was late the tourists had time to register at the La Fonda, be assigned to their rooms, freshen up a bit and visit the Cathedral before eating dinner. Such a picturesque church as is the Cathedral! Through the courtesy of Father Theodocious, one of the Franciscan fathers, the party was taken into the old church and shown the old, old vestments worn by the early missionary fathers, the old paintings brought over from Spain, the old, statues, with their unbeautiful faces and strange figures and the boarded crypt in which two early missionary fathers are buried.

The old cathedral is a place for musing and romancing, even though the additions built on it have robbed it of its original charm. The tourists who visited the church caught something of the old religious atmosphere and when they returned to the La Fonda for dinner, which was served promptly at 6 o'clock, their talk was mostly about the old missionaries. This mood was further augmented following the dinner, when the party were taken on a tour of the State Art Museum, where they were first shown the community auditorium built in monastic style with paintings depicting St. Francis of Assisi's influence in both the old and new world. The auditorium is delightful in that it preserves so truly the atmosphere of the country as well as the spirit of the Indian and the Indian's favorite saint. Its ceiling is a whalebone of aspen and its pillars are hewn out of giant pine trees.

"The Indian used live things for his architecture rather than marble and gold," the museum guide explained. "Trees were things of beauty to them, also things closely related to the Great Spirit. The Indian reverenced trees and used them reverently in his building endeavors."

Following the explanation of the auditorium architecture, the party looked at the Indian collection in the foyer and then admired the paintings hung in the museum gallery, all of which have been painted in this state. While none in the party claimed to be an authority on art, they all agreed that a group of pictures, as a whole, had never delighted them quite as well. The pictures of Sheldon Parsons were particularly interesting to them in as much as the artist, happening in the lobby of the La Fonda as they passed through for dinner, had been pointed out to them.

Thanks to Miss Halback's observant eye and detailed writing, La Fonda's dining room was colorfully described.

As the guests went back to the hotel for a game of bridge, following a walk about the town, they were pointed out as "the tourists" by many sidewalk groups. During the dinner hour, many persons passed by the tourists' dining room, a coolly furnished room with orange draperies and red spindle furniture, for a peek at the first tourists. This dining room was especially refitted for the tourists.

"I know how the Indians must feel now," several of party were heard to exclaim, as the curious grew in number outside the dining place.

The broad, colorful lounge faces the patio and Spanish
fountain. It is the center of the social life of the hotel
and a pleasant rendezvous for guests.

Spacious suites, consisting of living room and one or two bedrooms, each with private bath,
are delightful features of La Fonda. Many of these rooms are distinctive in their individual treatment of furnishings, decoration and color schemes.

Detour brochure page showing interior views of La Fonda

Apparently the first day's tour was enough to convince
the reporter she wanted to be part of the whole trip, and her
very complete description of every sightseeing detail must
have filled more than one notebook.

Sunday's trip, following upon a long night of sleep, started at 9
o'clock, after all the guests had breakfasted heartily in the dining room.
Instead of using the big detour bus, with which the trip to Santa Fe had
been made, the party was divided into three groups and taken in
Packard touring cars, specially made and provided with the most luxurious of comforts. These cars are provided with double windshields
and can easily accommodate six persons, three in the back seat, two in
the front and with a special chair in the rear of the car for the courier.

Tesuque was the first stop for the tourists Sunday morning. The old
church, as usual was the first place to be visited by the tourists, Miss
Matson telling interesting bits of the pueblo's history. Then followed

visits into the homes, some on the ground floor, and others on the second story. Here the party were also taken out to the corrals and shown how the Indian keeps his horses.

Tesuque with its twig fenced road into the pueblo proved very interesting to the tourists. The Rain Gods made here were of particular interest to them. One of the members bought one of these and when it started to rain sometime in the afternoon, she was threatened to be excluded from the party — "The Rain God had worked."

San Juan de Los Caballeros, a part Mexican and Indian village, the first capital of New Mexico, established in 1598, was the next stopping place. There were two churches here to interest the tourists and many, many children who stood off in a large circle and eyed the tourists, waving to them a bit pathetically as they left the pueblo. The tourists here wondered about the two braids some of the Indians wore. All the other Indians they had seen thus far had their hair braided in one braid with the front hair bobbed.

At Española the party stopped for luncheon, doing justice to the cooks. The stop here also included a brief rest before going on the rest of the journey to Puyé. Puyé reached, all save two members of the party, climbed up to the cliff dwellings — to the very top of them.

Several times a few members of the party vowed they had seen enough of how the Puyé Indians lived four or five hundred years before Christ, this writer among them, but always their curiosity overcame their timidity and on they went, climbing ladders, using the moccasin footpaths worn into the soft rock by the early Indians, to the top of the mesa. The ruins up here, at which archaeologists have been working for several years, were of sufficient interest to warrant the climb.

Several Santa Clara Indians, who claim it was their forebears who occupied these cliff dwellings, were idling about the top of the mesa and proved very friendly aids in telling the tourists their side of the story. They pointed out the kiva and found bits of log, which they claim, formed the roofs to the dwellings.

"I think the Indians who lived up here were very small in stature, because they had such little doors," said the Santa Clara Indian police, who assisted the tourists in gaining ascent to the top of the cliff. "Also their houses were not very high."

On the homeward journey the tourists were taken to the Santa Clara pueblo. As soon as they arrived here, the Indian women from the various houses came rushing forth, each with a basket of the beautiful black pottery, for which that pueblo is famous, and which they lined up before the tourists. While none of the houses were visited in this pueblo, the tourists all went in the church, where an old Indian pointed out the various "Santos" and the "Virgo," which stood on a shelf by themselves with many flowers before them.

Back to Santa Fe that evening, the guests were glad for a brief respite before dinner. Following the dinner they attend a stereoptican lecture in the art museum by W. W. Wiswalla. The lecture and pictures were about much of the country taken in by the detour.

Monday's trip did not start out until 11 o'clock. Before this the tourists were taken to the Governor's palace and San Miguel church. At noon they were served luncheon at Apache Inn in Valley Ranch. Though this writer could not go all the way of this trip, she gleaned enough information from the party of three tourists, traveling westward at Santa Fe Sunday night, who had just made the tour of the Pecos valley, to know that this part of the tour is perhaps the most worthwhile of the entire three days. Before arriving at Apache Inn for luncheon, the tourists were

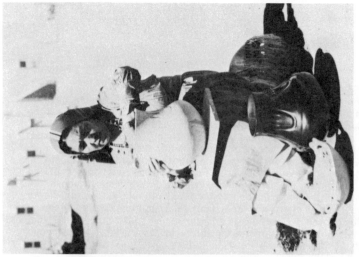

Tom Dozier's Aunt Severa at Santa Clara

Famous potter Maria and husband Julian

Santa Clara potter

shown the Pecos ruins at Cicuye and given a one hour stop. In the afternoon they visited San Jose, Tecolote and Kearney's Gap, arriving at the
Castañeda hotel at Las Vegas in time for dinner.

In addition to this three day Indian Detour, there are many special
side trips and tours, which any passenger on the Santa Fe can take by
getting a stop-over. Among these are those through Santa Fe canyon,
the one to San Ildefonso, to Taos, Indian pueblo and art colony; El Rito
de Los Frijoles, prehistoric cliff dwellings; Truchas and Cordova, old
Spanish settlements; Pecos canyon; Pueblo Bonito, Carlsbad Caverns
or the Rainbow bridge and Monument Valley country; Canyon de Chelly
or Blue canyon or Coal canyon and the August snake dance in the Hopi
villages; Montezuma's castle, the natural bridge and lakes and canyons
south of Flagstaff; the Petrified forests, the Roosevelt dam or the
streams of the White mountains.

There was only one incomplete item on the first trip.
Despite early attention to what was needed, the original
courier uniforms were not done in time. Part of this was due
to the short training period, and many of the couriers were
not chosen until just before the four week course started.
The only one dressed in what would be the official costume
for the 1926 trips was Erna Fergusson whose uniform was
borrowed by Anita Rose for publicity photographs.

The success of the May 15th Indian Detours reached
newspapers as far away as Los Angeles and New York and
the ensuing demand for additional sights to see meant constant updating of folders. The publicity department burned
a lot of midnight oil for the first six months of the Detours.
The large brochures were supplemented with many small
folders, designed to be picked up at train stations and tour
desks and tucked in a purse or pocket for future reading.

There was another company pushing Southwestern
sightseeing out of New York. Raymond and Whitcomb, a
travel agency in that city, put together what they called
"Seeing America First", a trip designed for the traveler with
nothing but money and time to spend it.

A special train of eight cars left New York on June 1,
1926, destined first for Chicago to pick up additional
passengers, then on to New Mexico for two days, next to
Arizona, where the Petrified Forest was explored, and eventually to California. The tours were touted as 'land cruise
liner travel', and the publicity pointed out the trip would
duplicate the luxuries of an ocean liner. And indeed, it just
about did. Besides the seven regular cars which carried
passengers, a dining and a lounge car, there was an enter-

tainment car which featured a gymnasium, a movie theatre showing silent films ('The Jazz Singer' was not made until the following year), a dance hall, a Victorian barber shop, a beauty parlor and a 200 volume library. Dancing was done to radio or Victrola music, and there was no reason for anyone to wish for hotels along the route.

The tour was one of four planned for that summer, and the passengers were loaded into hired jitneys at Santa Fe to visit Santa Clara and Tesuque Pueblos where they watched the Indians do their Eagle Dance. Then the tour proceeded to the Puyé Ruins and El Rito de los Frijoles. At the end of the two day New Mexico segment, the train took off at 11:00 P.M. for Adamana, Arizona for the Petrified Forest segment. The circle trip took a full month, with the first tour due back in New York June 29th after returning via the Northern United States.

The Raymond and Whitcomb tours were sporadic affairs, never attaining the permanent scheduling the Indian Detours had. They did make trips to New Mexico until the 1930's, using the Harveycars and buses whenever they could arrange for them.

Where previous Indian Detour brochures had brushed over Albuquerque with a sentence or two about a drive around town in the late afternoon of the last tour day, now additional trips were offered. The folders included a quick lesson in Spanish and Indian place names, complete with a pronounciation guide. Some of the tours were suggested as possible fill-ins for people with a half-day between trains after or before completing the Detours; others were of long enough duration to require the tourist to spend extra days in Albuquerque.

One trip took the dudes to the three extinct volcanoes West of the city, and lest the traveler have any doubts about this Harveycar trip being anything other than first class, they were assured they would be served an excellent basket tea in the open. The three hour trip cost $5 per person.

Longer trips included one of 130 miles, taking all day, and going to Jemez Springs and Soda Dam. Running north to Bernalillo, the route crossed the Rio Grande and then climbed into the Jemez Mountains, visiting several inhabited pueblos along the way. One of the few square kivas

Above: Soda Dam at Jemez
Left: Mesa Encantada

to be found was visited at Jemez Pueblo, and if the annual ceremonials were going on (Aug. 2, Nov. 12 and Dec. 25), time was allowed to watch.

The high point of that trip was Soda Dam, a weird dripping sculpture in stone, formed by the limestone from the natural hot springs in the area. If the tourist wanted to bathe in the hot springs and not rush back to Albuquerque, the trip could be extended to allow an overnight stay at La Esperanza Hotel in Jemez Springs. The price was $18 plus $7.00 extra for the overnight stay and a minimum of three people was required before the trip was scheduled.

Another proposed trip was slightly longer, 185 miles, still possible in one day, still offering an overnight stay if preferred. This went first to Acoma, called by the Indians, 'Sky City'. The folders described Acoma as "The most wonderful city on earth, built on the summit of a table rock 350 feet above the plain. It was already an ancient city when Coronado visited it in 1540. The old church in the village is of enormous proportion, the walls being 60 feet high and 10 feet thick, constructed of immense timbers, 40 feet long. All of the material had to be carried up from the plain on the backs of the Indians by way of a precipitous trail in the sides of the great rock and the task of building the church is said to have occupied about 40 years."

The Mission, rightly named San Estevan de Acoma, was originally built in 1629. Seventy years later it was either rebuilt or extensively remodeled, although no records re-

Above and Below: Two views of Acoma

main to tell what action was required nor why. Very likely it was burned in one of the recurring uprisings. Adjoining the mission was an artificial graveyard, built up by bringing earth from the valley below.

Like many Missions, the one at Acoma also had a legend. Inside the mission, there was a picture of St. Joseph on the wall, the largest painting ever made on elkskin, and the mission prospered because whenever the pueblo was threatened, the people would pray to the Saint

and he would intercede for them. Laguna had been experiencing a series of misfortunes and asked to borrow the picture. After a long council meeting that resolved nothing, it was decided to draw lots to determine the answer to the request, and the drawing came out negative.

The Laguna delegation didn't go along with the decision and stole the painting, whereupon the Acomas prepared for war. The padres persuaded the Acomas to leave the picture with the Lagunas to see if it truly had power, and war plans were put in abeyance. But the Lagunas prospered and the Acomas began to suffer a series of droughts, floods and sicknesses. Refusing to return the picture and fearing it would be stolen by the Acomas, for fifty years the Lagunas posted a guard over the picture 24 hours a day. The dispute finally was settled by the courts who ordered the picture returned to the Acomas.

Acoma was at one edge of the Enchanted Mesa, an enormous island of rock formed by erosion that rises straight up from the floor of a level valley, and Laguna was at the other edge. Both pueblos gave the viewer the comparison of inhabited villages, for Acoma was built long before the Spanish came in 1539, while Laguna was a later pueblo dating back to 1699. There the dudes could visit the pottery-making Indians and enjoy a basket lunch in the valley of the Enchanted Mesa before bedding down overnight at New Laguna.

One of the questions frequently asked of the couriers was what the design meant on the New Mexico State flag. The courier would explain this was a zia, a sun symbol, a sacred symbol to the Zia Indians whose pueblo was on the road to Jemez Pueblo, and then would go on to say this pueblo was not for visiting. For despite the friendly relationship between the majority of the Indians and the Harvey organization, a few, like the Zias, resented outsiders and were not only unfriendly but in some cases hostile.

For the traveler with a lot of time to spare, the Harveycars could be hired for a five day trip to see the Carlsbad Caverns and Gran Quivira pueblo. A minimum of a party of four paid $25 a day for the 750 mile tour. By now the Harvey organization had chosen a name for these independent tours, calling them Motor Land Cruises to separate them from the two- and three-day Indian Detours.

Tours of Carlsbad Caverns were popularized in 1925, and by the time the Motor Land Cruises scheduled them, the National Park Service had installed moderately easy walking trails and a guide corps.

This longer tour spent one night at Lincoln, the town made famous by Billy the Kid and infamous by the Lincoln County Cattle War of 1877. The Gran Quivira National Monument was an impressive sight on the tour with its 21 Indian pueblos dating back to 1300. It was abandoned in 1672 and the couriers filled the dudes in on the crop failures, the droughts, the Apache raids that brought an end to this communal area. The region was also colorful because of its small Mexican settlements, and Southwestern history came alive as the tourists walked through the streets of colonies named Torreon, Tajique, Chili and Tijeras.

During the first year of operation, many Detourists were writers who came to do independent pieces, or were sent by their parent publication to write a first-hand account of the new experience. Most reports were glowing; a few descriptions were somewhat sterotyped, as though they had been written after reading the brochure and left unchanged after taking the trip. One report was exceptional in its reaction to the pueblos. Francis McMullen of the New York Times Magazine wrote so well of his three day excursion, the story was picked up verbatim by the Kansas City Times of September 21st.

> Tourists have invaded the Indian country of the Southwest. Over roads once ridden by the conquistadores, the sightseeing busses now honk their way; and into even the remote fastnesses of the Pueblos penetrate these curious city folk. They seek no longer the gold sought of old by Spanish cavalier or Yankee sourdough, but merely the sight of a real live Indian in his feathers and paint, and, perchance, that priceless object of jaded nerves — a thrill.
>
> When formerly the motorless traveler wished to visit an Indian village, a taxi might be found, upon sufficient inducement, to undertake the trip from Albuquerque or Santa Fe, and a few years ago two young women went so far as to make a business of introducing special parties to the Indian section. But all this was a drop in the bucket compared to the tourist business of today.
>
> Bumpy roads, used by traders' carts and burros bringing firewood from the hills, are being widened, hard surfaced and straightened in preparation for heavy traffic routed to little frequented spots. Already

the valley is alive with long, slim cars bearing familiar trademarks and "rubbernecks" de luxe are carrying into and out of the Indian country crowds that have begun to vie with the American contingent on the boulevards of Paris.

Travelers headed for California leave the train at the little town of Las Vegas. The road over the hills is the same route the pack train and the covered wagon used. It is the route of the Indian fighters, the pony express and the Swaying Concord coach of the '50s, which carried passengers from Independence, Mo., to Santa Fe at $150 a head. The Easterner gasps at the unfamiliar landscape, the fluffy white primroses along the highway and the patches of purple verbena gleaming like lakes in the hollows. Mesas loom great truncated pyramids with the secrets of their strata boldly revealed. In the distance a hazy range of blue mountains outlines the horizon. One speeds through clusters of Mexican mud huts, their windows full of pink geraniums and strings of fiery chili beside their bright blue doors.

Eventually one draws up on a plateau crowned with ruins. The remains of its solid cruciform adobe walls bear testimony to the enforced labor of Indians more than three centuries ago, and to the ambition of religious enthusiasts that their mission there should last. Near by is the famous Pecos ruin, where archaeologists have been digging many years. Our guide tells the tale — a pretty young college girl in high boots and a 10-gallon hat, with enough Indian jewelry to open a curio shop.

The second day of the journey brings ladder-climbing adventures at the prehistoric cliff dwellings of Puyé. Then after considerable jolting over roads never intended for automobiles, one is landed in the midst of a sun-baked square. Adobe huts, studded with beams and laden with ladders at odd angles, are scattered around. Little bronzed boys in overalls rush up to see the visitors, and little straight-haired girls stand and gape; while papooses tied by shawls to their backs solemnly blink. Forthwith a tom-tom is heard, and across the plaza advances a formidable array — warriors in feathers and paint and (spirits of their ancestors!) some in striped silk shirts and others in anything they could get together.

In front of the tom-tom orchestra two eagle dancers keep time with the drums, their bodies stripped to the waist and painted a brilliant yellow. Their heads are covered with white down; yellow beaks hook over their blackened faces. Around their waists pieces of skin are knotted and rows of eagle feathers and red fringe extend down their arms and spread out into fan-shaped tails.

Bells jingle at their belts and ankles as they beat the ground in movements surprisingly eagle-like. They keep at it until perspiration drips from their chins; then the bonneted warriors take their turn, tomahawks in hand, and the plaza re-echoes their barbaric little yelps. Even in these civilized times one's blood runs cold. Perhaps this spectacle is put on for the visitors' benefit, but fiesta days are so numerous that, as likely as not, the Indians are dancing primarily to entertain themselves.

Next day, if one follows what is now becoming the beaten path, he reaches San Domingo, with its five broad avenues of adobe huts, set in the shadeless plain not far from the railroad tracks then, having cut through mesas and plunged down La Bajada Hill to Isleta, beside the Rio Grande, the tourists make their way even to the sky city of Acoma, to distant Taos and precipitous Frijoles, for the most remote spot is no longer beyond sightseeing reach.

Settlers in this region recall the time when to pass a day in a pueblo

Garage for storing and repairing Harveycars

was to drop out of sight of the white man's world. They used to wander off to the Indian ruins when they wished to be absolutely by themselves. To harbor such a fancy nowadays is a mistake. Almost at any moment the solitude may be broken by the tuneful bellow of the sightseers' bus; and New York, Chicago and San Francisco are dumped like a carload omelette at one's feet.

All sorts come, the couriers agree, but a special peculiarity distinguishes the typical tourist in the Indian country. Everything must be "wild" or at least outlandish. What was the surprise of one of the tourist service people, an Albuquerque woman, 100 per cent American, to overhear speculation as to whether she looked more Indian or Mexican. The party she handled that day had put her down as half and half.

As a group made its way up through the mountains recently an animal was glimpsed on the side of a hill.

"Isn't that a goat?" a woman whispered to the courier, who replied that it was.

"My dear," she turned to her companion, "do you see that wild goat?" Words cannot picture her disappointment when the courier felt obliged to tell her that the animal was one of a farmer's herd, such as one might see even in the East. But not so easily was the sightseer to be downed. Arriving at Frijoles Canyon, she suggested somewhat dubiously: "This country doesn't seem to be inhabited."

"No one lives near here," the courier admitted.

"Well, then!" the woman exclaimed, "aren't you afraid of bandits?"

"What do you mean?" asked the courier.

"Bandits!" fiercely came the reply. "Wild men. Isn't this Mexico?"

The traveler who comes to the Indian country, if he lingers more than a day, finds out many contradictory things about the pueblo dwellers. They have been described as a people of two languages, two religions, two sets of laws and two sets of implements. They have their own guttural utterances for communication with each other and a form of Spanish for trade and outside contracts. Many of the older generations know no English at all. Every pueblo has its quaint little adobe mission church, possibly hundreds of years old, and 90 per cent of the Indians, it is said, are nominally Catholic.

But the mission is generally on the outskirts of the village, removed from the throbbing life of the plaza, and the people are unmistakably still pagan at heart. They go to mass when the itinerant priest comes, but when the drought has lasted many weeks and it looks as if the corn will be ruined they turn to the kiva, their underground chamber in the heart of the village, and try the methods of their ancestors for inducing rain.

Rainey Bartley leads the climb up to Acoma

For days magic procedures go on there — where medicine men train youth in rites that have survived from times too remote for words; where women come only to serve, where strangers are never allowed. And presently the plaza is filled with weirdly attired figures dancing fervently in a prayer for rain. No amount of missionary work has ever dissuaded the Indians from the conviction that this is the most effective way to save their crops.

One does not stay in the pueblo long without hearing some mention of its "governor," and from what one hears one may judge he is the supreme power for all practical purposes. The title sounds grand enough but rarely does it designate a "big chief" holding himself in state apart. Perhaps you pass him, driving his wagon into town. Or he may be found at home making bead necklaces. Once when some visiting officials stopped to call on the governor of a village, they were told he was out stringing telephone lines.

If you follow Indians to the field you will find them operating modern farm machinery, supplied by the government and paid for on time. But if you go into their villages you will find them crushing grain by hand under a shed, from the edge of which sides of beef, perhaps, are hung to dry. Meals are cooked on stoves, but baking is still a community enterprise, done in outdoor adobe ovens, heated by embers that are raked out before the large flat cakes are put in.

Turquoise for beads is clipped by hand, with modern pliers, while the holes are bored with a most primitive sort of hand-operated drill. Their pottery knows no wheel. It is fashioned altogether by hand and polished with a rubbing stone. It is painted with bits of yucca leaf, in lieu of a brush, and baked in blazing dried manure. Yet the Indians are not unacquainted with the white man's ways of doing things. Where once there were only bedding rolls, tin trunks and baby's hammocks for furniture, the mail order house has left a trail of brass beds, sewing machines, lace curtains and kerosene lamps. Even a jar of beauty cream is sometimes to be seen on a window sill.

If the Santo Domingo Indians want silver with which to ornament the moccasins their women still wear, they take brown paper bags full of turquoise and go trading with the Navajos, as their ancestors have

Above: Detourists leaving the Hotel Castañeda
Below: Rest stop on La Manga Pass

always done. But how differently the modern Indians go — not on foot, for miles and miles over the plains, nor even on horseback, but by train as far as possible, and then by automobile, which the Navajos send to meet them.

Just what mark the increasing tide of tourists will leave on these people of mixed standards and mixed customs is not yet clear. The older men, it is said, hardly know what to think of the strangers. They eye them from a distance, shake their heads and turn their backs at sight of cameras.

The more enterprising, however, were not long in taking a new tack. They found that it was no longer necessary to sit for hours by the highway to market their wares; the market was coming to them. Women busy laying grains of corn out to dry in the sun hear the approaching motor's call and disappear into their huts. Presently they emerge with an apron full of lumpy things; then, squatting down on the ground, they spread around them bowls, vases, necklaces and rings, and wait for trade to begin. In the ensuing bargaining the Indian is seldom worsted, the visitor usually deeming it worth something extra to buy a bowl in its native pueblo.

If word is passed out in advance just when tourists are to arrive and a large party is expected, the plaza is alive with women in white doeskin leggins, wrapped to the knee, and with bright colored calico draped over their heads. Oilcloth covered tables are set in place and the goods are carefully laid out. Some of the men hasten to don feathers and beads, thereby the better to advertise themselves as subjects for the cameras that come with every tourist party. Some of these put such services at not less than 25 cents. Others get as much as $1.

Indians do not fail to realize on tourist possibilities to the limit. Having resisted temptation all day, the traveler alights at his hotel to find a couple of blanket wrapped figures with red rags around their heads lying in wait. They extend handfuls of fascinating things, with a persistent, "Buy! Buy!"

An aged vendor with a handsome war bonnet and a drum strolled into the hotel at Santa Fe one night. After a slack half hour sudden inspiration came. He suddenly commenced pounding on the drum with a variety of whoops and jumps that prompted hotel guests to gather exclaiming, "Come, watch the war dance!" Of course he passed around the drum for the cash his goods had failed to bring.

Gold such as these simple people have never seen before has come within their grasp this year. In one day one tourist was seen to spend more than $100 on Indian curios, giving $40 for a single set of bow and arrows. The same day another member of the party invested $400 in Indian rugs. Still another left a girl courier gasping at his proffer of a $50 tip.

She may have gasped, but if she wanted to remain a courier, she didn't grasp.

The Indian Detours were off and running.

8

THE WHERE OF IT — 1927

Besides the press releases that found their way into the newspapers around the country, and the folders that were placed for the taking in travel agents' offices, in information racks at railway stations and on the trains and mailed out to anyone who asked for them, the publicity for the Indian Detours was included in special bulletins at regular times to all station agents.

The first of these bulletins was furnished to agents in February, 1927. The Detours had proven to be successful; now one of Ford Harvey's better ideas was to interest groups as well as individuals in the special trips, and this was set forth in the February bulletin.

It was decided a maximum number that could be adequately housed, fed and taxied around with present facilities was 25 persons. Such groups as the Chicago Athletic Association (who included this tour in a circle trip from Chicago to Los Angeles to Hawaii and home) needed more reservations than this; an immediate decision was made to enlarge La Fonda. But this took time, so an interim idea was born. The travelers who wanted to come in groups too large for present accommodations would be housed in railroad Pullmans, left on the siding at Lamy.

*1927 bulletin designed
by Roger Birdseye*

Some of the first tour groups handled on this basis were the American Association of Railroad Ticket Agents and the American Banker's Association. On October 11, 1926, five special trains carrying 556 members of these two associations, vacationing at the same time, were taken care of in the Pullman 'Hotels.' The question of handling this number on the three-day Indian Detours was no problem because by this time fleets of Harveycars and Harveycoaches were standing at the ready outside La Fonda. Nineteen big White buses had been added to the original Yellow Coach fleet, and because of the number of passengers to be shuttled back and forth between Lamy and Santa Fe, they were pressed into service to supplement the railroad spur line which was designed for small numbers of people. Some roadsters had been brought out of the Grand Canyon to carry tour officials; local car owners willing to drive conventioneers around had been contacted.

All this expansion of service was not without its price, and a whopping $5 increase was made in the tour prices on May 1, 1927. But this was justified by the announcement in

Seven sections of the California Limited leaving Los Angeles for Lamy

the 1927 agent's bulletin that from that point on all rooms would be with private bath. Before, the $45 price for the three day all-inclusive tour was for room without private bath, with the option for passengers to pay $5 extra for a private bath. Now there would be no choice.

Although the Detours had been in effect less than a year, there were already many repeat guests. Ninety percent of the demand for winter tours had come from residents of the East and Middle West who found the infrequent snows of New Mexico more pleasing than the roof busters of the Eastern sections. Folders stressed that the cars and buses were heated, so sightseers need experience no discomfort, and the printed warning to bring a coat and other warm clothing was superfluous, since most of them left home bundled to the eardrums. The holiday season in December and January was one of many colorful fiestas in the pueblos, including the seldom seen Dance of the Sword Swallowers at Zuni, the Buffalo Dance at Taos, and the Eagle Dance and Hunting Dance at San Ildefonso.

The roads had been worked on during that first year until the narrow twisting road to Puyé was now wide enough and straight enough for the larger buses to use it without trouble. Bridges had been built over rivers so no unexpected flash flooding would trap sightseers in Santa Clara canyon.

Since the whole conception was in a trial and error situation that first year, the closing of the Detours for December, January, and February had been considered. But while it was under discussion, reservations poured in so fast the question was never answered, just abandoned. Business was 24% better in December than in November, and the first eighteen days exceeded any one of the preceding three months. January ran June a close second for reservations, and February promised to be the biggest month yet. Without further discussion, the Detours were on a year-round basis.

A few changes had been made in eating arrangements, too. Where 1926 travelers to Puyé had lunched at the hotel in Española, the growing size of the tours and the dissatisfaction of the Harvey Organization with the hotel had changed the plans so a basket lunch in the piney country around Puyé was substituted. For the Winter when outdoor eating was not feasible, two Indian homes had been brought up to Harvey standards and luncheon was served in the pueblo. This was a temporary arrangement, undoubtedly more pleasing to the Detourists than the Santa Clara squaws, and as soon as possible in the Spring, lunch was served outdoors again.

The basket lunches were so delicious they recruited one of Harvey's most reliable drivers. Tom Dozier was born in Santa Clara Pueblo and went to work for the Indian Forest Service, a government branch under the Interior Department. His ranger duties took him through Santa Clara Canyon and to Puyé. One day he arrived at the same time as the Harvey cars and was invited by one of the couriers to join them in lunch and talk about the history of the Puyé ruins. The chicken sandwiches and hot coffee brought him back day after day in time to connect with the tours, and after a few months of enjoying the free lunch, he decided to apply for a job as driver.

In an expansion of their regular schedule of places to see in their three-day cruise, a brochure was hastily put together called 'Roads to Yesterday.' A portion of the Harveycars, not buses, was set aside for the tourists who would want to extend their Detour on their own, yet be assured they would travel first class all the way, just as they had on the three-day Detour. Hotels were Harvey Houses, guides were Harvey couriers, cars were Harvey Packards, and Indians were Harvey friends. Who could ask for anything more?

Interest in Taos had blossomed when a writer for the Kansas City Star had made a trip out to the pueblo in 1921 and returned to write about it in the October 16th issue.

AT THE WESTERN END OF THE SANTA FE TRAIL

There is a popular idea that when the ox trails with much cracking of whips, shouts of greeting and creaking wheels rumbled into the historic plaza of Santa Fe, the trail had ended. For all commercial purposes, it had. The trail, however, did in fact lead on up through the mountain pass, ending entirely at the Indian pueblo of Taos, New Mexico. This place has no commerce to attract the trader, and those who visited it made the 65-mile journey purely for reasons of curiosity or romance. In those days macadam roads were not known and the trip meant a good three days' work. If the traveler, however, had a measure of appreciation, he was amply rewarded.

Taos is claimed by some to be the oldest American city, disputing the claims of St. Augustine, Fla., and Santa Fe. If we consider the Indian

Roads to Yesterday

Motor Drives
out from
Old Santa Fé

Harveycars

Reprinted July 1, 1927

inhabitants of Taos, then the settlement, the people and their dwellings, antedate any other existing community in the country by many centuries. If it be the oldest American city, it is still the least American, for it is totally unlike any other place in the United States. With the exception of an itinerant movie show and a half a dozen motor cars, the life of Taos today moves almost exactly as it did four hundred years ago.

Forty-eight years after Columbus first sighted land in the western world, the first white man entered Taos. Long before that, an Indian seer named Bah-ta-ko had led his peaceful followers away from the burning desert and the ravaging Apaches and Navajos of the far West. The promised land entered by these people was the verdant valley and fertile plains in the shadow of what are now known as the Taos mountains. Seldom a warlike people, this tribe has led a peaceful existence in its oasis. Their customs, their laws, their lives, despite occasional buttings-in by the white man's government, remain the same. These Indians claim kinship with the Toltecs and the Aztecs and probably immigrated from the south.

There is a Catholic mission church in the center of the reservation, emblematic of the European culture brought there, but the tribal questions, tribal laws and ancient religious rites still are held in the 'estufas', or underground council chambers near the pueblos. On the reservation are evidences of a well laid out town site, but the pueblos housing the 800 members of the tribe are the only dwellings that are now occupied. These two big tenements or community dwellings are known as the north and south pueblos, separated by a crystal-clear river of snow water, which supplies the Indians' needs for laundering, drinking, and for the more rash ones, bathing.

Most pueblos live on hillsides, on mesas or on the top of steep declivities. Taos is the only one lying in a valley. It is built beehive fashion with room for one hundred families in the one structure, and in this respect is different from other Indian settlements where the houses may adjoin but are not formed into a structure of more than one story.

There are usually three or four rooms occupied by a single family and these are kept spotlessly white with a coat of 'Terra Blanca', a whitewash found in a natural state and dug near the pueblo. The general living room usually is found upstairs over the sleeping rooms. Off the living rooms are the corn and meal bins and stones with which the grain is ground in primitive fashion. In this living room is to be found the peculiar arched fireplace where the cooking is done. These fireplaces are the only examples of arches used by the Indians. The beautiful simplicity of these interiors is a relief to the eye, tired by civilization's habit of cluttering up all available space with senseless things. The suites are entered by ladders which can be pulled up after dark, thus forming a simple yet effective nightlatch. The natives are rarely seen out after dark; perhaps these ladders account for it.

There are no half-breeds among the Taos Indians. Racial intermarriage does not exist. They keep their blood as pure as did the ancient Israelites. Though many of the older Indians are not what could be termed 'well-read', they are neither ignorant nor stupid. The Taos Indians all speak fluent Spanish in addition to their own language, and some of the younger generation surprise the visitor with a command of crisp English.

The women, as is the custom with Indian people, do the major share of the drudgery, attending to the house building and repairing, in addition to their housework and cooking. The sight of two dozen squaws on baking days, kneeling before the community bake ovens

Mission of Ranchos de Taos

great dome-shaped adobe affairs, is a novelty to the occasional tourist.

The main labor of the men is the cultivation of the fields. The grain is threshed in kralls, or fenced-in enclosures, by tramping it out or by beating it with flails.

Thus the Indian, steeped in an ancient civilization of his own, lives on, unmindful of the encroachment of the white man or modern culture.

The Spanish pioneers built three miles south of the pueblo and named the town Fernando de Taos, and there Spaniards live today much as they did in 1600. The 1-story dwellings, built to form a hollow square with their inevitable patios or courts, and their profusion of flowers, are the same now as then. The houses are built flush on the crooked streets of the drowsy village and entrance to some of the yards is through a gate or door painted a gay blue or green. Windows are often barred, but close examination often reveals the bars are made of wood. Sometimes the entrance is through massive arched doors, swinging on formidable iron hinges, extending clear across the woodwork. The courts inside usually give off to half a dozen apartments and a number of families inhabit the same dwelling.

Taos Valley contains some 7,000 inhabitants, of whom only about 500 speak or understand the English language. The place is as yet unspoiled by the coming of the railroad. It is a bit of the old world set down in the midst of the new.

*The road into
the Sandia Mountains*

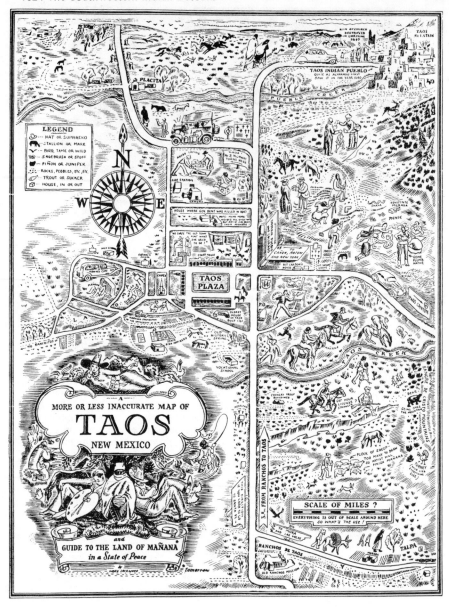

The Taos road, which began at the Hidalgo Bridge, so named because it was the crossing place of the river when the Spaniards forded the Rio Santa Fe, had been graded late in 1926. Taos was considered the granddaddy of all pueblos to visit. The mission there had been built before 1617, was burned in 1680 and a new church built in 1695 which continued in use until 1847 when the Taos Indians, incited by a group of Mexicans had rebelled against the

Hidalgo Bridge

United States. They fortified themselves in the church and in the ensuing bombardment, the church was completely ruined. Instead of rebuilding on the ruins, a new church was built, a massive edifice that fascinated the dudes unused to pueblo architecture.

They were equally fascinated by the five-terrace pueblo, highest in the Southwest. The pueblo was divided in half by the river running through the middle of it. After exploring the communal homes, the couriers loaded up the dudes and moved them on to the old Spanish-American village of San Fernandez de Taos, once the home of Kit Carson. They stopped to view his grave, reading he had lived in Taos from 1858 to 1866.

San Geronimo de Taos

Taos was an art center, and tourists went shopping for paintings to take home showing the canyon views, the ancient pueblo, properly called San Geronimo de Taos, the Indian ceremonials and the winding town streets.

If they were there in the Easter season, they could watch with well-bred horror the rites of the Penitentes as they flogged themselves bloody in the Flagellation Rites, and occasionally crucified one of their members. There was always a festival of some sort in Taos, not all this spectacular, but in January they could watch the Buffalo Dance, in February the Turtle Dance, in May the Relay Races, in September a general Fiesta, and the usual celebrations of Christmas in December.

The trip could be a one-day excursion from Santa Fe, but the Don Fernando Hotel, at which they lunched, provided first class overnight accommodations. The one day trip was $20 and the overnight all-inclusive rate was $35. The trip covered 150 miles and no minimum was required.

Another one- or two-day trip was a 95 mile drive to see the prehistoric cliff dwellings in the canyon of El Rito de los Frijoles, or Little River of the Beans. Part of the Bandelier National Monument, the drive in itself was enough to sell the trip. The road wound up Otowi Canyon over the Culebra Hill Road. Other Indian ruins could be visited on the way, Tsankawi, meaning 'place of the round cactus,' and Tyuonyi. The trip was not for the faint of heart and unsound of wind because it entailed a strenuous climb to visit the Great Ceremonial Cave and the kiva, reachable only by ladders and steep rock-cut steps. But there was enough to see on the valley floor without the physical fitness ladder climb.

Those frightening climbs provided some of the comic relief that made the Indian Detours memorable to the couriers and drivers. Margaret Wennips was dutifully following a puffing Chicago matron up the ladder when she noticed a black stocking, oddly misshappen with stuffing, dangling between the knees of the lady as she would move up each rung. When the group reached the top and stopped to rest, she discreetly mentioned having seen it and wondered if the woman was losing something. The woman assured her everything was fine, then proceeded to reach up and unpin the hose. Shielding it from view of the other dudes, she started to unwrap newspaper balls; inside of each was a diamond ring, each larger than the last. Margaret urged her to replace them and not say a word to anyone in the hotel about it.

Ann Cooper had a Frenchman in her party whose highest experience had been climbing up the steps from the boat dock on the Seine. He got partway up the ladder and literally froze with fright. With only a high school working knowledge of French, she kept yelling "haut, haut" at him, and he kept saying, "non, bas, bas." With other people on the ladder behind them, Ann finally solved the problem by taking his ankles one at a time and bodily moving them up to the next rung. And the climb down was accomplished in the same way.

One of the most colorful of New Mexican towns, Chimayo, was another 'Roads to Yesterday' trip. For a change, it was not an area of Indians and pueblos, but rather of the Mexican settlers. The tourists could watch the weaving of colorful Chimayo blankets growing before their eyes on clackety 100-year-old foot looms; they could walk the streets admiring the whitewashed homes decorated with huge strings of brilliant red peppers, drying in the sunshine; they could visit a Mexican church, called Sanctuario and spoken of as the Lourdes of New Mexico, and on Sunday watch the long line of pilgrims inching their painful way to the shrine on their knees.

The adobe chapel had been built in 1816 by a farmer, Bernardo Abeyta, who was instructed in a vision to dig beneath his plow for earth endowed with healing powers, and in so doing uncovered a cross and some pieces of cloth belonging to two priests who had been martyred there. He placed the cross where the chapel was to be built. Pilgrims came to dig for handfuls of the curative earth, which they made into a sort of tea. Those who came from a distance took back bits of the earth to act as a safeguard against future illness, and then a extra pinch to protect against possible storms en route home. Once home, if a violent storm occurred, they threw a few grains of the earth upon the fire, believing the smoke from the fire would travel up the chimney carrying the power to divert the storm.

When Don Bernardo died, the chapel passed to his daughter, Carmen Chaves. She and her husband continued

The Chimayo Sanctuario

to allow pilgrims to dig for earth with the blessings of the old priests of the village. Finally a young priest moved to the village and demanded the shrine be given to the Church. Carmen refused, and for years she was excommunicated with no one in the family being baptized, married or buried by the Church. The priest was finally transferred and harmony was restored by an older, more understanding Fray.

By the time the Harveycars stopped there, there was a large pit in the center of the chapel, the only shrine of its kind in the United States. The wall niches were full of unusual native wood carvings and the walls festooned with castoff crutches and braces. The dudes were greeted and shown around by a descendant of Carmen. (In 1929, an anonymous alumnus of Yale University who had been on the 1926 Indian Detour trip possibly, donated a check for $6000 to purchase the Sanctuario and present it to the Church. It is protected today under the Spanish Colonial Arts organization.)

Outside of Chimayo, two other Spanish settlements were on the tour route, Truchas and Cordova. At the latter, the old church was a highlight as the dudes walked through its bleached wooden door into its dim interior decorated in religious frescoes. The round trip was 90 miles, the cost only $13 per person with a minimum of three people.

The next auxiliary tour choice was San Ildefonso, a Pueblo that would be included on future Indian Detours. The round trip was only 50 miles and it was offered twice a day for $10 per person. If it happened to be January 23rd, tourists had a chance to see the Hunting Dance, but the Indians were eager to show off their black or red pottery anytime as they sat around the large plaza. To enlighten the tourists a bit puzzled by the pottery, the couriers explained the red pieces were made of the same clay as the black and it was polished and decorated in the same manner, but the difference was due to the mode of firing. The black pottery was fired with air entirely excluded from it by manure so that it smoked black, while the red had air circulating around it as it fired.

San Ildefonso had been a very prosperous village at one time, big and several storied. The reason for its demise was another Indian legend. The people of the village knew it was bad luck to move north, (a superstition that possibly

San Ildefonso pottery maker and dude

grew up because of the wintery weather in Northern New Mexico), and agreed they would move south and relocate the pueblo. But the village sorcerers insisted it be 'moved north. It was finally agreed the outcome would be settled by a gaming contest, which the sorcerers won by witch-craft. The pueblo moved north, which was held to be the reason the pueblo had decreased in population, had suf-fered famine and disease, and could not have homes higher than one story.

The dudes were then taken on to see the nearby Black Mesa, after having been told the difference between a mesa and a plateau was largely a matter of size. The mesa, it was explained, was usually smaller and more properly a table-shaped body of land in the midst of a lower plain with slopes extending downward on all sides. In contrast, a plateau is a great table close to the wall of a higher moun-tain range.

That bit of education over, the tourists explored the hundreds of pit dwellings built and used by the San Ildefon-so Indians when they were beseiged by the Spaniards in 1694.

A natural cave had been deepened by people looking for mineral wealth, and like many such places, an Indian legend told the story of a child-eating giant using it for his home. There are several versions of the legend, but the most popular is one told by the Indians themselves.

"The Pojoaque Giant was really a lizard. You see, long ago the children of Pojoaque pueblo were so bad their parents could not control them. The elders called a council to decide what to do about the naughty children, and one of the council members who was a wizard suggested he be shut up in a hole in the ground and fed deer meat for four days, and then he would have wisdom to punish the children. At the end of the four days, he was double his original size and was so hungry for meat he caught the children who disobeyed their parents and baked them one by one in a nearby oven.

When he had eaten all the bad children, be began to eat the good ones as well, and when all children were gone, he started to eat all the adults. When he had eaten all the Pojoaque people, he started to feed on the San Ildefonso children. The frightened parents sealed their children into their cold bake ovens, but the Giant rapped on each oven with a cane and if the oven did not sound hollow, he knew he had found another meal.

The people of San Ildefonso finally held a council to learn how to kill the Giant. They decided to appeal to the Twin War Gods and they donated gifts for the Twins. Sacred meal, beads, tobacco, buckskin robes, moccasins, clothing were all collected and taken to the Twins, who agreed to slay the Giant. But when they reached the Black Mesa, the Giant swallowed them along with the last San Ildefonso boy.

The Twins nauseated the Giant and he started to vomit, but the Twins were left inside along with the last boy. Walking around inside the Giant, the Twins found his heart and shot their arrows through it. When the Giant fell dead, his mouth flew open and the Twins came out carrying the little boy. The Twins then cut out the Giant's heart knowing it was the only way to destroy him for good, stuffed his stomach with cacti and pushed him into his own oven, lighting it.

The watching villagers saw the black smoke coming up from the Mesa and knew the Giant had been burned and they were happy again."

In many of the pueblos in the area, there is an annual pageant when naughty children hide from the Giant. If the child has really been bad, the mother allows the man representing the Giant to use a whip on the child. If she feels the child does not deserve punishment, she hands the Giant bread to eat instead.

There were other trips offered, including an afternoon tour of Santa Fe, a dinner drive up to Lamy, an all day drive through the Pecos River Canyon and a half day tour of Cochiti Indian Pueblo which was especially popular on July 14th, the Day of San Buenaventura, when the Corn Dance could be observed.

One of America's noted artists, John Sloan, attended the Corn Dance and carried in his mind all the impressions he set down in a satirical 1927 etching entitled "Indian Detours." The Harvey cars are rounded up in a tight circle, the dudes, drivers and Indians are doing their own thing, while Harvey chefs prepare food on a draped banquet table.

One of America's great poets, Witter Bynner, poet laureate of Harvard University, returned from watching the Rain Dance at Cochiti to write of his experience in verse.

A DANCE FOR RAIN

You may never see rain, unless you see
A dance for rain at Cochiti.
Never hear thunder in the air
Unless you hear the thunder there,
Nor know the lightning in the sky
If there's no pole to know it by . . .
They dipped the pole just as I came,
And I can never be the same
Since those feathers gave my brow
The touch of wind that's on it now.
Bringing over the arid lands

Butterfly gestures from Hopi hands
And holding me, till earth shall fail,
As close to earth as a fox's tail.
    I saw them, naked, dance in line
Before the candles for a leafy shrine;
Before a saint in a Christian dress
I saw them dance their holiness.
I saw them reminding him all day long
That death is weak and life is strong
And urging the fertile earth to yield
Seed from the loin and seed from the field
A feather in the hair and a shell at the throat
Were lifting and falling with every note
Of the chorus-voices and the drum,
Calling for the rain to come.
A fox on the back and shaken on the thigh
Rain-cloth woven from the sky,
And under the knee a turtle-rattle
Clacking with the toes of sheep and cattle —
These were the men, their bodies painted
Earthern, with a white rain slanted;
These were the men, a windy line,
Their elbows green with a growth of pine.
And in among them, close and slow,
Women moved the way things grow,
With a mesa-tablet on the head
And a little grassy creeping tread
And with sprays of pine moved back and forth,
While the dance of the men blew from the north,
Blew from the south and east and west
Over the field and over the breast.
And the heart was beating in the drum,
Beating for the rain to come.
    Dead men out of earlier lives,
Leaving their graves, leaving their wives,
Were partly flesh and partly clay,
And their heads were corn that was dry and gray.
They were ghosts of men and once again
They were dancing like a ghost of rain;
For the spirits of men, the more they eat,
Have happier hands and lighter feet,
And the better they dance the better they know
How to make corn and children grow.
    And so in Cochiti what day
They slowly put the sun away
And they made a cloud and they made it break
And they made it rain for the children's sake.
And they never stopped the song or the drum
Pounding for the rain to come.
    The rain made many suns to shine.
Golden bodies in a line
With leaping feather and swaying pine.
And the brighter the bodies, the brighter the rain
As thunder heaped it on the plain.
Arroyos had been empty, dry,
But now were running with the sky:

John Sloan's satirical etching "Indian Detour"

And the dancer's feet were in a lake,
Dancing for the people's sake.
And the hands of a ghost had made a cup
For scooping handfuls of water up;
And he poured it into a ghostly throat,
And he leaped and waved with every note
Of the dancer's feet and the songs of the drum
That had called the rain and made it come.
　　For this was not a god of wood,
This was a god whose touch was good,
You could lie down in him and roll
And wet your body and wet your soul;
For this was not a god in a book,
This was a god that you tasted and took
Into a cup that you made with your hands,
Into your children and into your lands —
This was a god that you could see,
Rain, rain in Cochiti! *

*Used by permission of the Witter Bynner foundation.

A short drive that was extremely popular was the trip to San Cristobal ruins. The pueblo had been a one-story building of many rooms, the inhabitants having been driven out around 1680 by the warlike Pecos Indians. The church ruins were typical of many others the dudes had visited, but the most interesting attraction was found on the rock wall back of the pueblo ruins. There they could read the prehistoric newspaper rock of the people of San Cristobal. Hunting scenes, sun symbols, plumed serpents, birds, animals, people were all set out for display in the pictographs.

For those who wanted to keep right on going once they started, the Harveycars could be hired with the understanding they would average 100 miles a day. A service offered by the Santa Fe Transportation headquarters would gladly line out tours of any desired duration, provide the cars, arrange accommodations and meals, provide a personal courier and a capable driver and show the tourist more than he really had wanted to see when he left home. Hunting and fishing trips could be worked in, and even camping out could be included along with pack saddle trips fanning out from ranches along the way. In fact, if a tourist wanted to start in New Mexico, see Arizona and end up in California, all by Harveycar, it would be arranged. Including all charges other than the camping trip, the fee was $65 a day

Sierra
Verde

Circle
Cruise

1—On road to Durango. 2—Balcony House ruin, Mesa Verde.
4—Looking into New Mexico at 10,000 feet—Cumbres Pass.
3—Pueblo Bonito—fortress home of ancient Americans.
5—The glorious climb up Mesa Verde.
59
60

for one, $70 a day for two, $25 a day per person for three to five people. A flat fee of $10 a day covered camping service, required to pay for the truck needed to carry the camping equipment.

One major factor instrumental in the rapid expansion of the boundaries of the Indian Detours was the repeat business. Many of the tourists would arrange business trips across the country so they could stop off and take advantage of the Detours, and once having seen the places scheduled in the first year of operation, they clamored for more. So the Fred Harvey system gave them more.

By July of 1927, a new detour added 900 miles of scenery which was mostly new. Still divorcing these

The July 1927 Brochure

special trips from the basic Indian Detours, this itinerary was called the Sierra Verde Cruise. It required eight days and followed a regular pattern of departures. This trip had one big difference in timing, though, because the possibility of snow-clogged roads made it necessary to run it only in the summer months. It was announced there would be a set schedule leaving La Fonda in Santa Fe at 2:30 P.M. on the 7th, 14th, 21st, and 28th of each month, and from the Alvarado Hotel in Albuquerque on the 8th, 15th, 22nd, and 29th of each month from June to September, with the final trip leaving Santa Fe and Albuquerque on the 7th and 8th of October.

The trip was the most expensive to date; $150 per person included all meals, accommodations, transportation, driver, courier and any entrance fees or tolls. There was no minimum, and no more than four people were assigned to a Harveycar, whether open or closed, and a choice of touring or sedan was offered.

Designed to offer the best variety of scenery possible, the schedule included a sweeping circuit of Northwestern New Mexico and Southwestern Colorado. Visits would be made to two National Monuments and four National Forests as well as a National Park.

Leaving in the early afternoon from La Fonda, the tourists spent time at two mountain mining towns, Madrid and Golden, and then traveled on to spend the night at Albuquerque, where the rest of the tourists would join them.

The next day the cars left the Alvarado at 8:30 after an early breakfast and visited the more popular pueblos on the original Indian Detour, Pueblo Bonito at Chaco Canyon National Monument, stopping briefly at Isleta and Laguna. A new oil field had been developed at Hospah, and Easterners who thought oil came out of a can at the filling station were treated to the pumps working like thirsty birds to bring up the black gold. The night was spent at Pueblo Bonito Lodge where rooms might not be luxurious, but they lived up to the Harvey rules of cleanliness and comfort. Arrival was planned early enough to allow a guided tour of the ruins, an excavation project of the National Geographic Society.

The next morning, the ruins of Chetro Kettle, Penasco Blanco, Pueblo Alto and Pueblo del Arroyo were poked and probed, and in the afternoon the tourists were swept off to Farmington, with a few chosen stops at Indian trading

Prehistoric ruins, Aztec National Monument

Cliff Palace, Mesa Verde, might be a dream city

Puyé, pitted with cliff dwellings

Pueblo Bonito, in Chaco National Monument

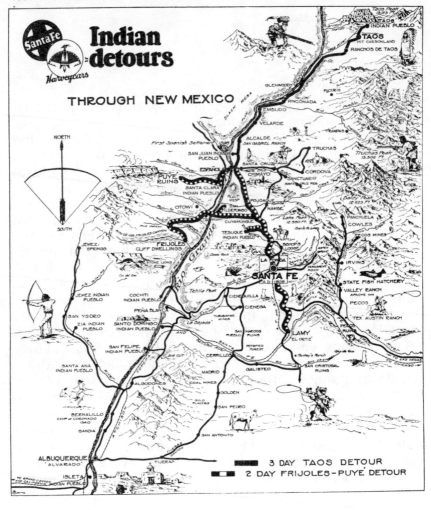

posts so the Easterners could begin their collection of silver and turquoise jewelry.

The dudes had been given a crash course in the buying of Navajo jewelry by the couriers, who were seldom seen without at least one necklace decorating their velvet blouses. One of the nightly talks in the lounge was on the use of coins for the silver, with an explanation that since United States laws forbade the defacing of coinage, the Navajo silver came from Mexican silver coins. They were told that the Navajos first made jewelry for the American officers and soldiers stationed at Ft. Wingate, having learned the basic craft from Mexicans. This surprised a lot of tourists who thought it was an ancient American Indian craft.

The dudes were then told how to distinguish handmade pieces from the machine-stamped silver. For those who couldn't distinguish the difference in color between the slightly grayish sheet silver that was stamped, the difference in irregular designs that marked the handcrafted pieces was pointed out in a slide show. Having learned about the silver, they were told the really fine old pieces did not use turquoise for adornment and were therefore more valuable as collectibles.

After that, the subject of turquoise was covered, with the claim that the finest American turquoise was mined near Cerillos. The potential buyers were then warned about sunlight, perspiration and grease damaging the stones. They were given a guideline for prices which were seldom a subject of haggling because the Indians priced their pieces low enough to satisfy all but the most greedy purchaser. Many a Navajo was able to redeem his pawned masterpieces after the Harveycars left, the dudes having exchanged money for native handwork. The overnight stop was at the Avery Hotel in Farmington.

The fourth morning they began the highlight of their trip, a day spent at Mesa Verde National Park. There they learned from the couriers that Pueblo Indians had settled in the area about 1 A.D., building pit houses on the mesa top. Later they would build homes of rock, tucking the rooms, towers and storehouses under the protecting overhanging ledges. Tourists would stand in awe at the accomplishments of a people who vanished mysteriously in 1200 A.D. while the Park guides told them of its discovery, first by the Spaniards who undoubtedly had stopped to look at the ancient pueblo in the mid 1700's, then by a pioneer photographer, William H. Jackson, who located the ruins in 1874 and went on to produce the first black and white pictures of the area.

The tourists, weary from climbing, enjoyed a good meal at the Spruce Tree Lodge, learning more facts about the ruins from an after-dinner fire talk, and then retiring to recharge their climbing batteries for the next day's tour.

There was plenty of time for exploring the ruins they had missed before setting off again on the afternoon of the fifth day for the Wrightsman Hotel at Mancos, Colorado. The Indian ruins were left behind; now the trip would show

The old and new transportation meet

them some of Colorado's most beautiful Rocky Mountains.

The sixth day was a driving day from Mancos to Durango, then to Pagosa Springs where a basket lunch gave time to stretch legs before dipping back into New Mexico to visit the railroad town of Chama, where a narrow gauge railway chugged alongside the road over 10,260 ft. Cumbres Pass into Antonito. The night was spent at the Lodge in Conejos Canyon.

The trip was almost over and on the seventh day an early start saw the Harveycars headed for Taos by way of Cerro, Questa and the Carson National Forest. Views of the Sangre de Cristo range and the Taos Mountains were admired and lunchtime found the group at the Don Fernando Hotel in Taos. The afternoon was devoted to a walking tour of the famous pueblo and the artist colony and the Don Fernando was headquarters for the night.

The next day the return to Santa Fe and Albuquerque completed the circle and the group rested up before boarding their transcontinental trains the following day to head for home, their enthusiasm bubbling over into letters sent to the couriers, the Santa Fe and the Fred Harvey headquarters.

I believe this Indian-detour was one of the most delightful trips I have ever taken. One of the things which appealed to me most was the personal touch that is given. One feels like a personal guest rather than just a tourist on a sightseeing tour. Taos, of course, was the climax of the trip, for I shall never forget the beautiful drive along the Rio Grande Canyon.

Miss Beulah N. Stapp,
6150 Kenwood Ave.,
Chicago, Ill.

To any thoughtful, intelligent observer it would prove a most delightful excursion.

R. E. Culver,
407 Tootle,
St. Joseph, Mo.

Truchas Peaks

I think this trip very enjoyable, and certainly one of the most interesting and unusual one could take here in the United States. This brief visit fascinated me with New Mexico, and I am planning to come back and see Acoma, the Enchanted Mesa, Frijoles, and other places I did not see this year, and also some of the Indian ceremonials.

Miss Edna Scheid,
605 Lake St.,
Hobart, Ind.

I thoroughly enjoyed my trip over the Indian-detour. Everything was most satisfactory. The hotel accommodations and the meals were of the best. I want to mention particularly the courier service, which I found a delightful change after the guide service which one usually has on sightseeing trips.

Miss Vivian Duthie,
224 Pine St.,
Berlin, N.H.

Some months ago it was my privilege and pleasure to take the Indian-detour. It was a perfectly delightful experience — unique, educating, full of beauty, and in every detail perfectly planned and executed.

I should like especially to mention the delightful courier service, as well as the comforts of the La Fonda.

Mrs. John W. Cadberry. Jr.,
12 High St.
Morristown, N.J.

I wish to express to you my enjoyment and appreciation of Santa Fe and the Indian-detour country. The combination of ancient civilization, colorful Indian Pueblos, and Mexican villages in their setting of most beautiful scenery makes it an unforgetable trip.

Miss Jennie L. Weaver.
231 West Race St.,
Somerset, Pa.

We often talk of the New Mexico part of our trip, which in many ways was the most enjoyable part of it all. From the standpoint of service to the traveler, it was head and shoulders above all the rest. The Santa Fe may well be proud of the Indian-detour.

Albert E. Seibert,
49 Wall Street,
New York City

My recent first-time trip into New Mexico was far too short, but most interesting. That country certainly possesses a charm which is unescapable. The Indian-detour is a happy memory and I hope to come again.

Miss Alice B. Cunningham,
Glens Falls, N.Y.

I consider it a privilege to heartily recommend this unique trip to any who may be touring the west. The days spent on the Indian-detour are not merely sightseeing days, but days of leisure and untold fascination.

Miss Elizabeth A. Taylor,
1328 W. Main St.,
Barnesville, Ohio

I found my visit to Santa Fe and the state of New Mexico one of the most enjoyable as well as most educational parts of my western tour.

Mrs. A. Forck,
4737 Parker Ave.,
Chicago, Ill.

I have just returned from a trip to the Coast and am writing you to express my appreciation of the service extended to me on my visit through the Indian country in New Mexico. It was a very interesting and instructive two-day journey and your Couriers added much to my knowledge of Indian customs and history. I really had a very lovely time and enjoyed every minute I was in New Mexico.

Miss Margaret Dun,
393 Seventh Ave.,
New York City

Harveycar leaving the hotel at Taos

The west is changing rapidly and I know of no short trip where one can see so much of the old life of the Southwest.

Forest C. Overton,
CASTLE & OVERTON, Inc.
200 Fifth Ave.,
New York City

The Indian-detour was one of the most delightful experiences my sister and I have ever had. Every trip we took was most interesting and gave us an idea of Indians and their life that we, at least, had never had before. The Couriers, who are all most attractive young women, were very thoughtful of our comfort and added much to the pleasure of the trip. After we finished the detour we stayed in Santa Fe a week longer which enabled us to go to Santa Clara to see one of the Indian dances, which we would not have missed for anything. After leaving Santa Fe we returned to Albuquerque and took the trip to Acoma, which seemed to be the climax.

Miss Christine L. Munger,
420 West 118th St.,
New York City

It is with the greatest enthusiasm that I review my short trip to New Mexico in September, which included the Indian-detour. My desire now is to go again as soon as possible and stay much longer. The thoughtfulness and helpfulness of everyone in making the Indian-detour a success is no small part in the pleasant memory.

Miss Florence M. Weaver,
2410 Terrace Road,
Des Moines, Iowa

Our visit to New Mexico is a very delightful memory to us both. We found something unique, absorbing and fascinating.

W. B. Getty,
228 N. LaSalle St.,
Chicago, Ill.

Petroglyphs
at
Pajarito Park

I thoroughly enjoyed the entire three days. The country is wonderful. Visiting the many pueblos and seeing the Indians in their natural environment was a most delightful experience. I consider this trip an outstanding feature in looking over my itinerary of several weeks of travel. From the time one steps off the train until train time again the service is complete.

Mrs. Chas. L. McAleer.
206 Clark Road.
Brookline. Mass.

A second Land Cruise was rapidly put together, this one totaling 750 miles, requiring four days and visiting Carlsbad Caverns. Twice a month, on the 1st and 15th, the Harveycars were programed to leave La Fonda at 8:00 A.M. starting in May, 1927. Tourists staying at Albuquerque would be picked up along the way, as the cars wound their way through Encino, Vaughn and Roswell, cutting a long diagonal path Southeast to the Caverns. The cost was $80 and a two person minimum was required.

The first day was pure driving, absorbing the sometimes spectacular, sometimes boring scenery of a portion of New Mexico the tours had not covered before. A lunch stop was taken in Vaughn at the Gran Quivira National Monument once inhabited by Piro Indians, and the tourists bedded down for the night at the Crawford Hotel in Carlsbad.

The next day was solely for exploring. Wearing stout walking shoes and warm sweaters, the couriers led the Harveycar passengers to the Cavern entrance. The Caverns had their own guides who filled the dudes in on the history of the National Monument. They told of its discovery by cowboy Jim White, who found the cave when he traced what he believed to be smoke from a volcano and found instead thousands of bats swarming out at twilight to feed. Having heard tales of bats getting entangled in hair, the dudes glanced fearfully at the ceiling, and then relaxed as the guide said the bats were so useful in pest control that a man in Colorado had written requesting he be sent a shipment of them to help destroy coddling moths that were ruining his apple orchard. Naturally the request was refused.

Occasionally, Jim White himself would go along on the tour with the dudes, couriers and drivers. He liked to talk about his discovery and the way he let himself down on a rope for his first exploration. More than likely, the courier at the head of the tour group would be Dorothy Raper whose degree in geology gave her an advantage in the question and answer department.

She remembers once when the sights were a little more spectacular than expected. Since there were no lights and no elevators, the groups would walk down the inclined pathway with the leaders of each small grouping carrying lanterns. When everyone was assembled in the King's Palace, a huge circular room, the official guide would order all lanterns turned off, then light a magnesium flare and run around the entire perimeter of the room. That was spectacular enough, but on one Land Cruise the flare exploded,

A White Coach loading dudes at Las Vegas

knocking the guide unconscious and plunging the room in darkness. Jim White was on this particular tour. Sending the couriers back up the pathway with the dudes, he made his way to the opposite wall, gathered up the burned guide and carried him out on his back for treatment. Then the balance of the rooms open to visitors was explored with a new guide.

City-bred people whose experience with underground caverns had been the New York or Chicago subways, panted their way up and down ladders, along dripping shafts to stand in awe in the King's Palace, the Queen's Chamber and the Big Room. To give the winded sightseers a chance to relax, the couriers and drivers packed in basket lunches which were served partway through the trip. The couriers had to know as much about the history, geology and discovery of the Caverns as the official guides, and they clued the tourists so they could immediately identify the stalactites ('they hang *tight* to the ceiling') and stalagmites. When lunch was over, the walking tour continued, the couriers carrying out the soiled linen napkins, empty thermos bottles and enamelware cups and plates in the wicker picnic baskets. That night, again, the tour stayed at the Crawford Hotel.

The next morning the cars headed toward Mountainaire, going through Roswell to Lincoln, where the couriers explained the confusing details of the Lincoln Country Cattle War of 1877. They poked around the jail where Billy the Kid was imprisoned in 1881, and from which he made an unspectacular escape. The couriers talked about the volcanic lava flow of Carrizozo, but the more than 400 acres had not been made a State Park at that time and the cars stopped only long enough for the tourists to marvel at the rough black rocks tumbled like an abandoned play pile along the road. And the cars continued into Mountainaire where the ruins of pueblos stood chuck-a-block with ruins of the Mission Church that had been abandoned in 1672 after repeated Apache attacks. They looked at Indian pictographs and then retired to the hotel to have dinner and sleep.

The fourth day, they returned to Santa Fe by way of Gran Quivira National Monument. Again, lunch was a basket affair and the long trip back was broken up with

Type 53 White buses; Harvey Motorcoaches on tour

visits to the ruins at Quarai and little Mexican villages along the way.

Quarai, now a State Monument, started as a little mission Church of the Immaculate Conception in 1630. It survived 42 years of repeated attacks by the Apaches until it was finally abandoned in 1672 to crumble quietly into ruins.

By December, another Carlsbad Caverns Cruise had been put together, running only three days, costing only $60, but leaving out a lot of the sightseeing along the way, and cutting short the cavern exploration so only part of the caves were visited, but tailored to fit the time budget of busy transcontinental tourists.

By December 1, 1927, the Indian Detours and the Land Cruises, were, as the bulletin issued to agents proclaimed, "563 days old, without a single day being missed because of inclement weather." The bulletin went on to point out, "there is not one month in the calendar year when Indian Detour guests do not express surprise and pleasure on the climactic conditions encountered." And it concluded with "there is no off season for the Indian Detour. Spring is a delight in the mountain valleys. Summer nights call for blankets. Fall brings ten straight weeks of sunshine. The volume of winter travel speaks for itself."

New Mexico, anxious to keep its reputation as a sightseers' wonderland, spurred its Highway Department into a flurry of road building; the Santa Fe/Harvey operation, knowing it had a winner on its hands, kept the board meetings going overtime, planning new trips to satisfy the growing number of people choosing the Southwest over any other attraction, not only in the United States, but in much of the world.

A new rest house had been built at Puyé, giving non-climbers the opportunity to stand in warm comfort looking at the ruins through glass walls and the climbers a chance to warm their ladder-exposed portions to the roaring fireplace. Hotel personnel were relaxed having gone through the baptismal fire of a daring experiment. Couriers and drivers had the self-assurance of experienced experts. There was no end of money to be made in the mid-twenties and the mystique of the Southwest was at its height.

1927 was a good year, for everything including the Indian Detours.

9

THE WHERE OF IT — 1928

1928 was a good year, too. Babe Ruth was at the height of his money-making career, the Graf Zeppelin flew some very wealthy tourists from Germany to New Jersey in four and one half days and before the year ended, Herbert Hoover would be elected President.

In 1926, Stutz cars had been equipped with an experimental 'shock-proof' glass. It had wire running horizontally through the glass to give it stability. A different version, using a sandwich of transparent celluloid between two sheets of glass was used on the Rickenbacker car, but it wasn't until 1928 that Cadillac introduced a regular safety plate glass on cars. Determined to make Harvey vehicles a model of safety, Clarkson had the new safety glass installed on all cars as fast as it could be done.

The Indian Detours, less than two years old, had attracted many famous travelers from wide points in the country. In Los Angeles, W. F. Alder, an author and lecturer who talked of his travels to anyone who would pay his fee across the U.S., devoted an entire broadcast over radio station KNX to the Detours.

Another well-known author, New Yorker Amos Parrish, wrote in a magazine he published, "Next time you go to Los

One of the fleet of Harveycars

Angeles, take the Santa Fe. Stop off on the Indian-detour.
Three days. Three thousand years." He went on to describe
some of the sights that had most impressed him, and gave
special attention to the couriers, in particular Dorothy
Raper.

> "Each car has its courier. If they are all as good as ours — the trips are
> surely all pleasant ones. This courier is not the blatant, wise-cracking
> guide that New York sightseeing trips are burdened with. A Wisconsin
> graduate, she has trained for this interesting work by specializing in
> geology and other things that fit her for it. And she knows what she's
> talking about. She answers questions, no matter how foolish."

Mr. Parrish even had a few things to say about the
Indians.

> "The Indian gets a great laugh out of the rushing white man. He sees the
> humor in the situation when the white man madly races against time.
> His people found out centuries ago that time is merely a relative thing in
> that it is endless — so why the clamor? His mountains — his blue sky —
> his sweep of sand land — all are endless, and like time itself, timeless.
> Just as this Indian country erases time, so does the Indian sell you the
> idea that today is only a single grain of corn in the acres of the ages."

All this free publicity did more to promote the Detours
than any amount of advertising could do. And the Santa Fe
added new club cars to its trains that brought the
Detourists to New Mexico. A publicity shot shows Mr. W. J.
Black, the passenger traffic manager with four Indian
chiefs, three of them appropriately dressed in their
customary tribal wear, and one resplendent in a white
cowboy outfit.

Such tactics lived up to what the dudes who had never
been West expected. Courier Ann Cooper was shopping in
a Chicago department store while on a publicity trip . When
she asked to have the items mailed, the clerk said she

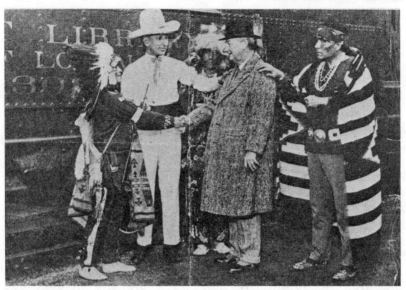

would need to know what customs forms were required. This was not an isolated incident; in fact, the State of New Mexico added the letters 'U.S.A.' to their license plates for many years.

Once on the Detours, the Easterners still found the West was the wilderness they expected. One New York traveler was vociferously extolling the complete satisfaction he had experienced at the end of the Isleta tour and one of the couriers suggested he plan to take in the Grand Canyon the next time. He was adamant; that was one place he would not visit. He had read of the numbers of people who went there every year and he had had enough of hordes of people back home. No amount of explanation about the size of the Canyon convinced him it would not be wall-to-wall tourists.

Some of the tourists had never seen farm animals before, let alone grazing stock. Driving to Carlsbad, two Philadelphia dudes were riding with Dorothy Raper when one lady noticed a cow or two on the open range. She asked why they didn't see more cows and was enlightened about the amount of pasture needed for one cow in the desert regions of the West. Her companion had been unable to hear Dorothy's explanation and asked her seat companion what the reason was for so much land, and so few cattle. Coining a new meaning to the word, the lady said, "Oh, it takes that much land for pasteurizing in New Mexico."

Some of the comments got into notebooks the couriers carried, partly to get answers to some unexpected questions they couldn't field, and partly to be referred to when writing friends about their experiences. Margaret Wennips drew a circle around one dude question as the funniest of the year when one of her dudes wanted to know why in the world the Indians at Puyé had built their pueblo so far from the railroad. She then went on to say the schedules could include more sightseeing if they had only built closer to the stations.

The experimental schedules had been proven workable and popular by early 1928, and the division was clearly made between the Indian Detours, the original two and three day trips for tourists with little time and lots of questions; the Roads to Yesterday, which substituted more scenery for less history; and the Motor Land Cruises designed for tourists with plenty of time and money and a desire to spend most of their vacation in cars rather than on trains. It was expected — and hoped — the dudes who had signed up for an Indian Detour at home would sign up for a Land Cruise in the lobby.

People were still taking most of it with them when they went traveling in the days before drip-dry clothing, and the steamer trunks that traveled in the baggage cars of the trains had become somewhat of a problem for the handlers. Even the scheduling of transfer could be a problem, especially on Motor Land Cruises where people often did not return to the starting point. It was fine to say "bags out at seven, you out at eight," but the Harveycars were equipped only with a rear trunk and one running board carrier, that often was partially occupied with picnic baskets. It was necessary for rules to be laid down, and the first rule was that the cars would carry only hand luggage. Other baggage was tagged with a special identifying card to assure tourists their baggage wouldn't go to Chicago or Los Angeles without them. A limit of 100# was put on all steamer trunks, and if the tourist insisted life could not go on without the trunk being delivered to La Fonda or the Alvarado, it was brought in a special baggage truck. But the tourists were encouraged to check the major portion of their luggage at the terminals where it was held in a special section reserved for Detourists. For a minimal fee of 15¢,

Above: Harveycar with luggage carrier
Below: Taking a scenery break

the trunk could be forwarded, at the proper time to the
departure terminal, and for people who left the train at Santa Fe and rejoined it at Winslow, as an example, they could
rest easy knowing the trunk would be on the same train
they were when it came time to continue their journey.

Certainly some of the Detourists must have grumbled
a bit, being used to dressing for dinner in many vacation
spots. But it was soon apparent that their motoring garb,
regardless of whether it cost a few dollars at Sears

The Indian-detour

2 Days $40.00

Schedules

The Puyé Detour

Westbound

EFFECTIVE MAY 15, 1928

(Cancels all previous schedules)

Day of Arrival at Lamy

TRAIN No. 3	TRAIN No. 23
1st California Limited	2nd California Limited
9:15 a. m. Arrive Lamy	9:50 a. m. Arrive Lamy

Guests met at trains by Couriers

(PASSENGERS FROM BOTH TRAINS)

10:10 a. m. Leave El Ortiz Hotel by Harveycar
11:15 a. m.-12:00 noon Cicuyé (Pecos Ruins)
12:15 p. m. Arrive Apache Inn (Valley Ranch) for lunch
1:45 p. m. Leave Apache Inn (Valley Ranch)
3:00 p. m. Arrive La Fonda Hotel, Santa Fé
3:30 p. m. Drive about Old Santa Fé, visiting Governor's Palace, Old Museum, San Miguel Church, etc.
6:00 to 7:00 p. m. Dinner, La Fonda
8:00 p. m. Informal Lecture, La Fonda
Overnight, La Fonda*

Second Day—Puye Detour—Westbound

(PASSENGERS FROM BOTH TRAINS)

7:00 to 8:00 a. m. Breakfast, La Fonda
8:45 a. m. Leave La Fonda by Harveycar
9:10- 9:25 a. m. Tesuque Indian Pueblo
10:10-10:30 a. m. Santa Clara Indian Pueblo
11:15 a. m. Arrive Puyé Cliff Ruins
12:00 noon Lunch, Puyé Rest House
1:15 p. m. Leave Puyé Cliff Ruins
3:00 p. m. Arrive La Fonda, Santa Fé
6:00 to 8:00 p. m. Dinner, La Fonda
Overnight, La Fonda*

Day of Departure—Puye Detour—Westbound

7:00 to 8:00 a. m. Breakfast, La Fonda
8:15 a. m. Leave La Fonda by Harveycar
9:30-9:55 a. m. Santo Domingo Pueblo
11:15 a. m. Arrive Alvarado Hotel, Albuquerque

11:45 a. m. Train No. 3 (1st Cal. Limited) leaves westbound
12:15 p. m. Train No. 23 (2nd Cal. Limited) leaves westbound

*Due to heavy increase in Indian-detour travel, it is possible that La Fonda, the Harvey hotel in Santa Fé, will have insufficient rooms with private bath to meet all Indian-detour requirements pending completion of additions tripling the capacity of the hotel. Temporarily, therefore, guests may on occasion, be allotted rooms at the De Vargas hotel, one block distant. These rooms will in every way be up to the high standard of Indian-detour accommodations provided at La Fonda. All Indian-detour guests will continue to take their meals at La Fonda whenever in Santa Fé.

2

Eastbound

EFFECTIVE MAY 15, 1928

(Cancels all previous schedules)

Day of Arrival—Albuquerque

TRAIN No. 2	TRAIN No. 4	TRAIN No. 24
THE NAVAJO	FIRST CALIFORNIA	SECOND CALI-
	LIMITED	FORNIA LIMITED
2:00 p. m. Arrive Al-	Lunch 3:10 p. m.	Arrive Al- 6:15 p. m. Arrive Al-
buquerque.	buquerque	buquerque
Alvarado Hotel		
3:30 p. m. Isleta Drive.	3:30 p. m. Isleta Drive	

Guests met at trains by Couriers

PASSENGERS FROM TRAINS 2, 4 AND 24 JOIN AT DINNER

6:30 p. m. Dinner, Alvarado. Evening free: Attention is drawn to Indian Museum at Indian Building, Alvarado
Overnight, Alvarado Hotel

Second Day—Puye Detour—Eastbound

(PASSENGERS FROM TRAINS 2, 4 AND 24)

8:00 a. m. Breakfast, Alvarado Hotel
9:00 a. m. Leave Alvarado Hotel by Harveycar
10:45-11:45 a. m. Santo Domingo Pueblo
1:00 p. m. Arrive La Fonda Hotel, Santa Fé
1:30 p. m. Lunch, La Fonda Hotel
3:30 p. m. Drive about Old Santa Fé, visiting Governor's Palace, Old Museum, San Miguel Church, etc.
6:00 to 7:00 p. m. Dinner, La Fonda
8:00 p. m. Informal Lecture, La Fonda
Overnight, La Fonda*

Day of Departure—Puye Detour—Eastbound

7:00 to 8:00 a. m. Breakfast, La Fonda
8:45 a. m. Leave La Fonda by Harveycar
9:10-9:25 a. m. Tesuque Indian Pueblo
10:10-10:30 a. m. Santa Clara Indian Pueblo
11:15 a. m. Arrive Puyé Cliff Ruins
12:00 noon Lunch, Puyé Rest House
1:15 p. m. Leave Puyé Cliff Ruins
3:00 p. m. Arrive La Fonda, Santa Fé

3:35 p. m. Passengers for Train No. 2 (The Navajo) leave La Fonda for Lamy by Harveycar
4:45 p. m. Train No. 2 leaves Lamy, eastbound

4:45 p. m. Passengers for Train No. 4 (1st California Limited) leave La Fonda for Lamy by Harveycar
5:50 p. m. Train No. 4 leaves Lamy eastbound

7:50 p. m. Passengers for Train No. 24 (2nd California Limited) leave La Fonda for Lamy by Harveycar
8:55 p. m. Train No. 24 leaves Lamy, eastbound

NOTE: Passengers for Train No. 4 take dinner after boarding train at Lamy.
Passengers for Train No. 24 take dinner at La Fonda at 6:00 p. m., before departure for Lamy by Harveycar.

3

SUBJECT TO CHANGE WITHOUT NOTICE

A motor-link unique in transcontinental rail travel

Schedules

3 Days $57.50

The Taos-Puyé Detour

Westbound

EFFECTIVE MAY 15, 1928

(Cancels all previous schedules)

Day of Arrival at Lamy

TRAIN No. 3	TRAIN No. 23
1st California Limited	2nd California Limited
9:15 a. m. Arrive Lamy	9:50 a. m. Arrive Lamy

Guests met at trains by Couriers

(PASSENGERS FROM BOTH TRAINS)

10:10 a. m.   Leave El Ortiz Hotel by Harveycar
11:15 a. m.-12:00 noon   Cicuyé (Pecos Ruins)
12:15 p. m.   Arrive Apache Inn (Valley Ranch) for Lunch
1:45 p. m.   Leave Apache Inn (Valley Ranch)
3:00 p. m.   Arrive La Fonda Hotel, Santa Fé
3:30 p. m.   Drive about Old Santa Fé, visiting Governor's Palace, Old Museum, San Miguel Church, etc.
6:00 to 7:00 p. m.   Dinner, La Fonda
8:00 p. m.   Informal Lecture, La Fonda
Overnight, La Fonda*

Second Day—Taos-Puye Detour—Westbound

(PASSENGERS FROM BOTH TRAINS)

7:00 to 8:00 a. m.   Breakfast, La Fonda
8:45 a. m.   Leave La Fonda by Harveycar
9:10- 9:25 a. m.   Tesuque Indian Pueblo
10:10-10:30 a. m.   Santa Clara Indian Pueblo
11:15 a. m.   Arrive Puyé Cliff Ruins
12:00 noon   Lunch, Puyé Rest House
1:15 p. m.   Leave Puyé Cliff Ruins
3:00 p. m.   Arrive La Fonda, Santa Fé
6:00 to 8:00 p. m.   Dinner, La Fonda
Overnight, La Fonda*

Third Day—Taos-Puye Detour—Westbound

(PASSENGERS FROM BOTH TRAINS)

7:00 to 8:00 a. m.   Breakfast, La Fonda
8:30 a. m.   Leave La Fonda, proceed via Rio Grande Canyon and Ranchos de Taos to Taos
11:30 a. m.   Arrive Don Fernando Hotel, Taos
12:00 noon   Lunch, Don Fernando Hotel
1:00 to 3:00 p. m.   Visits to Taos Pueblo, Kit Carson House and Grave, Artist Colony, etc.
3:30 p. m.   Leave Don Fernando, Taos
6:30 p. m.   Arrive La Fonda, Santa Fé
6:30 to 8:00 p. m.   Dinner, La Fonda
Overnight, La Fonda*

Day of Departure—Taos-Puye Detour—Westbound

7:00 to 8:00 a. m.   Breakfast, La Fonda
8:15 a. m.   Leave La Fonda by Harveycar
9:30-9:55 a. m.   Santo Domingo Pueblo
11:15 a. m.   Arrive Alvarado Hotel, Albuquerque

11:45 a. m.   Train No. 3 (1st Cal. Limited) leaves westbound
12:15 p. m.   Train No. 23 (2nd Cal. Limited) leaves westbound

*See bottom page 2

4

Eastbound

EFFECTIVE MAY 15, 1928

(Cancels all previous schedules)

Day of Arrival—Albuquerque

TRAIN No. 2	TRAIN No. 4	TRAIN No. 24
THE NAVAJO	FIRST CALIFORNIA LIMITED	SECOND CALIFORNIA LIMITED
2:00 p. m. Arrive Albuquerque. Lunch Alvarado Hotel	3:10 p. m. Arrive Albuquerque	6:15 p. m. Arrive Albuquerque
3:30 p. m. Isleta Drive	3:30 p. m. Isleta Drive	

Guests met at trains by Couriers

PASSENGERS FROM TRAINS 2, 4 AND 24 JOIN AT DINNER

6:30 p. m.   Dinner, Alvarado. Evening free: Attention is drawn to Indian Museum at Indian Building, Alvarado
Overnight, Alvarado Hotel

Second Day—Taos-Puye Detour—Eastbound

(PASSENGERS FROM TRAINS 2, 4 AND 24)

8:00 a. m.   Breakfast, Alvarado Hotel
9:00 a. m.   Leave Alvarado Hotel by Harveycar
10:45-11:45 a. m.   Santo Domingo Pueblo
1:00 p. m.   Arrive La Fonda Hotel, Santa Fé
1:30 p. m.   Lunch, La Fonda Hotel
3:30 p. m.   Drive about Old Santa Fé, visiting Governor's Palace, Old Museum, San Miguel Church, etc.
6:00 to 7:00 p. m.   Dinner, La Fonda
8:00 p. m.   Informal Lecture, La Fonda
Overnight, La Fonda*

Third Day—Taos-Puye Detour—Eastbound

The schedule for this day is identical with that shown on previous page for the Third Day Taos-Puyé Detour Westbound.

Day of Departure—Taos-Puye Detour—Eastbound

7:00 to 8:00 a. m.   Breakfast, La Fonda
8:45 a. m.   Leave La Fonda by Harveycar
9:10- 9:25 a. m.   Tesuque Indian Pueblo
10:10-10:30 a. m.   Santa Clara Indian Pueblo
11:15 a. m.   Arrive Puyé Cliff Ruins
12:00 noon   Lunch, Puyé Rest House
1:15 p. m.   Leave Puyé Cliff Ruins
3:00 p. m.   Arrive La Fonda, Santa Fé

3:35 p. m.   Passengers for Train No. 2 (The Navajo) leave La Fonda for Lamy by Harveycar
4:45 p. m.   Train No. 2 leaves Lamy, eastbound

4:45 p. m.   Passengers for Train No. 4 (1st California Limited) leave La Fonda for Lamy by Harveycar
5:50 p. m.   Train No. 4 leaves Lamy, eastbound

7:50 p. m.   Passengers for Train No. 24 (2nd California Limited) leave La Fonda for Lamy by Harveycar
8:55 p. m.   Train No. 24 leaves Lamy, eastbound

NOTE: Passengers for Train No. 4 take dinner after boarding train at Lamy.
Passengers for Train No. 24 take dinner at La Fonda at 6:00 p. m., before departure for Lamy by Harveycar.

5

Roebuck, or a few hundred at Abercrombie & Fitch, would see them through the trip with possibly a change to a simple dress or suit and lighter shoes for dinner, plus of course the usual change of underclothing and toiletries.

For men, the recommended clothing of the Detours and Cruises were Bedford cord or corduroy breeches with matching belted jacket. High hose was used with stout shoes and often, especially in the colder months, laced puttees. The whole outfit at Sears cost under $20, even with a vest and matching cap thrown in.

The ladies could choose either a knife-pleated skirt, or with the thought of climbing into Indian ruins and remaining modest, it was suggested she also wear breeches. These could be the riding type with flared styling or the recently introduced blousy knickers. Riding boots, or high heavy hose with sturdy walking shoes were advised. With this, the ladies could select either a tailored shirt, or feel more feminine in one that was pleated; and a cloche hat was a must, especially when riding in an open car. A sweater or jacket was warm enough for all but the winter months, when a heavy coat was added. And the bill at Sears on all this, minus the coat, was a mere $15.

The baggage problem disposed of, the Santa Fe moved on to charges for the transfer from Lamy to La Fonda, deciding a 90¢ charge for the 18 miles was necessary. After all, passengers had been given a free ride ever since 1916 and where there had been only four trains daily in each direction in 1916, now there were twelve. A corresponding number of baggage runs were made to assure the dudes their luggage wouldn't be delayed reaching their rooms.

Charges for the tours were increased to keep up with the changing expenses. The shakedown had shown the starting price was too low, so the three-day Indian Detour trip which had been $45 per person in 1926, and had been increased to $50 on May 1, 1927, was finally set at $57.50 on May 15, 1928. It was expanded to include Taos and to cover 100 more miles so the increase did not appear to be a rate boost. This trip was listed as the Taos-Puyé trip.

The Taos trip on the 'Road to Yesterday' schedule was increasingly popular. There were so many things to see along the way, the dudes had little time to worry about the primitive road. First, the cars paused to take a quick look at

Santa Niño, a small settlement on the way to Española. Small ranch houses along the way were pointed out and their Spanish names spelled out. The Mormon settlement of Fair View was sometimes driven through if time permitted.

Having heard of the Penitentes, the dudes were most curious about the village of Alcalde and would whisper to each other as the car drove slowly through the dusty streets. Next, they exclaimed over the postoffice at one of the many settlements along the road, surprised to find a letter would be delivered in such hinterlands.

The railroad station was pointed out at Embudo, and then the courier drew attention to the safety glass feature of the car they were riding in and explained that here a crusher and revolving drum made fine particles of the ore called lapidolite, mined nearby. The powder was then placed in shipping containers, loaded onto freight trains and sent to Philadelphia where it was used in making the strong windshield glass.

In rapid succession they were shown Ciénega, La Bolsa, Rinconada, with the English translations of 'meadow', 'the pocket', and 'corner'. A stop was made at the last village to examine the two gate posts at one of the houses. They were capstans, one marked 'David Havre' and the other 'Mercury'. They were from a Mississippi river boat that had been retired and shipped to New Mexico to work as a dredge on the Rio Grande by a New York company mining for gold. Before it could be used, a cloudburst sent a wall of water down the canyon that tore the boat from its mooring, smashing it into kindling. Parts of the boat were found along the highway for miles, including the two capstans, the only parts still intact.

If the dudes felt in need of a short walk, they were given a brief chance to explore some pictographs before being given a tour of 'Woody's Mill', a gold mill that had been turned into a wheat grinding operation.

The last village before the spectacular drive through the Taos canyon was Ciéneguilla, 'Little Marsh'. There was an old church with a shiny new roof and an old story which this time was not a legend, but an historical fact.

At the time when Kit Carson was living in Taos, a band of Apaches laid siege to the town. In the dark of night, a messenger from the village went to Taos to ask Carson's help, and he obliged by sending a group of soldiers to the village the next morning. When they arrived, they found only a camp fire at the approach to the village, with an aged Apache squaw crouched beside it. They killed her, hung her to a tree limb and rode back out of the canyon to a mesa.

Before they could regroup, a band of warriors who had been hiding in the brush at the canyon mouth took bits of broken mirrors, reflecting the rising sun into the eyes of the horses. The horses stampeded and plunged over the cliff, killing all the soldiers, six of whom fell down the cliff banks into the Apache ambush. Word of the rout reached Carson before nightfall, and he sent another platoon with wagons to bring the bodies back to Taos for burial.

Taos Pueblo

The dudes were shown seven mounds just outside the village, said to be the six soldiers side by side, with the seventh mound slightly removed and presumably that of the squaw.

The trip then proceeded to the Taos Pueblo where the cars spent an hour before going on to visit Carson's home.

There had been a small problem arise at the pueblo late in the Fall of 1927. The governor had sent word to Clarkson that he wanted to charge admission to the

Young Eagle Dancers

pueblo. Feeling this would be commercializing the trip, Clarkson met with their council to listen to their complaints. He learned the problem stemmed from the fact the other pueblos were doing a brisk business in pottery and jewelry. This left Taos Pueblo out in the cold, since it had nothing but utilitarian pottery; their clay would not polish, they were not craftsmen and neither wove nor worked silver.

Clarkson's suggestion that they open small stores in some of the homes selling items other Indians made was met with underwhelming enthusiasm. Never daunted by problems, Clarkson then suggested they dress up one of the small boys, since the dudes especially enjoyed seeing the children, and have him dance. The suggestion pleased everyone, and it became the pattern for the tourists to walk around the pueblo, following the sound of a beating drum and undulating chants into one of the homes. There one of the young boys in dance costume would put on a showy routine, passing his drum around at the conclusion so the dudes could drop coins on the head. All this pageantry made the repeat customers of the Indian Detours overlook the small price increase.

To compensate for this increase, a new two-day Puyé Tour was introduced. This outing covered 200 miles and was priced at $40 per person. Picking up passengers from Westbound trains in Lamy, the drive was made first to

Cicuyé Ruins. It was an impressive sight for first-timers. The digs had been thoroughly explored and much was known about them. Each of the two communal houses had been four stories in height and had accommodated a total of 2500 people. The church had been built in 1617 and was properly called Pecos Mission since the pueblo had been built by the Pecos Indians. The name Cicuyé was a derivative of the Isleta name for the pueblo, Sikuye. Shards of the eight different types of pottery made there could be kicked up in the sand, and the dudes grasped broken bits for souvenirs as they headed for lunch at the Valley Inn before being driven to La Fonda.

Giving the guests 30 minutes to stash luggage and wash up, the city tour kept them busy until 6 o'clock, when dinner was served. After dinner, the lectures and slide shows which had proven popular, were given in the small lounge.

The following day the tour visited Tesuque Pueblo, Santa Clara Pueblo and finally the Puyé ruins before returning the dudes to La Fonda for a good night's sleep.

The next morning a brief stop was made at the Santo Domingo Pueblo before reuniting the passengers with their forwarded baggage on either the first California Limited which left at 11:45 A.M., or the second one which left at 12:15 P.M.

Eastbound passengers were met at Albuquerque where they spent the first night at the Alvarado Hotel before being escorted to the same places of interest listed, rejoining one of the three Eastbound trains at Lamy, the first and second California Limiteds or El Navajo.

If returning passengers wanted to stay over a day or two and see more sights, they were encouraged to take a later train. One of the side trips suggested was to Belen, less than an hour's drive south of Albuquerque.

There the dudes were welcomed into the home of the DeBacas, a gentle Spanish family who knew no reason why their house should be chosen for a miracle. Hundreds of people had seen the fabulous window by the time the 1928 Detours were in progress and the dudes were more than anxious to see a miracle rather than hear about one.

The strange phenomenon appeared in the glass of the window on the East gable of the house. The distinct figure of the Madonna could be seen floating in clouds, as in a church painting. The image was visible only in daylight and the glass had been certified as being a pane of ordinary window pane purchased from a local Belen merchant. There was no picture near the window that might have been reflected in the glass, nor anything across the street that could have been mirrored in it. The Madonna could not be seen from inside the house, but after viewing the window from inside, the curious stood outside to see the clear apparition, visible from any angle, intensified if dark material was held against the inside of the pane. Intrigued and convinced there was no chicanery in the miracle, the dudes thanked the DeBacas and returned to the folder map to see what more could be visited if they lingered.

With so many folders flying around, revised folders that replaced already revised folders, the Indian Detour bulletins became a colorful item in the pamphlet racks of train stations and travel agencies. A large 72-page folder was introduced with many photographs and maps bringing the reader up to date. The usual small schedule folder was also reprinted and revised, and where old folders had all been printed in red-orange and black, the new folders were in blue and dull green to avoid confusion, and enable agents to destroy old issues. One point hammered home was that the tours had never failed to go on schedule in the 730 days the Indian Detours had been offered.

The new 1928 folders were once more the product of Birdseye's enthusiastic pen.

> In Northern New Mexico, the Santa Fe follows the line of least resistance across a region of concentrated interest unique in America or abroad.
> Behind the narrow train horizons are hidden primitive Mexican villages, Spanish missions, Indian pueblos, prehistoric cliff dwellings, and buried cities — all set in the matchless scenery and climate of the Southern Rockies.
> New Mexico's mystifying ruins were left by the oldest races in America. Her changeless inhabited Indian pueblos were rooted in antiquity before Columbus sailed. Her picturesque adobe villages have been built by the descendants of the Spanish Conquistadores who fought their way northward from Old Mexico nearly four centuries ago. Many of her quaint Mission churches antedate those of California by 150 years. Here history is the thrilling, little-told record of a remote and endless frontier.

Everyone connected with the Detours was pleased

La Fonda in 1928

Projected expansion

with the response to the folders, except possibly David Cole, manager of La Fonda, who found the gracious hostelry was bursting at the seams. It was decided the only solution was to enlarge the hotel as quickly as possible. Immediate plans were drawn up for the expansion and the drawings of the projected tripling of capacity were reproduced in an agents' bulletin and sent out at once, even though the remodeling would not be finished for another year.

The expansion would bring one wall close to the End of the Santa Fe Trail marker, and excavators dug up such early relics as a cannon ball and an old Civil War Colt revolver. Even a human skeleton was unearthed and hastily transported to a more hallowed grave.

One of the planned expansions was the building of a special lounge in the lobby for the couriers. The pamphlet-littered desk was the focal point of the tours, and it was felt it would be better to have the couriers occupy a room apart in the lobby. Erna Fergusson breathed a sigh of relief, sat down at her desk, and wrote a story of the Indian Detours for the October issue of The American Motorist.

A 1928 Packard ad

Indian Dances of the Southwest

Southwestern Indians are a dancing people. Whether they live in mud-hut villages and till the fields for a living, or wander the plains with flocks and herds, they love to dance. Indians dance for pleasure, to be sure, but primarily they dance for prayer. For centuries they have been Christians, converts first to the Catholic Church and later and more sketchily to Protestant churches. When matters of importance arise, however, the Indian is at once a pagan, appealing to his ancient gods for the real things of life. For rain and sun and the successful hunt and especially for water he goes to the tribal gods. With the Indian it is water, water, either everywhere or nowhere. He lives in an arid land which is subject to occasional devastating floods. Usually the land is dry and it is only by means of repeated and persistent dance-prayers that he gets from the gods enough rain and snow to mature his crops or to supply enough grass for his herds.

White people, impressed with their own importance and that of their dollars, often assume that Indians dance only for white spectators. This is emphatically not so. Many of the dances are strictly secret and no whites are permitted to see them. Many of them are not announced in the white man's towns and often a hundred or more men and women, beautifully costumed, and carefully trained, will dance all day with only their own people as audience.

Motorists crossing New Mexico and Arizona are often literally within a stone's throw of such a fine ceremony and, not knowing of it, they pass by. Usually the Indian village is a mile or more off the highway, and the motorist does not even know that he is crossing a country of marvelous primitive pageantry and that, by lowering his proud record of three hundred miles a day, he may see a ceremony much older than history.

Where to go and what to do when there are the two problems. First, it is usually worth while to visit every Indian village. Even if no dance is in progress other things will repay the time. Potters and basketmakers and workers in turquoise are interesting to see. It is worth while, too, just to make friends with a shy, proud people in their homes. The crude white tourist who looks upon Indians as animals in a zoo meets with very little attention. Poking his head into an open window with "Is there anything worth looking at in here?" he is apt to be met with a gently closed door and silence.

The visitor who approaches with courtesy and with quietness gets a very different reception. A very wise gesture is to call first upon the governor. Every village elects its own governor, usually a dignified man who appreciates an attitude of respect and consideration. Ask anyone for the governor and call at his house. He will smoke your cigarettes. His wife and children will accept candy. Scatterings of small coins are apt to offend. If they do not offend they will certainly finally corrupt a people who are now very proud of being self-supporting. No more winning gift can be offered than feathers. Green or blue feathers are preferred, as they are like the parrot feathers which are the choicest possession of every tribe and which probably have come through from Central America. Feathers for the governor, candy for the youngsters, or a brilliant silk handkerchief for the governor's lady will show that you are a friend understanding the ways of courtesy.

This is how to see the dances. When is another question. Oddly enough, many Indian pueblos celebrate their ancient festivals on Catholic saints' days. This is due to the Indian's pleasant disposition to pay respect to all religions. He is quite willing to make a polite and distant bow in the general direction of whatever church is handy — and powerful. Each village celebrates the day of its own patron saint. The canny traveler will watch the Catholic calendar and arrange his tour in such a way as to reach San Juan on Saint John's Day or Santa Clara on Saint Clara's Day. All important festivals like Christmas and Easter and even lesser ones are celebrated in nearly every village. Bearing this in mind, one may count on seeing a dance somewhere at almost every season.

Among the pueblo, or village people the year's dance cycle may be said to begin in the spring. When the melting snows begin to roll in brown floods down the streams, the ditches are dug out to receive them and the people dance their prayer for plenty of water to last all summer. Such a dance is largely pantomimic. In the pueblo of Isleta the motions of the dancers indicate the slow spreading of waters over the fields, the ploughing and harrowing, the falling of the summer rains. This ceremony is followed by a long series of similar ones which are practically the same in all pueblos. The white man calls them Corn Dances and the Indian accepts his name. In Taos the growth of the corn is typified by the successive dancing groups. Every few weeks a dance takes place. First children dance, then youths and maidens, then young married people, and finally when the corn is ripe, mature men and women.

There are differences in different villages, but on the whole such a day follows certain lines. The day begins, as in all Catholic towns, with mass sung by a Franciscan monk, most likely, in the adobe mission church. All the Catholic Indians, and that is the bulk of the population, attend mass. Then the image of the patron saint is carried in procession around the village and placed in a shrine. Here appears the odd comingling of Christian and pagan. The saint, set behind candles on a simple altar, is guarded by two long-haired Indians with rifles across their knees, and surrounded with the best examples of Indian work that the village affords. The monk prays, the rifles are fired, the people kneel and then, just as the Catholic atmosphere is thickest, far off is heard the beat of the tom-tom.

Soon a group of old men comes pounding in, chanting to the beat of the tom-tom, their old faces lifted in the song, their hands moving rhythmically, their long hair swinging in braids or chignons. Following them come the dancers from the kiva. The kiva is the ceremonial lodge. It is sacred and secret, it is the center of the village life, and its standing shows no signs of yielding to the importance of the church. The dancers come up from within and pour down the ladder in a brilliant stream. The women, demure with dropped eyes and long hair, wear simple black wool garments and brilliant crown-like structures of turquoise blue. They carry tight bouquets of flowers or evergreen to symbolize eternal life. The men are stripped to the waist and painted. Their hair is worn long and fox skins hang from the waist behind. On their kirtles and sashes are embroidered the symbols of water and growth — black for clouds, green for crops, red for sun. Men and women enter in two long rows, the men beating on the ground with their feet, shaking their gourd rattles, insistently demanding the attention of the gods. The women shuffle, keeping their feet on the ground to get from it a reproductive power and bring forth many children. The rhythm is queer and exciting with tricky changes. The figures shift with the changing beat. Usually one dancer in the middle of the line begins to turn. He is followed by the others in succession until, like wind moving through corn, all have turned. Sometimes the women dance each meekly behind her man; sometimes they weave in and out in intricate patterns. With the exception of the rhythm, which is more complicated than it looks, the dance is simple enough. It lasts all day, two teams taking part. Occasionally there are strange lonely dancers, the Koshare, who represent the spirits of the dead. They are supposed to be invisible to the dancers and having absolute license they are often very funny.

As autumn comes on and the crops are gathered, the ceremonials are in gratitude for a successful season with pleas for more of the same, or better. The most magnificent of these autumn ceremonies is that of the Shalako at Zuni. This is a masked dance. All the pueblos undoubtedly have masked dances, but they are held secretly. Only at Zuni and in

Top: Along the Rio Grande between Santa Fe and Taos
Center: The Hoop Dance of Taos
Bottom: Harvest Dancers at Santa Clara

the Hopi villages may the casual visitor see these amazing rites.

It is the culmination of the religious year of the Zunis. Even the gods come to the village where new houses are prepared for their reception. Only seeing this dance can give an idea of its compelling fascination. About thirty figures appear. The Shalako, numbering four are tall, weird beings, draped in skins and hand woven garments. They wear monumental masks, which make them about nine feet high. Attendant figures are almost as huge and quite as magnificent in garments of white deer skin, heavily beaded moccasins, and masks in black and white and turquoise blue and orange. It is a riot of color. Lesser characters are the cardinal points, east, north, west, south, the zenith and the nadir. A small boy, messenger of the fire god, carries a burning brand and his little body is spotted with the colors of the flame. Beginning in the late afternoon, a bewildering series of dances and formal ceremonies goes on until the next noon. Visitors tramp from house to house all through a long cold December night. They stand in the cold or sit in a house redolent of many Navajos, and they bring back word that nothing the Russian ballet has ever done is so brilliant, so full of color, so weirdly magnificent. As one said, "It is the most gorgeous thing in the world and all you have to do is to hold on and not smell too much."

Christmas brings another sort of dance. Then it is important to bring back the sun which, as has been noticed, grows weaker and weaker until it almost slips away. Indians know how to bring it back and every year they do so. In some places, with the broad tolerance of the Catholic priests, pagan dances are permitted in Catholic churches. First the midnight mass and then the pagan dance. "We dance," the Indians will explain, "in honor of the Christ Child." "Why not?" said one old priest. "After all, it is their religious expression, they do it reverently, and it does not offend me." So Christmas and New Year's are times of dancing, too. On twelfth night there are dances in honor of the newly elected governors who that day take office. Finally, to bring the year back to the spring, every village has its hunting dances.

These are the most definitely dramatic of all. In some cases, an entire drama of the hunt is played out. Deer, antelope, mountain goats and buffalo, dressed in skins and with real antlers or horns, prance and lumber through a forest symbolized by a dozen little cedar trees stuck in the ground. With every animal in character the whole is still a harmonious dance. Even the hunters with bows and arrows move in perfect rhythm with the varied steps of the animals. Only the comedy character has absolute license. In these dances he is the white man. Usually an old frock coat, a straw hat, and a blunderbuss of a gun are his properties. He falls awkwardly over his own feet or he rides a stick for a horse and is ignominiously thrown. He startles the game. He impedes the dancers. He brings roars of mirth from his Indian audience. The white who thinks of the Indian as a stolid being with no sense of humor should see an Indian take him off some day!

All of these ceremonies take place in New Mexico and belong to the pueblo people. It only begins the list of ceremonies, however, for there are the Navajos with their wealth of mysticism, the Apaches who go in for wild, blood-curdling yells, the Hopis of Arizona, who are world-famous for their Snake Dance. Navajo dances occur in the winter. "After the thunder sleeps," they say — which means after the season of thunder storms is over and frost has come — they hold great sings which are often attended by more than a thousand Navajos. The ceremonies last for days, are surrounded with deep mystery; and they permit outsiders to see only an occasional part. Eastern conjurers would be interested in the feather dance in which a feather stands upright in a basket and, untouched and alone, dances in time with a dancing man. Weirder and wilder than any is the fire dance. Old men sing in their typical, complaining note, while young men, smeared with gray earth, leap and bound through the flames, beating themselves and each other with burning brands, and trilling high mad calls.

Motorists crossing the southwestern States are nearer to the primitive than anywhere else on the continent. They are crossing a land in which a foreign people, with foreign speech and foreign ways, offer them spectacles which can be equaled in very few Oriental lands. Fortunately most travelers are naturally courteous and they will witness these dances without offending the simple people who perform them and without feeling obliged to stamp out reverent ceremonies because they are different.

Most of the spectators were reverent and very few unpleasant episodes occurred. The couriers were instructed to lay down the ground rules of dude behavior before arriving in the pueblos. There were a few instances when the dudes forgot. Usually open hostility could be avoided, but this depended on the individual pueblo.

At Santa Clara, the Tewas were a gentle people. Dorothy Raper had told her group not to climb on any buildings in the pueblo, to stay away from the dancing ground and not say anything in the belief they would not be understood. She turned around to speak to some of the Indians she knew and one of them suddenly pointed to one of the rooftops. Standing there were two people from San Francisco and she called for the driver to get them down at once, making her way to the governor who was standing impassively watching them. She started to apologize for the dudes' behavior when the governor raised his hand stiffly for silence and said solemnly, "some people have no breeding."

The Indians at Santo Domingo were the hardest to deal with and were often unpredictable. Many of the dudes wondered why there were three men standing on each kiva when they drove up. It was explained these men were called look-outs and they were there because they had knowledge that a large number of 'White Skins' were coming into the village. Because they knew the 'White Skins' did not obey the Indians' admonitions, they were there to guard the kivas from intrusion.

Clarkson's assistant, Ellis Bauer, was once called upon to drive a party of Italian Air Force members, 20 men

Left: "White Skin" Lookout on Santo Domingo Kiva

Below: Harveycar on the highway near Chapelle, N.M.

and General Italo Balbo, on the three-day Detour because he knew how to handle a bus and a regular bus driver was unavailable. Loading up the men in the early evening, the trip was a special one. The moon was full, making day out of night in the crystal air, and a 'Happiness Dance' was going on at Santo Domingo. It was November and a time of gift giving when everything from live chickens, rabbits, canned goods and dead field mice — a great delicacy to the Indians — would be exchanged.

Eagle Dance at Santa Clara. Note similarity to John Sloan's etching

The men were warned not to attempt to take any pictures, even though the bright moon would permit it. There were two busloads on the tour, and as they drew up to the pueblo, fully half the men grabbed their cameras, jumped off the bus, and started snapping away at the dancing Indians. Without a sound, Indians poured out of every doorway, all carrying clubs. The two drivers lit out at a dead run to round up the scattering men, but before they could get them back on the buses, there was a general smashing of cameras that started by knocking them to the ground with the clubs and then jumping up and down on them.

Before that episode, the Santo Domingans had imposed a head charge on the groups, but the next day notice was sent to Clarkson's office that no more groups would be allowed to stop at the pueblo. It took a heap big powwow to open the pueblo to visitors again.

Shortly after the Harveycars were allowed in Santo Domingo again, a group of dudes was taken to see the January 6th 'Day of Three Kings' celebration when animal dances were performed. One lady feeling the call of nature was searching frantically for something that looked familiar to her and finally resorted to hiding behind one of the hogans. Busily engaged, she was interrupted by a squaw who held out a hand and said "that 10¢." Not inclined to argue, the lady paid off.

Many of the dudes objected to being charged a fee for photographing the Indians at work and play, and the couriers were instructed to soothe the irate tourists by saying, "after all, they must interrupt their work dozens of times a day to pose for pictures. This is simply to defray the cost of lost worktime."

A Harveycoach at Tesuque. Bake ovens in foreground, church at left

The couriers, one and all, grew to hate cameras. Rainey Bartley was asked by one of her friends if she had trouble telling the Chinese dudes from the Japanese, for there were many Orientals on the trips. She replied it was easy; the Japanese all had cameras. But they weren't the only ones, so did the Germans and the Dutch and the British and the Americans.

One of the Couriers learned to hate cameras when a dude had her jump off the same cliff ruin at Puyé a half dozen times because he forgot to wind the film right. Another made the driver wait two hours for a second train to round the bend because he had double exposed the first shot.

When publicity photos were needed by Birdseye, a special trip was made in slack time, using couriers and drivers dressed as dudes, and at no time was there an official photographer on trips other than large convention-type excursions; then the photographer was usually one of the convention employees.

Long before Erna Fergusson's 1928 story appeared, many magazines carried coupon ads for information on the tours, and apparently these had a wider circulation than originally expected. Inquiries came from over 50 foreign countries and territories. On the first tour in May, 1928, Detourists were registered from Australia, Germany, Panama, Ceylon, Holland and Japan. Total participants for the twelve months of May 1927 — May 1928 was up 24% from the first year, yet rail traffic in general had been falling off at an alarming rate, mainly because of the increase in personal motor travel. It was projected the final 1928 Indian Detour figures would show a 50% increase over the previous year.

The Indian Detours were alive and well.

10

THE WHERE OF IT — 1929

By the beginning of 1929, the new trips being offered were growing so fast the folders were hard put to keep up with the changes. By the writing standards of today, the brochures were too full of flowery promises; judged by the writing styles of the period, they were just the kind of description needed to get tourists to sign on the dotted train ticket. And that's exactly what they were handed, a dotted train ticket on which could be entered any tour or combination of tours the train traveler might decide on while en route across the country. A lot of the travelers did decide as they read the deluxe 86 page folder they were handed at the train station. The first five paragraphs hooked the reader with romance.

Of the beaten paths in our Far Southwest, few are of the kind we all know. More are of a very different sort.

The few are the steel ribbons of the railroads, following lines of least resistance across immensity. The many are the paths of the Indians, worn inches deep in solid rock by moccasined feet; the ways of the sandalled padres and steel-clad soldiers of Spain; the trails of the fur-capped mountain men; and the broad tracks blazed by those in buckskin and deepened under the dust clouds of plodding pack trains and Covered Wagons.

It is with the latter that this folder has to deal. They lead away into the hinterlands of New Mexico and Arizona, far from the familiar beaten path of the railroad. They criss-cross a last frontier that has taken 350 years to subdue. They find out buried cities that flourished when Britons crouched in caves, reach medieval Spain dreaming away the centuries in the mountains of America, and string together age-old Indian pueblos where one may "catch archaeology alive." They seek out the mines, the lumber camps, the open ranges and the painted canyons of the least-known and most fascinating corner of the United States.

Those who are passing on into the setting sun made the Southwest safe. The railroad made its gateways accessible. It needed only the automobile, dragging better roads behind it, to let down the last barriers of time and distance, discomfort and inconvenience, that for so long barred the Southwest to any but the pioneer.

During nearly fifty years, transcontinental travelers have been familiar with the high ideals of efficiency and service maintained by the Santa Fe Railway and the Fred Harvey System. Those ideals now find new expression in a Southwestern motor service for the most discriminating traveler.

The folder went on to explain the courier corps and their duties. Knowing the folder would be around for awhile, a section was devoted to the remodeling of La Fonda. It was pointed out the building would be a stepped back design, patterned after the famous Taos pueblo, rising to five stories. The fifth floor would offer four- and five-room suites with private balconies to give the resident a view of the surrounding mountain ranges. Fireplaces of the adobe Indian style were in each suite. A total of 160 rooms, almost all with private bath, would mean no one had to be turned away from a New Mexico holiday. Outside single rooms with bath were priced at $6.00, double rooms with bath were $8.00. And when it opened formally in the Spring of '29, it was booked solid.

In true Spanish style, the new wing was built to enclose a flagstone patio, glass enclosed for winter use, the glass removable for summer. A new lounge was exclusively for the couriers, and included a library filled with books on the Southwest and photographs of places to be visited. Colored slides were available to any viewer who wanted to see the attractions in living hues.

A new lecture lounge had been built to relieve the overcrowding in the original room where evening talks, dance programs and plays were presented. Moving pictures were thrown on a large screen, placques of the various ceremonials hung on the walls, and a large fireplace was kept burning.

A museum-type room, the Indian Room, housed part of

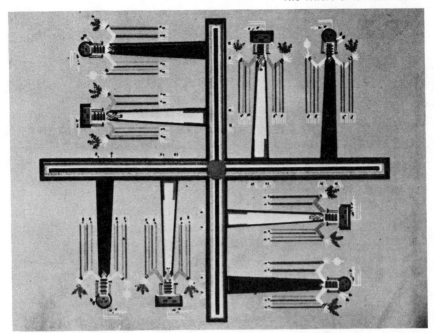

One of the controversial Sand Paintings

the Fred Harvey Indian collection and many pieces of his Mexican artifacts. Antique chimayos shared space with colorful serapes, church relics from old missions were in niches flanked by Navajo rugs, basketry and pottery were accented by Spanish mantillas and rebozos.

To keep the Spanish flavor of the area, a special room, The New Mexican Room, was the dance center with a Mexican mariachi band playing every weekday evening for dinner and dancing. On Sunday, the gay songs and swinging strings were replaced with a decorous chamber music program. The new Fonda was everything the folder had promised it would be.

The folder gave adequate if not equal time to the Alvarado Hotel in Albuquerque and El Navajo Hotel in Gallup, assuring the tourists no matter where they stayed, Harvey would see they were pleased.

El Navajo had been an old hotel, built originally in 1895, but it was one of the Harvey Houses that was completely renovated. In the updating of 1922, replicas of Indian sand paintings were made to hang on the walls. The Navajos objected to the use of what to them is a sacred symbol and the Harvey system ordered them removed at once. It was a lack of communication more than a grievous error, for once the Navajos learned it would create a hardship for a company they had always been on good business and personal terms with, they suggested a proper dedication to their gods would remove any stigma from the decoration. The paintings were hung, and a proper 'sing' was held by Navajo medicine men.

Since the Harveycars were not stationed at Gallup, it was necessary for the folder to point out there was a charge of $24.75 to deadhead the car, driver and courier from or to Albuquerque, but the importance of Gallup as a headquarter point for tours into Arizona had been realized for some time. In the past, train passengers had left the train at Adamana, West of Gallup, hurried into tour cars, dashed around the Petrified Forest, snapped fast photos of the Painted Desert, and hurried back to the station at Adamana to catch the next train for their destination.

The Arizona tour had not been touted very loudly, taking second place to the New Mexican tours, and leaving the sightseeing in Arizona to those who still flocked to the Grand Canyon as they had for the past 30 years. Letters like the one a Dr. Watkins wrote the Santa Fe System caught Hunter Clarkson's attention enough to schedule trips to the Forest and Desert beginning in 1929.

> . . . While I am writing, I want to say a word to you in regard to the Petrified Forest. When we went to the Petrified Forest from Santa Fe and left the train at Adamana, there was only one other person stopped off there to see the Petrified Forest. That was three from the whole train and as the conductor said, there should have been twenty-five or thirty leaving the train at that place and I am sure that if the Fred Harvey system was to start a hotel near there and advertise the Petrified Forest, there would be one hundred people a day at least stopping off to see it. As I consider it one of the most marvelous things I have ever seen and am thoroughly enthusiastic over it I am spending a good deal of time in telling all of my friends about it . . .
>
> Yours very truly,
>
> (Signed) Dr. G. C. G. Watkins

The inclusion of this region as a Land Cruise was received with enthusiasm and takers, but there were still some who felt the trips should have been made an Indian Detour type of outing, with a set party fee. One of the many who expressed their feelings was a Mr. H. H. Winn, who wrote:

"I hope to make another trip with you next Fall to take in the Painted Desert region, providing I can join some small party. The trip is too expensive for a party of one."

Mr. Winn had a point. While the folder listed twelve Indian Detour cruises with prices very much the same as the previous year, the balance of thirteen Land Cruises escalated according to the rate card at the end. By the time the traveler figured it out, it was a fairly costly vacation, especially when one or two people were the only interested parties. For instance, the Cruise from Santa Fe to the Grand Canyon was $386 for one person, $404 for two, $422 for three and $540 for four.

Interior of a typical Harveycoach

Courier Henrietta Gloff wrote a report of her first Land Cruise assignment to the Grand Canyon.

Report on a Harveycar Motor Cruise Through the Navajo Country.

April — May 1929

Friday, April 26, 1929.

Left Grand Canyon 9:00 a.m. — took Navahopi Road to Tuba City. This road is always interesting from a scenic standpoint. Pass through

Trailing in to Rainbow Bridge

Elephant's Feet, near Red Lake

The gigantic arch of Rainbow Bridge frames the distant snow-clad slopes of Navajo Mountain. Note horses in lower left corner.

Page from the 1929 brochure showing scenes from the Rainbow Bridge Tour

Gas was available at Kayenta, (Ariz.) Trading Post, the farthest place (168 miles) from a railroad in the U.S.

The Lee's Ferry bridge over the Colorado River

Tusaya forest, stop at the Canyon of the Little Colorado, visit the Melgosa Petrified Forest. At this time of year the Navajo flocks of sheep and goats are especially interesting. It is the lambing season and the whole family is out with the herd. The San Francisco Peaks can be seen in the distance.

Stop at Cameron for lunch. Cross the Suspension Bridge across the Little Colorado and continue on across the Painted Desert to Moencopi. Stops can be made to see the dinosaur tracks and hard sandstone pumpkins. Cross the Moencopi wash and climb a hill to the top of Moencopi Mesa. Moencopi means running water and, indeed, there are so many springs and streams that it is hard to believe this is a Hopi settlement. The Moencopis are an offshoot of the Oraibis. They came to this spot on account of the water but they did not have real homes here until 1879, when the Mormons settled in Tuba City nearby and protected them from the Navajos. The Moencopis make baskets and they are more prosperous than the other Hopi villages.

Tuba City was named for an old Moencopi Chief, Tuba. The government purchased the water rights from the Moencopis and made Tuba City a part of the Navajo Reservation. It is now called the capital of the Navajo Reservation. Here there are a large government hospital and a school for the Navajos. Mr. C. S. Walker is the superintendent and he will be glad to help us at any time. It will not be necessary to call on him though, because Mr. and Mrs. J. B. Stiles, who run and own the Trading Post, have very comfortable rooms and very good food. We reached Tuba City at 4:30, which gave us time to rest and dress for dinner.

Saturday, April 27, 1929.

We left Tuba City at 9:00 o'clock and took the Kayenta Road to the Wetherills. This road is very good in dry weather and the surrounding country beautiful and interesting. Lunch must be taken because there is no cook at Red Lake and while a Trading Post lunch can be eaten along the way, Mrs. Stiles' lunch from Tuba is more appetizing. Take lower road at the left to avoid sand and pass large body of water that looks like a lake and is called Sheep Dip. Cross sandy Mesa to Red Lake where the sand in the lake bottom looks red. Mr. Skeet Stiles is the manager of the Red Lake Store.

Pass through formations that look like elephant's feet and are so called. Take right road to Kayenta (left to Rainbow Lodge). Pass Cow Springs, where Mr. and Mrs. J. B. Smith have a Trading Post and they are most cordial and helpful. From here on the road passes through a region filled with ruins — pottery and arrow heads can be picked up almost anywhere. Pass large groups of rocks, call Thief Rocks, and then down on to the Calamity Flats, so called because they are almost impassable in wet weather. Pass two groups of hogans and then go down into Long House Valley. There is a large ruin on the left side of the road. (We ate our lunch there). Cross Marsh Pass and pass the mouth of the Segi Canyon. Segi Canyon is filled with the ruins of prehistoric Pueblo Villages. The famous Betatakin and Keet Seel Ruins are in Segi Canyon. Pass group of peach trees — which show the Spanish influence. Then around the head of the pass to Kayenta.

Kayenta means bottomless spring. Mr. and Mrs. Wetherill settled here in 1910 because of the spring water on the hill behind their home. Kayenta Lodge is very comfortable and one of the most interesting, if not the *most* interesting spot in the southwest. Here Mr. and Mrs. Wetherill have collected and arranged a very valuable collection of western specimens. It is an education to be here with the Wetherills.

Sunday, April 28th.

We took mules and with Mr. Wetherill as our guide we rode into the Segi Canyon to the Betatakin Ruins. Betatakin is something like Cliff Palace in Mesa Verde, but even more spectacular. Betatakin means hillside house. The Betatakin Indians came from Chin Lee and went to Oraibi. The ceremonial Cave above the main village is not unlike that of Frijoles but is several times larger. Very few tourists have been here and so there are great numbers of arrow heads and shards. This is a very interesting trip and no one will be sorry for having made it.

Monday, April 29th.

An Indian came to Mr. Wetherill and said that he had found a skeleton in Kaykugay Canyon so we drove to the spot and Mr. Wetherill discovered 4 skeletons. He did some digging and we had the privilege of seeing dippers, beads and fetishes brought out of the old burials.

After lunch, we rode to Dine Hutso, a Trading Post about 30 Miles north of Kayenta. This road runs through old Indian grounds and skirts the edge of Monument Valley. The groups of Navajos passed here are very interesting. Plenty of dead pawn can be picked up at Dine Hutso because very few traders get up there. Mr. Ashcroft is the manager of this Post.

Tuesday, April 30th.

We spent the day in Monument Valley. The formations in this Valley are probably the most beautiful and the most interesting in the world. We took our lunch and ate it at the foot of Mitten Rock. The Henry, Carriso and the Ute Mountains can be seen in the distance on this trip. One can continue north to Mesa Verde on this road.

Wednesday, May 1st.

We took our lunch and spent the day in an old Indian battlefield where we found pottery and arrow heads. The glimpses of the Navajos and the scenery are all fascinating on this trip.

Above: Navajo women in Monument Valley

Left: Hopi girls

Thursday, May 2nd.

Spud (Milam) took Col. Blank back to the Grand Canyon. Mrs. Blank and I spent the day with the Wetherills. Mrs. Wetherill knows more about the Navajo than anyone in the world. She has made a collection of Indian herbs and flowers and she has the Indian story and use for all of these plants filed in such a way that anyone can understand them. She has an excellent collection of Sand Paintings and the story that goes with each one. Navajos come into the Wetherill home and hold their council meetings. There are no locks on the Wetherill doors and it is not unusual to find a group of Navajos in the room.

Friday, May 3rd.

Mr. Wetherill took us to the Black Mountains, which is about 12 miles east of Kayenta. The Black Mountain is filled with prehistoric ruins.

Saturday, May 4th.

Spud returned from the Canyon. Mrs. Blank spent the day purchasing clothing for the Navajos, and in buying supplies for the Kayenta Hospital. We also went over the Wetherill library. Mrs. Blank took Mr. Wetherill's books to California with her to have them rebound. She is also planning to have the Plant legends and the Sand Paintings published so that more people may have the opportunity of getting some knowledge of the Navajo.

Sunday, May 5th.

We took the Wetherills to their old home at Ol Jeto, which is just across the state line in Utah. Ol Jeto means Moonlight Waters. It has a lovely location on a stream and among a group of cottonwoods. Trees and water are unusual in this sandy desert country. Mr. and Mrs. Taylor have charge of the Trading Post and will always be glad to see Harveycars. From Ol Jeto we drove to Guilding, which is a Trading Post in Monument Valley. We drove back to Kayenta through Monument Valley just as the sun was setting. This is a very beautiful experience.

Monday, May 6th.

We took lunch with us and started for Rainbow Lodge. This road led through some of the most beautiful country we had seen and we thought we had seen all there was to be seen, by this time. We drove on a hogsback between Piute and Navajo Canyons. The coloring in these two Canyons is as glorious as that in the Grand Canyon. Stops may be made at Inscription House and a visit made to the Inscription House Ruins. (This must be done on mules). We reached Rainbow Lodge at five o'clock and the clean, comfortable cabins were most welcome. Mr. and Mrs. Wilson have charge of Rainbow Lodge and are hospitable and eager to please.

Tuesday, May 7th.

We took mules and a guide and rode to the top of Navajo Mountain. This is a beautiful trip and not too hard for the inexperienced. Mrs. Blank took this trip to see if she thought the mules would be comfortable enough for the Rainbow Bridge trip. (She found them most uncomfortable). The view at the top of Navajo Mountain is wonderful; one can see down into Monument Valley, the Ol Jeto wash, the Carriso, Henry and Clay Hills. It is well worth while.

Wednesday, May 8th.

We left Rainbow Lodge and drove back to Tuba after lunch.

Thursday, May 9th.

We took lunch with us and drove to Lee's Ferry to see the new bridge across the Grand Canyon. This trip is interesting from a scenic standpoint. The road runs along the Painted Desert and the Echo Cliffs. A few miles out there is a spring and a number of willow trees. This spot is called Willow Springs. There is a Trading Post here. The Gap comes next, where Mr. Joe Lee, descendant of the old Mormon Elder, John D. Lee has a Trading Post. He is an interesting talker and he knows a great deal about the country. Guests will find him entertaining. Then on to Cedar Ridge to another Trading Post. After Cedar Ridge the road follows the Echo Cliffs to Marble Canyon. The Vermillion Cliffs are immediately in front of the car and Marble Canyon runs between the Vermillion Cliffs and the Echo Cliffs. The Bridge is really a marvellous piece of engineering and it gave us a thrill to take the first Harveycar across the Grand Canyon. Mr. and Mrs. Buck Lowrie have a Trading Post and Hotel at the Ferry. It is a worth while trip. The round trip covers about 130 miles.

Friday, May 10th.

We spent the morning at Tuba City and drove back to the Grand Canyon in the afternoon. It was a great pleasure to walk into the cool El Tovar and find clean rooms with refreshing baths awaiting us, after two weeks in the desert.

The road from Chin Lee to Kayenta is in good condition and a very interesting loop trip can be made with this in mind: Gallup to Keams, Keams via the Hopi Villages to Tuba, Tuba to Rainbow Lodge, Rainbow Lodge to Kayenta, Kayenta to Chin Lee, Chin Lee to Gallup. Another interesting trip would be from Chin Lee to Kayenta, Kayenta to Rainbow Lodge and Bridge, Rainbow Lodge to Tuba, Tuba to the Canyon.

The 1929 folder was the most complete that would be printed for the tourists; the number of trips was the most that would be offered; the prices were the highest that would be charged. Before the year was out, most people wouldn't have the money for the train ticket, let alone for the frills. But the frills were neatly spelled out.

No. 1.   TAOS — one day *$20.00*

Taos is an Indian pueblo of five terraces, the highest in the Southwest. It is split into two parts by the Taos River, a clear stream that never fails. For background it has a range of forested peaks 12,000 feet high. Its superb setting, splendid Indian types and changeless, picturesque life have made Taos a mecca for artists of national reputation.

The Rio Grande is muddy and sluggish in its lower reaches. On the way to Taos from Santa Fe it is a blue mountain river full of white water. For twenty miles the road follows its rugged canyon and the still deeper one of the Taos River.

The white mission church at Ranchos de Taos, built in 1772, is buttressed like a fortress. Kit Carson is buried at Don Fernando de Taos, where the home of the famous scout from 1858 to 1866 still stands. Here Cruise guests are cared for at the Don Fernando, a new and uniquely interesting hotel. The winding streets of the old frontier town are dotted with studios of well-known artists. The surrounding country is a stronghold of the strange religious society of the Penitentes.

The pueblo of Taos is a few miles beyond Don Fernando de Taos and there is no season of the year when it is not full of interest. The Taos Indians, also, are famous throughout the Southwest for the beauty of their ceremonial dances.

En route to or from Taos, Tesuque or San Juan Pueblos or San Gabriel Ranch may be included without extra charge.

Rate, $20.00 per person, including luncheon. Round-trip 155 miles. Minimum of three fares is required.

No. 1-a.   TAOS VIA THE INDIAN-DETOUR **$15.00**

Cruise No. 1, excepting the slight variations noted in the last paragraph, made in comfortable 11-passenger Harveycar coaches as a part of the regular three-day **Indian-detour**, when seats are available.

No. 2.   TAOS — overnight **$35.00**

Taos Cruise (No. 1) extended overnight. The return to La Fonda is made on the afternoon of the second day.

Rate, including four meals and overnight accommodations with private bath, at the Don Fernando, $35.00 per person. Minimum of three fares required.

No. 3.   TAOS — two days............................... **$38.50**
via Puyé Cliff Dwellings and Santa Clara

Interesting variations in routes are possible on the two-day Taos Cruise. One of the simplest and pleasantest is to leave the main highway near Española, cross the Rio Grande, visit Santa Clara Indian pueblo and climb up Santa Clara Canyon to the great prehistoric cliff dwellings at Puyé, thus including some of the most popular points on the **Indian-detour.**

Rate, including four meals and overnight accommodations, with private bath, at the Don Fernando, $38.50 per person. Round trip, 185 miles. Minimum of three fares required.

No. 4.   TAOS — two days............................... **$40.00**
via Puyé, Santa Clara, Black Mesa, San Ildefonso

The Puyé variation in Cruise No. 3 extended to continue on from Santa Clara down the scenic west bank of the Rio Grande. The road passes close under the Black Mesa of San Ildefonso, recrosses the river at Otowi Bridge and passes through the pueblo of San Ildefonso, famous for its beautiful black pottery. In Tewa mythology Black Mesa, once stormed by the Spanish conquerors, is the center of the universe.

Rates, including four meals and accommodations with private bath, at the Don Fernando, $40.00 per person. Round-trip, 200 miles. Minimum of three fares required.

No. 5.   TAOS — two days............................... **$40.00**
Via Chimayo, Sanctuario, Truchas and Cordova

Still a third variation of the Taos route is to include Chimayo and Sanctuario, on the eastern flank of the Rio Grande Valley, and Truchas and Cordova, high up in the foothills of the Sangre de Cristo Range. *(See Cruise No. 10.)*

Rate, including four meals and accommodations with private bath, at the Don Fernando, $40.00 per person. Round-trip, 200 miles. Minimum of three fares required.

No. 6.   TAOS — two days............................... **$45.00**
With combined variations of Cruises Nos. 4 and 5.

An exceptionally fine two-day cruise may be built up by including, either going to or coming from Taos, the swing to Puyé, Santa Clara, Black Mesa and San Ildefonso, outlined in Cruise No. 4, and on the reverse Chimayo, Sanctuario, Truchas and Cordova, referred to in Cruise No. 5, and described under Cruise No. 10.

Rate, including four meals and accommodations, with private bath, at the Don Fernando, $45.00 per person. Round-trip, 235 miles. Minimum of three fares required.

Above: and Center: Otowi Suspension Bridge

Otowi Rocks

No. 7.   EL RITO DE LOS FRIJOLES — one day **$13.00**

The prehistoric cliff dwellings in the canyon of El Rito de los Frijoles, or The Little River of the Beans, are included in the Bandelier National Monument. The ruins are among the most remarkable in New Mexico, the canyon itself is beautiful and the road to it is unusually interesting.

The latter traverses the valley north of Santa Fe to the pueblo of San Ildefonso, crosses the Rio Grande at the Otowi Bridge and climbs up Otowi Canyon over the scenic Culebra Hill Road. It then passes the ruins at Tsankawi, where a stop is made if desired, and continues on through a forested canyon country to the rim of Frijoles Canyon. There the car is left for luncheon at El Rito Ranch, on the canyon floor.

The communal ruins of Tyuonyi are just below the ranch. The cliff dwellings are hollowed from the base of the soft volcanic cliffs and stretch from the foot of the trail on up the canyon. In many the ancient plaster clings to walls and floors and the ceilings are darkened with the smoke of fires dead a thousand years. Still farther up the canyon is the great Ceremonial Cave and kiva, reached by ladders and rock-cut steps.

Rate, including luncheon, $13 per person. Round trip, 95 miles. No minimum number of guests required.

No. 8.   EL RITO DE LOS FRIJOLES — overnight **$18.00**

Cruise No. 7 extended overnight with the return to La Fonda in time for lunch on second day.

Rate, including three meals and accomodations at El Rito Ranch, $18.00 per person. No minimum number of guests required.

Note. Any Taos Cruise previously outlined may be lengthened to include El Rito de los Frijoles. Delightful combinations are possible.

No. 9.   PECOS RIVER CANYON — one day **$13.00**

The source of the Pecos River, northeast of Santa Fe, is surrounded by five giants of the southern Rockies, each more than 12,000 feet high. Thence the river tumbles southward through its upper canyon to the Santa Fe Trail.

The drive along the old Trail from Santa Fe to Valley Ranch and on up the Pecos is a delightful day's run. Above the Ranch the road follows the windings of the main canyon, crossing back and forth over the clear, swift stream. Indian Creek, Holy Ghost and lesser side-canyons slash back through the mountain wall. The familiar cedar and pinon of the lower elevations give way to alder, aspen, scrub oak and heavy pine.

Usually it is possible to motor up the Pecos as far as the Ranger Station above Cowles Ranch, where a basket lunch is served. In every direction stretches an unspoiled wilderness famous for its excellent hunting and fishing.

Rate, including luncheon, $13.00 per person. Round-trip, 95 miles. Minimum of three fares required.

Note. Courier offices will gladly suggest short variations of this drive, which may also be inserted on itineraries of long Cruises starting or ending at Las Vegas, New Mexico.

**No. 10.   CHIMAYO, SANCTUARIO, TRUCHAS, CORDOVA —
one day** **$13.00**

Chimayo is an historic Mexican village some 35 miles north and slightly east of Santa Fe and away from main traveled routes. Here the Chimayo Rebellion had its inception. Chimayo blankets, woven on century-old foot looms, are noted for their color and design.

Near Chimayo is Sanctuario, often called the Lourdes of New Mexico. Pilgrims from as far away as Colorado, Arizona and Old Mexico come to worship at the shrine. The little 'dobe chapel, screened by great trees, was built in 1816 by Bernardo Abeyta and is embellished with quaint native wood carvings.

Truchas and Cordova are old Spanish settlements — interesting, primitive types of the really remote Mexican towns. Truchas, stretched along a bare ridge in the foothills of the Sangre de Cristo Range at an elevation above 8,000 feet, commands tremendous views of mountain and valley. Cordova clings to the wall of a deep, hidden valley some miles away.

Rate, including luncheon, $13.00 per person. Round-trip, 90 miles. Minimum of three fares required.

For combination of Cruise No. 10 with Taos itineraries, see Cruises Nos. 5 and 6.

No. 11   JEMEZ SPRINGS AND SODA DAM — one day.

The interesting Cruise to Jemez Springs and Soda Dam (No. 21 from Albuquerque) also may be made from Santa Fe.

Rate, including luncheon, $25.00 per person. Round-trip, 200 miles. Minimum of three fares required.

No. 12.   JEMEZ SPRINGS AND SODA DAM — two days.

Cruise No. 11 extended to a more leisurely two-day drive.
Rate, including four meals and accommodations at Jemez Springs, $35.00 per person. Minimum of three fares required.

No. 13.   TAOS AND RED RIVER LOOP — three days.

Any variation of the two-day Cruise from Santa Fe to Taos Pueblo and return (Nos. 3 to 6), extended to three days by including the Red River Loop. Two nights instead of one are spent at the Don Fernando Hotel, Taos, the second day of the Cruise being devoted to an exceptionally scenic 90-mile swing through the Cimarron and Red River canyons, the Mexican villages of Questa and Arroyo Hondo, the Carson National Forest and the upper Taos Valley.

No. 14.   PAGOSA SPRINGS, WOLF CREEK PASS, CONEJOS VALLEY, CUMBRES PASS
Three days — 470 miles.   **June 1st-October 15th.**

First Day — Santa Fe to Pagosa via the primitive Mexican settlements and painted cliffs of Chama Valley, Chama and the Continental Divide. At Pagosa there are immense hot mineral springs. **Second Day** — Pagosa to Conejos Valley, via Wolf Creek Pass, 10,860 feet, and Alamosa and Antonito, Colorado. Overnight at LO Ranch on the Conejos River. **Third Day** — LO Ranch to Santa Fe, via the Cumbres Pass, which straddles the Colorado-New Mexico line at 10,260 feet, and Chama Valley.

This Cruise is one of extraordinary beauty, in part following white water streams through virgin forest and crossing the two loftiest passes in Cruise territory.

No. 15.   PAGOSA SPRINGS, WOLF CREEK PASS, CONEJOS VALLEY, TAOS PUEBLO
Four days — 500 miles.   **June 1st-October 15th.**

The first two days are identical with those of Cruise 14. **Third Day** — LO Ranch, Conejos Valley, to Don Fernando de Taos, New Mexico, via

Above: Harveycars and coaches at Pecos Ruins
Below: Stopping to view the Sangre de Cristo Range

Sunshine Valley, Questa, Carson National Forest, and Sangre de Cristo mountains. Overnight at Don Fernando Hotel, with visits to Taos Pueblo, artists' colony, etc. **Fourth Day** — return to Santa Fe, via Ranchos de Taos, Taos Valley and gorge of the Rio Grande.

The previous folders had not included the coverage of Arizona's Indian country; this one did.

Above: Wolf Creek Pass
Below: Approaching Mesa Verde

Cruises to or from Grand Canyon

There is an increasing demand for special Harveycar Cruises bridging the northern Southwest between such convenient starting points along the Santa Fe main line as Trinidad, Colorado, and Santa Fe and Albuquerque, New Mexico, on the east, and Grand Canyon, Arizona, on the west.

The minimum time required for such one-way Cruises is about seven days from Trinidad, five days from Santa Fe, and four days from Albuquerque. They may, however, be extended to any length. Numerous unusual routes are available and varied itineraries and cost will be submitted on request. The following are examples of short Cruises only:

No. 16. SANTA FE TO GRAND CANYON — five days.

One person $386.75		Three persons $422.25
Two persons $404.50		Four persons $540.00

First Day — Leave La Fonda Hotel, Santa Fe, at 2:00 p.m., proceeding to Albuquerque via Cerrillos and the mountain route through the Sandia and Ortiz ranges and Tijeras Canyon. Overnight at The Alvarado, Albuquerque. **Second Day** — Albuquerque to Gallup via Isleta, Laguna and Acoma Indian pueblos. Basket luncheon near the Enchanted Mesa before visiting Acoma, the Sky City. Overnight at El Navajo, Gallup. **Third Day** — Gallup to Keam's Canyon, in the Navajo Country, via the trading post at Ganado. Overnight at Keam's Canyon, Arizona. **Fourth Day** — Keam's Canyon to Tuba City, via the Hopi Villages and Blue Canyon. Overnight at Tuba City. **Fifth Day** — Tuba to El Tovar Hotel. Grand Canyon, via the Painted Desert, Cameron trading post and Navahopi Road.

Several of the many features of this delightful Cruise deserve special mention. Laguna, Acoma and Enchanted Mesa are the objectives of the most popular one-day Cruise made from Albuquerque (No. 22). Blue Canyon, still little known even to Arizonans, is among the most beautiful in America. Tuba City, an old frontier Mormon settlement, is now headquarters of the Western Navajo Reservation. The Painted Desert is crossed for 22 miles between Tuba City and Cameron Trading Post, while thereafter the route approaches the 3,000 foot gorge of the lower Little Colorado, climbs to the Coconino Plateau and for 30 miles follows the South Rim of Grand Canyon to El Tovar Hotel.

The rates quoted above cover every expense from time of departure from Santa Fe to and including luncheon at El Tovar on day of arrival at Grand Canyon, with cost of dead-heading Harveycar, driver and private courier from Grand Canyon back to nearest fleet base at Albuquerque.

No. 17. GRAND CANYON TO SANTA FE — five days

Eastbound patrons of the Santa Fe stopping at Grand Canyon may cover the same fascinating country by Harveycar, by taking Cruise No. 16 in reverse, and resuming the rail journey from Santa Fe. In this case the Cruise will start after lunch at El Tovar on the day of departure, the first night being passed at Tuba City, the second at Keam's Canyon, the third at Gallup and the fourth at Albuquerque. Cruise ends with arrival at La Fonda before luncheon on the fifth day.

All-expense rates are identical with those quoted for Cruise 16. Ample advance notice should be given, however, to permit of dead-heading equipment from Albuquerque to Grand Canyon.

The four-day Carlsbad Cavern trip made a point of the constant improvements being made in the trails and lighting.

No. 18. CARLSBAD CAVERN CIRCLE CRUISE
Four days — 750 miles.   **$100.00.**

New Mexico's Carlsbad Cavern, acording to Willis T. Lee, leader of the National Geographic Society's 1924 expedition of exploration, is "the most spectacular of underground wonders in America" More, in the length of its galleries and passages, in the height and size of its enormous chambers, in the delicate coloring and bewildering variety and beauty of its formations. Carlsbad Cavern is without a peer among the famous caves of the world. It is unique, as well, in the cool purity of the air and the unvarying temperature of 56 degrees found throughout its miles of fascinating windings.

Carlsbad Cavern is now a National Monument with excellent approach roads and a National Park Service guide corps. The entrance is 26 miles from the town of Carlsbad, in the foothills of the Guadalupe Mountains of southeastern New Mexico. Underground there are miles of well-engineered trails and a constantly expanding system of lighting.

This featured all-year Cruise from Santa Fe covers 750 miles, made comfortably in four days, with ample time allowed for Cavern exploration. The Cruise, diagonally across New Mexico, is in itself exceptionally interesting.
First Day — La Fonda Hotel, Santa Fe, to Carlsbad, via Lamy, Encino, Vaughn and Roswell. Lunch at Gran Quivira, Vaughn; overnight at Crawford Hotel, Carlsbad. **Second Day** — Carlsbad to Carlsbad Caverns. Basket luncheon underground. Return to Carlsbad for night. **Third Day** Carlsbad to Mountainair via Roswell, Lincoln, Carrizozo. Overnight at Mountainair. **Fourth Day** — Mountainair to Santa Fe, via Gran Quivira National Monument and Willard. Luncheon en route, visiting ruins at Quarai and quaint Mexican mountain villages when feasible.
Rates — *For special Circle Cruises, $100 per person, with a minimum of three fares required. Regular Carlsbad Cavern Circle Cruises also leave La Fonda on the 1st and 15th of every month, with no requirements for a minimum number of guests. Rates, routes, accommodations and service are identical with those of special Cruises.*

IMPORTANT NOTES

1. The Carlsbad Cruise, in whole or in part, may be worked into longer Cruise itineraries.

2. Special three-day Carlsbad Circle Cruises may be arranged from either Santa Fe or Albuquerque at any time, at a rate of $75 per person, with a minimum of three full fares required. However, owing to the mileage involved, the three-day Cruise is recommended only where the saving of a single day is important.

3. As the underground trails of Carlsbad Cavern are necessarily covered on foot, guests should provide themselves with comfortable walking shoes.

4. The Carlsbad Cavern is fully described in a large illustrated folder gladly sent on request.

After listing the Sierra Verde Circle Cruise, with specific details of sights to be seen and food to be eaten, emphasis was placed on the trip being not only offered on a regular schedule, but subject to being tailored for the individual vacationer.

No. 19 **SIERRA VERDE CIRCLE CRUISE**
Eight days — 900 miles $150.00
June 7th — October 8th

It would be impossible to arrange another Circle Cruise by motor, of

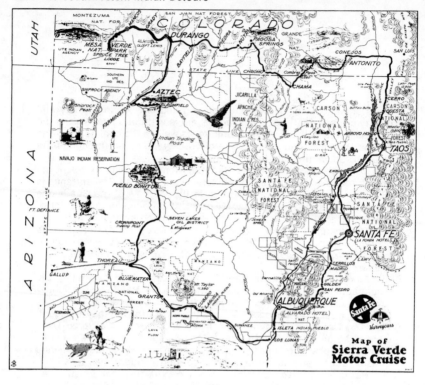

Map of
Sierra Verde
Motor Cruise

similar length and cost, to provide a more complete cross-section of the varied interest of the Far Southwest.

In a sweeping circuit of northwestern New Mexico and southwestern Colorado it includes a great National Park, two National Monuments, and four National Forests; seven magnificent mountain ranges and a score of rivers and white-water streams. It reaches our greatest prehistoric ruins. It crosses the strange Navajo country and touches Mexican hill villages and three ancient Indian pueblos.

SIERRA VERDE HIGH LIGHTS

MESA VERDE NATIONAL PARK. Magnificent mesa country, forested and slashed with canyons, set aside for the preservation of hundreds of the most remarkable prehistoric cliff ruins in the Southwest.

CHACO CANYON NATIONAL MONUMENT. Major prehistoric communal ruins showing extraordinary architectural skill, and including Pueblo Bonito and Pueblo del Arroyo, excavated by expeditions of the National Geographic Society.

AZTEC NATIONAL MONUMENT. More great prehistoric ruins, different in many points of environment, architecture and construction.

FOUR NATIONAL FORESTS. Long reaches across the Manzano, San Juan, Rio Grande and Carson National Forests, wilderness mountain playgrounds covering millions of acres.

MOUNTAINS. The Cruise picture is framed in mountains — the Sangre de Cristo, Jemez, Sandia, Ortiz, San Mateo, La Plata and Taos ranges. There are a score of peaks from 11,000 to over 14,000 feet.

RIVERS. Rivers and mountain trout streams in endless succession, including the Rio Grande, San Juan, Mancos, Florida and Las Animas; the Chama, Conejos and Red rivers; La Manga and Elk creeks and many others.

INDIANS. The pueblos of Isleta, Laguna and Taos, continuously inhabited for centuries. Between Thoreau and Farmington the Navajo country is crossed for 120 miles.

THE CRUISE DAY BY DAY

First Day. Afternoon run from La Fonda Hotel, Santa Fe, to Albuquerque, via Cerrillos, the mountain mining towns of Madrid and Golden and a magnificent new route through the Manzano Forest and Ortiz and Sandia ranges. Dinner, overnight and breakfast at Alvarado Hotel. (Parties starting from Albuquerque cover the portion of the Cruise on the afternoon of their seventh day.)

Second Day. Alvarado Hotel to Chaco Canyon National Monument (Pueblo Bonito) via Isleta and Laguna Indian pueblos, Thoreau, the great red rim cliffs of the southern Navajo country, and the trading post and Indian School at Crown Point Agency. Overnight at Pueblo Bonito Lodge. Escorted visit to Pueblo Bonito ruins, excavated under direction of National Geographic Society.

Third Day. Further opportunity to inspect nearby ruins of Chetro Kettle, Penasco Blanco, Pueblo Alto and Pueblo del Arroyo. Leave in afternoon for Farmington, New Mexico, via Indian trading posts and Navajo country. Overnight at Avery Hotel, Farmington, New Mexico.

Fourth Day. Farmington to Spruce Tree Lodge, Mesa Verde National Park, Colorado via Durango and Mancos. Morning visit to great ruins at Aztec, followed by drive through San Juan and Las Animas valleys and beautiful mountain scenery approaching Durango. The tremendous climb to the top of Mesa Verde, over splendidly engineered roads and revealing panoramas covering thousands of square miles, is made during the late afternoon. Dinner and overnight at Spruce Tree Lodge. Following dinner there is a camp-fire talk on the prehistoric cliff ruins within the Park.

Fifth Day. Both morning and afternoon there are escorted visits to some of the most extraordinary ruins in the United States before leaving Mesa Verde for Wrightsman Hotel, Mancos, Colorado, where the night is passed.

Sixth Day. Mancos to the magnificent Conejos Valley via Durango, Pagosa Springs, Chama and the Cumbres Pass. This entire day is spent in a region of the utmost grandeur and beauty. Basket lunch beside one of the white-water streams and the tangle of mountains east of Pagosa, the location of tremendous hot sulphur springs. Overnight at LO Ranch in Conejos Valley.

Seventh Day. Conejos Valley to Don Fernando de Taos, via Antonito, Sunshine Valley, Cerro, Questa and the Carson National Forest and high foothills of the Sangre de Cristo and Taos mountains. Luncheon at Don Fernando Hotel, Taos, followed by afternoon visit to the famous pueblo of Taos and the local artists' colony. Dinner, overnight and breakfast at the Don Fernando.

Eighth Day. Return to La Fonda Hotel. Santa Fe in time for lunch, via Taos Valley and the upper gorge and valley of the Rio Grande. *(Cruise guests starting from and returning to Albuquerque continue on to that point after luncheon at La Fonda, Santa Fe.)*

IMPORTANT NOTES

The Sierra Verde Circle Cruise is operated both as a regular and Special Cruise. The regular Cruises differ from Special Cruises only in that they are scheduled to start from definite points on definite dates; that on those dates the Cruise will be made, for a single guest if necessary, without increase in the per capita cost; and that individuals or small parties may be asked to share cars up to the limit of four persons per car.

Regular Cruises leave La Fonda Hotel, Santa Fe, at 2:30 p.m. on the 7th, 14th, 21st and 28th of each month between June 7th and October 7th, inclusive; The Alvarado Hotel, Albuquerque at 8:30 a.m. on the 8th, 15th, 22nd and 29th of each month between June 8th and October 8th, inclusive.

Special Cruises will be arranged at any time from these points for a minimum of three guests. It is often possible to operate these Special cruises earlier or later in the year, depending upon road conditions approaching Mesa Verde.

Mileage. Approximately 900 miles. Rate, $150 per person, including every expense. Per capita cost of this featured Circle Cruise is appreciably less than usual Cruise rates.

The balance of the schedule used an updated text taken from many previous folders and the rates for regular cruises were listed for easy reference.

No. 20.   THE SANDIA LOOP DRIVE
one day $13.00

The Sandia Loop from Albuquerque, opened to motor travel for the first time in the summer of 1928, already is recognized as among the finest short scenic drives offered by the Southwest.

From the Alvarado the route is east to and through Tijeras Canyon, thence north through forested Tejano Canyon, and then west in a beautiful climb to the crest of the Sandias, familiar by sight to every Albuquerque visitor as a succession of precipitous and treeless rock barriers rising above the city some 4,000 feet. From the brink, nearly 10,000 feet above the sea, green slopes and tangled mountains roll away to the east. To the south the eye travels clear to the Staked Plains of Texas. Albuquerque and the villages and pueblos of the Rio Grande valley become tiny details in a vast sweep hedged with distant blue ranges.

After leaving the crest the road for miles follows Ellis Creek through heavy timber and a profusion of wild flowers, with occasional sudden panoramas of the distant Estancia Valley, and the San Pedro, Cerrillos, Ortiz and Sangre de Cristo Mountains. The Cruise interest is heightened by a visit to the little native town of Placitas, hidden near the base of the Sandias, and numerous glimpses of the picturesque life of isolated ranchitos in the canyons.

Return to Albuquerque is from the north, via Bernalillo; the entire drive, including basket luncheon on the crest, consuming six or seven leisurely hours.

Rate, including luncheon, $13.00 per person, with a minimum of three fares required.

No. 21. JEMEZ SPRINGS AND SODA DAM
one day **$18.00**

The drive to Jemez Springs and the Soda Dam penetrates the Jemez Mountains northwest of Albuquerque, a region long considered one of the most beautiful in New Mexico.

Running north to Bernalillo, the road then crosses the Rio Grande and climbs the western slope of its broad valley through cedar-dotted hills and rock-walled mesas. The tremendous panorama broadens with every mile. One by one the Sangre de Cristos, the Sandias, the Manzanos, and the main bulk of the Jemez Range lift into sight.

The inhabited Indian pueblos of Santa Ana and Zia and the isolated Mexican village of San Ysidro are passed before Jemez pueblo is reached. In the latter there is an unusual square kiva and the terraced dwellings typical of the older pueblo settlements. The Indian ceremonials that occur at Jemez are often especially fine.

The country between this point and Jemez Springs is remarkable for brilliancy of coloring and the weird work of wind and water in sculpturing its sandstone formation. At Jemez Springs, widely known for its medicinal qualities, there is a ruined mission and pueblo. The natural Soda Dam, a mile distant, is an unusual sight.

Rate, including luncheon, $18.00 per person. Round trip 130 miles. Minimum of three fares required.

Couriers and Drivers dig in (and out)

No. 22. JEMEZ SPRINGS AND SODA DAM
overnight **$25.00**

As above, but remaining overnight at La Esperanza, Jemez Springs.

Rate, including three meals and hotel accommodations with private bath, $25.00 per person. Minimum of three fares required.
Note. The Jemez Cruise is one of exceptional interest. It may be made from Santa Fe as well, in either one or two days (Nos. 11 and 12), or used as a one- or two-day link between Santa Fe and Albuquerque, or the reverse.

No. 23   ACOMA, LAGUNA, ENCHANTED MESA
one day **$25.00**

The large pueblos of Acoma and Laguna, inhabited by more than 1,000 Indians, lie far to the westward of Albuquerque, in broken, scenic country. Between them in the Mesa Encantada, or Enchanted Mesa — an enormous island of rock, formed by erosion, that rises sheer from the floor of a level valley.

Acoma is well named the "Sky City" and its people the "People of the White Rock." It occupies an almost sheer-walled mesa, 400 feet high, whose rocky cliffs have been freakishly carved by wind and weather. The pueblo itself was old when the Spanish Friar Marcos first heard of it in 1539. Its massive Franciscan mission was established nearly three centuries ago.

The interesting pueblo of Laguna, founded in 1699, clings to the crest of a barren rock hill near the main highway. The old Mission church, built in the same year, is still in active use. Laguna women, like those of Acoma, are adept in the manufacture of pottery.

Rate, including basket luncheon, $25.00 per person, with no minimum number required. Round trip distance, 185 miles.

No. 24.   ZUNI PUEBLO AND INSCRIPTION ROCK — one day

Thirty miles south, through highly scenic country to ancient Zuni pueblo, discovered by Marcos de Niza, a Franciscan friar, in 1539. Thence eastward to Inscription Rock and the Ice Caves and lava flows. Return to El Navajo via Grants and the red rim cliffs of the Navajo country.

No. 25.   PETRIFIED FORESTS AND PAINTED DESERT — one day

An exceptionally fine view of the southern tip of the Painted Desert is included on the way to Adamana, south of which the route passes through many thousand acres of the Petrified Forests National Monument. Here are the world's greatest known groupings of petrified trees, both in extent and beauty. Millions of tons of jeweled fragments and massive trunks litter the tattered surface of a painted Bad Lands. Basket lunch is carried, with return to El Navajo for dinner.

No. 26.   CHACO CANYON VIA SHIPROCK — two days

The objective is the Chaco Canyon National Monument, where National Geographic Society expeditions have spent many years in excavating the prehistoric ruins of Pueblo Bonito, Chettro Kettle, etc. These immense ruins reflect the highest achievements of the ancient pueblo civilization.

The route is north from Gallup via an excellent new road through the Navajo Country to Shiprock, a detached pinnacle rising 1,700 feet. Lunch at Farmington, in the San Juan Valley, and overnight at Chaco Canyon. The morning of the second day is free for inspection of the ruins, with return to Gallup via Crown Point Indian Agency and Thoreau.

Satirical impressions of the Detours

No. 27. HOPI VILLAGES — two days

The route is northwest from Gallup through the Navajo Country to Keam's Canyon, where the night is passed. Several of the famous Hopi towns, the fabled "Seven Cities of Cibola" of early Spanish explorers, are visited. These are the most isolated and primitive of all Southwestern pueblos and are built on the tops of sheer-sided mesas commanding immense desert panoramas.

No. 28. CANYON DE CHELLY — two or three days

The duration of the Cruise to Canyon de Chelly, which is seldom approached by motor except from Gallup, is largely a question of the time guests may wish to spend by saddle in the main canyon and its scarcely less interesting tributary, Canyon del Muerto.

Canyon de Chelly is in the heart of the Navajo Country to the north of Gallup. With an early start from El Navajo it is possible to reach McSparron's Ranch, where comfortable accommodations and good horses are available, during the afternoon.

When no trail trip is made into the canyons, return to Gallup by motor is made the second day. The supreme interest of this particular Cruise, however, lies in devoting the second day, and often the second night as well, to a leisurely exploration on horseback of points accessible in no other way, with return to El Navajo left for the third day.

The cost of saddle trips here taken is included in the regular all-expense Motor Cruise rates charged.

Note. The season for Canyon de Chelly trips is from about April 15th to December 1st and it may be included in long Cruises passing east or west through Gallup throughout that period, with rare exceptions.

RATES. Harveycar Motor Cruise rates are all-inclusive, covering every charge en route from the time of actual departure until termination of Cruise. Motor transportation, services and expenses of private Courier and driver-mechanician, guests' meals and hotel accommodations, fees, etc., are included.

Regular tariffs for Cruise parties of one or more are as follows. Children under 12 years of age are considered as half fares.

Guests in Party	Per Diem Party Charge
One adult	$65.00
One adult and single child	67.50
One adult and two children	70.00
Two adults	70.00
Two adults and single child	72.50
Two adults and two children	75.00
Three adults	75.00

Additional adults, $25.00 per person per day; additional children under 12, $12.50 per child per day.

The emphasis on trips into Arizona made little mention of the old trips by way of Flagstaff, Winslow and Williams; the emphasis now was on the use of the Harveycars from Santa Fe or Albuquerque. The American public wanted it that way; motoring was becoming the only way to go. Crossing the country by car was no longer an adventure, it was a routine.

The folder made a subtle attack on train travel by saying, "From Trinidad, Colorado, to Santa Fe, N.M., is a mountain run of seven or eight hours by rail, made for the most
part during the hours of darkness. Many Westbound Cruise
guests, therefore, will prefer to start their motor outing at
the foregoing point, reaching Santa Fe by a two-day
Harveycar Cruise of exceptional interest. The first day's
drive Westward from Trinidad includes Eagle's Nest Pass,
Ute Park and the Cimarron Canyon, ending at the Don Fernando Hotel in Taos." The tour gave the tourist a head start
on Indian Detouring by visiting Taos on the way to Santa
Fe.

Not that all the urging was to keep the tourist in a
Harveycar, as long as it took a Harveycar to get him to
where he was going. Whether he was headed for Navajo
country in general or had a specific destination such as
Rainbow Bridge, the folder told the whole story in an attempt to sell the traveler before he reached Santa Fe.

The Navajo Country
Including Hopiland

No visitor is apt to remain long in the Far Southwest without hearing of the Navajo Country. Nor may he feel that he really knows New
Mexico and Arizona without having made at least one excursion into the
extraordinary region so designated.

The Navajo Country blocks off the whole northeastern corner of
Arizona, in Coconino, Navajo and Apache counties; extends into
McKinley and San Juan counties of northwestern New Mexico, and
swallows the lower part of San Juan County in southeastern Utah. From
east to west it is approximately 200 miles across; from south to north,
nearly 150 miles. Its 25,000 square miles represent the greatest zone of
undeveloped Indian land in the United States.

Two adjacent but distinct reservations, the Navajo and Hopi, are included in the Navajo Country. A few Hopis live on Navajo land; nearly as
many Navajos as Hopis live in the latter's territory. Connecticut, Rhode
Island, Massachusetts and New Hampshire combined would disappear
in the region allotted to the two. Add the fringe lands utilized by the Indians and the whole is larger than West Virginia.

This enormous district lies just north of the Santa Fe main line from
Thoreau, New Mexico, to Canyon Diablo, Arizona. Yet within its boundaries there are no railroads. There are no cities. Its towns are the age-
old pueblos of the Hopi. Its motor roads, product of half a dozen years,
link isolated trading posts and Indian agencies. All told, perhaps 1,000
whites live among 35,000 Indians in 16,000,000 acres where the keynotes
are distance, silence, color — and the wonder working of natural forces.
Each element in the population adds interest for the visitor.

The Indian Trader. The present accessibility of the Navajo Country
is due almost as much to the Indian trader as to expanding roads. A few
years ago the chance visitor accepted his free hospitality without ques-

PROGRAM
Inter-Tribal
Indian
Ceremonial

August
28, 29 and 30
1929

Gallup, New Mexico

Left: Cover of 1929
program

Facing page: Program
schedule for final day

FRIDAY AFTERNOON
August 30, 1929

Review of Entertainers
Stick Race.
Continuance of the two previous days.
One and a Half Mile Relay Race for Ponies.
Half Mile Fast Horse Race.
Tug of War for Men.
Potato Race on Horseback.
Ring Tournament on Horseback.
Half Mile Horse Race for Squaws.
Tug of War — Squaws.
Moccasin Race — Squaws.
One and a Half Mile Relay Race.
On foot. Three men to the team.
One and a Half Mile Relay Race.
For fast horses.
Commanche Dance — Jemez Indians.
Exhibition riding throughout afternoon performance
Music by the Inter-Tribal bands.

FRIDAY EVENING
August 30, 1929

Music by the Inter-Tribal Indian Bands
St. Michaels Indian School and the Albuquerque Indian School Band.
Review of Entertainers
The greatest Inter-Tribal representation of the Indian ever attempted in the United States of America.
1. **War Dance of the Klamath Indian.**
Rendered in native Klamath tongue by Inter-Tribal Indian Quartet (mounted). A representation of four Indian tribes, Sioux, Ponca, Cherokee, Klamath. Encore? A surprise presentation.
2. **Antelope Dance by Hopi Indians.**
A religious ceremony.
3. **Basket Dance by San Juan Indians.**
The basket is the most used utensil in the sacred ceremonials and home life of the Indian. The wedding ceremony and Yei-bichai may not be performed without it. The Pueblo Indian uses it to carry his seed grain to the field, and the harvest, threshing of the grain and conveying of grain to the estates for grinding. After baking of bread it is again used to serve the bread at the table. The origin of the basket is unknown but it may safely be surmised it was originated by primitive women to store useful household items and personal trinkets. This dance is done by the Indian in appreciation of this useful article.
4. **Hoop Dance by Taos Indians.**
A pleasure dance enjoyed greatly by the Taos boys and friends. Requires much grace and agility. If you don't think so, try it.
5. **Zuni Fun Maker — Joe Crazy Horse.**
6. **Harvest Dance by San Ildefonso Indians.**
A dance of thanksgiving for bountiful harvest.
7. **Special by Announcement.**

8. **Eagle Dance by Santo Domingo Indians.**
In the dim past ages, centuries ago, a great and terrible plague, perhaps famine, infested the land of the Pueblos. In their distress the Indians made a dance of supplication to the Great Spirit for relief and in answer to their prayer an Eagle was sent to fly over the Pueblo, causing rain clouds to form. Then the thunder bird shot his Lightning Arrows into the clouds, causing the rain to fall and thus bring relief. As rain is so important to life, and the Eagle and Thunder bird so closely allied to the Rain God, the Eagle has a place of great veneration and this dance is performed to commemorate the time he saved the tribes of the Pueblos. Note the soaring, darting, graceful movements of the Eagles.
9. **Moo-Y-Ya. (Snow Dance) by Zuni Indians.**
10. **Cibolo Dance by Zia Indians.**
11. **Eagle Dance by Tesuque Indians.**
Performed in commemoration of relief from famine as in dances of other Pueblo tribes.
12. **Tribal Songs in native tongue.**
Inter-Tribal Indian Quartet. Solos — Sioux, Ponca, Cherokee and Klamath. Special by Announcement.
13. **Buffalo Dance by Cochiti Indians.**
A dance to the God of the Hunt that much Buffalo meat may be brought home.
14. **Yei-bichai Song by Navahos.**
Ten mounted singers of this powerful Indian tribe will render this beautiful weird song. A rare treat.
15. **Shield Dance by Jemez Indians**
A graceful dance for pleasure.
16. **The Why and How of the Inter-Tribal Indian Ceremonial.**
A short address by Homer P. Powers, Director of Ceremonies.
17. **The Fire Dance of the Navahos.**
The fire dance, a rare and impressive ceremony is a portion taken from the Mountain Chant, another of the Navaho's important nine day and night ceremonies. It is performed only after the Thunder bird is asleep and is a curative or healing ceremony for women. It is seldom performed off the Navaho reservation and only after much hard labor and preparation of the Corral and Medicine Lodges or Hogans. Many Medicine Men participate. The Navahos will present several sketches from the Mountain Chant. **The Growing of the Yucca Plant, The Feather Dance, and Fire Dance.**
18. **Good Night and Good Bye Review of Entertainers.**
The Inter-Tribal Indian Ceremonial Board of Directors, and all Indian Entertainers participating extend you a cordial welcome to be with us again in Nineteen Hundred and Thirty.

tion or excuse. Today many of the posts provide excellent meals and detached cabins with comfortable beds, piped water and electric lights, all at moderate cost.

The life of the posts themselves is always fascinating — the lounging bucks, silent squaws and wide-eyed children; the droop-headed horses at the rails; the sense of isolation from accustomed things; the primitive barter of groceries and dry goods for hides, wool, Navajo blankets and Indian jewelry.

The Navajos. The Navajos are in many ways the most remarkable tribal unit in America. They number about 35,000 and are increasing. They are virile, independent and pure blooded. They are superb horsemen, nomads living a primitive life in difficult country. They practice little agriculture but range successfully nearly 2,000,000 sheep, goats, horses and cattle.

Navajo dwellings are simple wickiups or domelike "hogans" built of cedar trunks, brush and mud. They have no villages and seldom gather in great numbers except for horse racing, "chicken pulls," or religious ceremonial, when they ride in from immense distances and seem to appear out of nowhere. Their ceremonials are weird and spectacular in the extreme and usually occur "When the Thunder Sleeps," or after the first frost. Weaving was learned long ago from the Hopis and Navajo rugs have become famous. Their skill in the handworking of silver and turquoise jewelry is equally remarkable.

The Hopi Villages. Navajo and Hopi have lived side by side for centuries, yet the two are utterly different in many important characteristics. The one is tall and slender, the other short and stocky. One wears his hair long, knotted up with string; the other in a short bob. The Navajo is essentially a free-ranging nomad, the Hopi a sedentary agriculturist living in ancient compact communal settlements or pueblos. Until his taming some 60 years ago the Navajo was warlike and predatory; the Hopi has always been peaceful, only resisting aggression.

There are about 2,200 Hopis and their villages occupy isolated and almost impregnable capes projecting out from Black Mesa, in the southwestern corner of the Navajo Country. Here the Spaniards, Pedro de Tovar and Juan de Padilla, of Coronado's expedition, found them in 1540. Living far from their related tribes in Zuni, Acoma and the Rio Grande Valley, the Hopis are the most primitive of all the pueblo peoples, whose highly developed cultures once covered the entire Southwest.

For centuries the Hopis have maintained themselves in face of incredible difficulties. Their dry farming and irrigation, in an arid land, are marvels of toil and patience. Their religious life expresses itself in elaborate ceremonies, an endless plea for the rain that spells life. *The Hopi Snake Dance, held each year in August, is the most extraordinary of American aboriginal ceremonials and is always accessible, through a series of special Harveycar Motor Cruises.*

Topography. Ninety-nine per cent of the entire Navajo Country lies between 4,000 and 9,000 feet above sea level. The average altitude is probably 5,500 feet. Precipitation varies but is generally very scant. Only the highest elevations are heavily forested. As a consequence the water run-off is rapid and the whole country is a gigantic laboratory for the play of erosive forces. Washes and arroyos network the land. Innumerable canyons expose brilliantly colored strata. Mountain flanks are carved and recessed. Immense and unscalable forms rise from valley floors.

Above: White 53 Harveycoach at spurline depot

Below: Indian medicine man at Santa Clara studies white man's 'horse'

Courtesy White Motor Corporation

The spur depot at Santa Fe was for freight only

Climate. Sunshine floods the Navajo Country the year round. Relative humidity is less than 50 per cent, tempering heat and cold and the daily swing in temperature of 40 degrees. Summer days are hot, the nights cool; winter days are bright, the nights sharply cold. Spring and fall are the dry seasons; snow falls in winter and rains in July, August and early September. The latter are highly local and seldom last more than a few hours: 24-hour rains are exceptional.

Hopi squaws weaving baskets at Grand Canyon

Cruises to the Navajo Country. Roads and accommodations throughout the Navajo Country are improving constantly and unusual Harveycar Cruises of any length and for any month, can be planned from Santa Fe or Albuquerque, New Mexico, or from any other point on the Santa Fe main line between Trinidad, Colorado, and Ash Fork or Grand Canyon, Arizona. Itineraries will gladly be suggested for such Cruises by motor alone, or combining motor and saddle trips, if desired. *(See also Cruises Nos. 16, 17, 19, 26, 27, 28.)*

THE RAINBOW BRIDGE

The Rainbow Bridge is the greatest of all known natural arches — as it is also the most beautiful and perfectly proportioned. Moreover, the story of its finding by white men helps to dispel any belief that in the Far Southwest the days of geographical exploration and the thrill of discovery have long since passed.

It was not until 1908 that an old Navajo informed Mrs. John Wetherill, wife of the famed guide and Indian trader at Kayenta, Arizona that a marvelous natural arch spanned one of the tangle of unknown canyons beyond Navajo Mountain, straddling the Arizona-Utah line.

Inquiry showed that knowledge of the arch had been current among both Piutes and Navajos for many generations. By the former it was called Barohoini — The Rainbow; by the Navajos, Nonnezoshe — The Arch. Yet apparently only two living Indians, a Piute father and son, had actually seen it or knew the way to it.

The next summer two expeditions set out to find the hidden colossus. Weeks of hardship in some of the roughest country in America followed. Eventually the parties joined under guidance of the Piute Nashja-begay and John Wetherill. On August 14, 1909, they stood in awed silence at their goal.

At their feet trickled clear water. Massive piers 278 feet apart carried a graceful buff-colored arch that swept overhead higher than the dome of the national capitol. The unbelievable whole was perfect in its symmetry and hued and tinted by shadows and the tricks of "desert paint."

Seen from a little way, men and horses at its base dwindled to insignificance, tiny details difficult to locate even on a photographic print. At a distance the arch itself seemed to shrink, a giant's masterpiece dwarfed by a setting greater still.

Rainbow Bridge spans Bridge Canyon, tributary from the south to Glen Canyon of the Colorado River. Actually it is in Utah but access is from Arizona. At present the nearest points on the railroad are Grand Canyon and Flagstaff, on the Santa Fe, 185 miles distant. For sixteen years after discovery the closest approach by motor was to Kayenta and less than 600 white men and women followed the difficult 12-day pack trip necessary from that point. The shorter combined motor and saddle trips now possible, however, are among the most remarkable of all American travel possibilities.

In 1925 a motor road was constructed to Navajo Mountain and Rainbow Lodge built on its southwestern shoulder. Here comfortable cabin accommodations, shower baths and excellent meals are provided. Rainbow Bridge is but 13 miles away by a new and spectacular trail and the saddle round trip covers either two or three days, as desired. Camp is made in Bridge Canyon, near the arch.

All-expense combination motor and saddle trips to Rainbow Bridge, requiring either four or five days in all, may be arranged from El

Tovar Hotel, Grand Canyon, at any time between May 1st and December 1st. Full details will be found in the Santa Fe folders "Grand Canyon Outings" and "Trails and Drives."

Harveycar Motor Cruise guests may make Rainbow Bridge an objective from Santa Fe, New Mexico, or any other desired starting point, covering intervening country of extraordinary interest. Or it may be included as a side trip on any long-range Cruise passing east or west through the northern Indian country between Santa Fe, Albuquerque or Trinidad, and Grand Canyon. In either case Cruise cars remain at Rainbow Lodge on a hold-over basis, guests settling with the lodge proprietors for meals, accommodations and saddle trips taken during their stay.

Rainbow Lodge charges are $3.00 per day for lodging and $1.00 for breakfast, $1.25 for luncheon and $1.50 for dinner. The two-day saddle trip to the Bridge, including guide, meals, and full trail and camp equipment, is $50 per person; for the three-day trip, $60 per person.

Rainbow Bridge has become known the world over, but the trail to it still holds the rare thrill of discovery. Few have actually seen it and there is today but one white man's house within 60 miles of Rainbow Lodge.

Included in the information was a month-by-month breakdown of what weather could be expected. This table had been compiled from a U.S. Weather Bureau 54 year record of Santa Fe. It held a magic lure for Arizonans suffering in 110 degree heat in July; it was impossible to resist for Minnesotans shoveling three feet of snow off the front walk in January.

One of the large 1929 tour groups

A Little Word Picture of An Ideal Year-round Climate — What Weather Old Santa Fe and the Northern Southwest has to Offer the Visitor in

January — Coldest month of the Santa Fe winter — and an exceedingly popular one. There is 72% of possible sunshine, against 50% in New York and 45% in Chicago. Average temperature is 29°, precipitation but .59" and the normal snowfall 5.9".

February — Warmer than January, the average climbing to 33°. Normally 6.4 inches of snow accounts for much of a precipitation less than one-quarter that of New York City. Again there is over 70% of possible sunshine. Indian-detour travel approaching a peak.

March — Light snows pass quickly and new growth starts in the upland valleys. Average temperature is 40° and precipitation less than one-fifth that for Boston or New York. Normally but one day in eight is overcast.

April — Spring reaches high into the mountains, with occasional showers and snow flurries. Mean temperature at Santa Fe climbs to 47°, with 73% of possible sunshine. Prevailing winds from the Southwest.

May — A perfect out-of-doors month throughout the Indian-detour country and for special Harveycar Motor Cruises, long or short. Maximum temperatures of the long, sunny days average 68°. Dense fog has never been recorded and protracted storms are almost unknown.

June — Another rare month for Harveycar guests. At Santa Fe, average relative humidity at 6 p.m. reaches the phenomenally low figure of 28%. Brief thunder showers account for the normal one inch of rainfall and there is 79% of possible sunshine.

July — Normally the wettest and warmest month of the Santa Fe year — yet both terms are only relative. Precipitation of 2.71" — contrasting with 4.54" for New York — falls in highly localized showers. Average temperature is but 69°, the mercury sinking into the low fifties at night.

August — Resembles July, though both rainfall and temperature are somewhat lower. The former is 2.36", the latter 67°, with the same cool, refreshing nights. With normally but three fully cloudy days, August is another pleasant revelation in summer Southwestern climatic conditions at lofty elevations.

September — Beginning of the crisp, clear Fall of the northern Southwest. Precipitation drops to 1.62", average temperature to 61°. Normally but three days in the month are overcast. Harvesting starts in the pueblos, with dance and fiesta.

October — The most brilliant month of the Southwestern year. Magnificent coloring in the high foothills and first snows above 10,000 feet. An average temperature of 50°, with 79% of possible sunshine. Roads everywhere at their best.

November — Another splendid month for the Indian-detour and long or short Harveycar Cruises. Days are clear and warm, the nights crisp and sparkling. Precipitation is but .76" and the percentage of sunshine equals that of El Paso, San Diego and Los Angeles.

December — Noo-pah-po, "month of fires and ashes." Precipitation .76", mean temperature 31°. Occasional light snowfall, between sharp nights and brilliant days unexpectedly mild. Magnificent Indian ceremonies during Christmas week and at New Year's.

The folder went on to describe the beauties of the Painted Desert, with the last sentence of the first paragraph a subliminal suggestion the motorist on his own would be sorry — he'd miss the best part.

The Painted Desert — Arizona

The Painted Desert of Arizona is another of the Southwest's contributions to the unusual scenic features of America. As such it is already known by name and reputation to millions. Comparatively very few, however, have seen more than glimpse of its southern tip, where it approaches close to the transcontinental motor highway some miles east of Holbrook. Fewer still are more than vaguely familiar with its actual extent. Even on many otherwise excellent maps the location given is faulty.

Roughly, the Painted Desert may be described as a thin crescent open to the northeast, lying in a great bow of the Little Colorado and Colorado rivers, and forming the western boundary of the Navajo and Hopi Indian country. The northern tip rests at Lee's Ferry, on the Colorado; the southern tip near Holbrook, on the main line of the Santa Fe. Between these points the outer curve of the crescent sweeps for nearly 200 miles, marked by river courses that are in part broad sandy washes and elsewhere follow impassable canyons from 500 to 3,000 feet in depth. The area is difficult to estimate but the width of the desert proper varies from less than three to more than twenty miles, according as the rim cliffs of the Indian country approach or recede from the rivers.

It is this curiously shaped region, a mile above the sea, that is aptly named the Painted Desert. The annual precipitation averages less than three inches and there are places where the Indians claim no rain has fallen for two years at a time. Elsewhere light rain and snows occur in winter and in midsummer black-browed little thunder storms break here and there without rhyme or reason. The sparse vegetation is insufficient to protect the drainage of the myriad arroyos and the water rushes fiercely and futilely away, aiding the wind-driven sand in its endless work of weird desert sculpture.

The Painted Desert is almost devoid of human settlement. Here and there along its borders — at Leupp and Cameron, at Tuba City, Cedar Ridge, The Gap and Lee's Ferry — there are picturesque trading posts. Except for the thin traffic of the roads and trails and an occasional Indian family camped among the rare cottonwoods, the desert itself lies silent and empty.

To its remarkable coloration, therefore, the Painted Desert owes both its name and fame.

The history lesson went on with the description of Inscription Rock and Canyon de Chelly.

Inscription Rock

El Morro National Monument

In eastern New Mexico, south of the Santa Fe main line and not many miles from the ancient Indian pueblo of Zuni, an enormous mass of reddish sandstone dominates the surrounding country. Erosive forces have worked upon it until from a distance it resembles a gigantic medieval castle — an impression recorded in the Spanish name "El Morro." It is perhaps better known locally, however, as Inscription Rock.

El Morro's northern face is sheer and the base of the cliff is in places almost as smooth as a blackboard. Here passing Indians recorded the events of war and peace in pictographs. Old Spanish exploring and punitive expeditions, following the Indian trails, chiseled a chronicle of their achievements. Still later, pioneers and military pathfinders registered significant names and dates.

The oldest of the Spanish records is that left by Don Juan de Onate, governor and colonizer of New Mexico, then a province of the Spanish crown. Returning from a tremendous overland march to the head of the Gulf of California in 1606 — over three centuries ago — Onate, in quaint Spanish, noted that the Indians "gave their obedience," for which they received favor "with clemency, zeal and prudence."

This and the many later recitals chiseled beside it give El Morro, now protected as a National Monument, a unique historical interest that is heightened by the scenic value of the surrounding country and of the great rock itself.

El Morro National Monument may be worked into through east or westbound Harveycar Motor Cruises by lengthening the run between Gallup and Albuquerque to two days. It may also be made an objective of a full one-day loop trip from El Navajo Hotel, Gallup. In either case visits to Zuni pueblo and to the Ice Caves and lava flows may be included.

Canyon de Chelly

No list of the most spectacular canyons of the Southwest would be complete without prominent mention of Canyon de Chelly, Arizona, and of its famous branch, Canyon del Muerto, or the Canyon of Death, so named from the massacre there by the Spaniards of many Navajos. In their grandeur and beauty, their prehistoric ruins, their place in early frontier history, and in their present-day interest as a center of primitive Navajo Indian life, these canyons have an unusual and many-sided fascination.

Riders in the canyons are dwarfed to pin-head size by the towering walls, lifting a thousand feet sheer from the white sandy floor. Scores of prehistoric cliff ruins attest the antiquity of human habitation, continued in more recent centuries by the nomadic Navajos, whose crude camps dot the green cottonwood brakes at the base of the brilliant cliffs.

It concluded with an appeal that was guaranteed to make the ones who had held out this far ready to cry 'uncle'.

The Far Southwest

A few terse facts may help to develop still further the immensity, the contrasts and contradictions, and the many-sided interests that have made of our Far Southwest perhaps the most written about and yet least known major section of the United States.

New Mexico and Arizona are respectively the fourth and fifth largest states in the Union. Combined they cover over 236,000 square

miles — an area considerably larger than that of France. They are our youngest states, yet were visited by Europeans over 70 years before the discovery of the Hudson River and had received permanent settlement well before the landing of the Pilgrims on the Massachusetts coast.

To the Southwest no less an authority than John Muir ascribed the most extravagant and varied grouping of natural wonders on the known globe. It is a far cry from the Grand Canyon to the Carlsbad Caverns, or from the Rainbow Bridge to the Petrified Forest.

Archaeologically, too, this region offers the richest and most inexhaustible field in our country. The definite count of its prehistoric ruins, whose builders attained the highest development found on the continent north of Old Mexico, already runs into the thousands. After thirty years of exploration scientists barely have scratched the surface and can only guess at the discoveries yet to come.

Today nearly one-quarter of all the Indians in the United States live in New Mexico and Arizona. On their immense reservations in these two states they have maintained, as nowhere else, their individuality, their purity of blood, their old virility, their picturesque tribal customs and religious ceremonial.

In American history the Southwest is a field apart. Elsewhere our frontier days came and went swiftly before the resistless march of the Anglo-Saxon across the continent. In the Southwest the frontier stood still for three centuries, adding endless pulse-stirring chapters to a record that finds only the barest mention in the text books with which most of us are familiar.

Here history is a strangely vital, living thing. Everywhere one goes it clamors for attention and explanation. In New Mexico today one may watch the religious pageantry of medieval Spain issue from age-greyed churches antedating by a century the earliest California missions — and yet know that beside him stands a man who remembers Billy the Kid, who took part in the bloody Tonto Basin War of Arizona sheepmen and cattlemen, who felt the hand of Geronimo and his Apaches, or who watched the coming of the first railroad.

An amazing proportion of the Southwest is still controlled by the Federal Government. The fact is significant, from the standpoint of the traveler. In the Southwest such ownership spells National Parks, National Monuments, National Forests and Indian reservations covering tens of millions of acres.

National Parks and Monuments. Grand Canyon National Park, nearly as large as Rhode Island, is entirely in Arizona. Mesa Verde National Park, sheltering scores of spectacular prehistoric cliff dwellings, is just over the New Mexico border in southwestern Colorado.

Of the fifty-seven National Monuments that have been set aside in all of the United States, including Alaska, twenty are located in the Southwest. In this manner are protected the Carlsbad Caverns, 20,000 acres of the Petrified Forest, the Rainbow Bridge, Inscription Rock, old Spanish missions, the twenty major prehistoric ruins in Chaco Canyon, and many others in the Bandelier, Aztec, Wupatki, Walnut Canyon, Montezuma's Castle and Casa Grande National Monuments.

National Forests. To those who may still think of the Far Southwest only as a desert land it comes as something of a shock to learn that here is to be found the greatest continuous sweep of virgin pine forest left in the United States; that in Arizona lumbering has gone on continuously since 1881; and that in Arizona and New Mexico there are fourteen National Forests, covering in the aggregate nearly 20,000,000 acres.

These immense wilderness playgrounds are divided almost equally between the two states in number area and timber resources and each year new roads and trails are creeping deeper into their magnificent fastnesses. As heavy timber in the Southwest normally occurs only above 6,500 feet, cresting the innumerable mountain ranges that criss-cross the country, it is apparent that these fourteen great forests provide ruggedly beautiful scenery of infinite variety. Already they are touched or crossed by Harveycar Cruise routes in a hundred places.

The Indian Country. Although largely remote from any railroad and until very recently inaccessible with full comfort, the Indian country of the Far Southwest is a source of endless attraction to those travelers who have found their way into it.

Squaws parade at Gallup Ceremonial

This attraction is not confined alone to the varied and primitive life of the different tribes and to the frontier atmosphere of the isolated trading posts, great as that is. Many of the outstanding scenic marvels of the country are to be found within the boundaries of Indian land. Rainbow Bridge, Monument Valley, Blue Canyon and Canyons de Chelly and del Muerto, the Painted Desert — these better-known points are merely indicative of the possibilities of great areas that run the whole gamut of scenic and climatic interest.

There are more than 50,000 Navajos, Pueblos, Apaches, Hualapais, Havasupais, Pimas, and members of other scattered tribes, occupying reservations in Arizona and New Mexico aggregating over 37,000 square miles. Belgium, Holland and Denmark combined could almost be contained in this single fascinating field for Harveycar Motor Cruises away from the beaten path.

Courier Wennips and Driver Sayre on a tour

All this 'on-the-spot' appeal made it necessary to give the conductors a set of rules confusing to everyone but the conductors (we hope).

Arrangements are now in effect whereby conductors of Trains 3 and 23, as well as sections thereof, into Dodge City, will inquire of passengers holding sleeping car accommodations to Lamy, whether they expect to make either of the tours, and will file daily at Dodge City, wire addressed to Fred Harvey, Lamy and Santa Fe, advising the total number of passengers for the tours, together with the number of the train and date of arrival at Dodge City.

On account of connection at La Junta between Train 25 and the Limiteds, conductor of Train 25 will file wire at La Junta daily, addressed to Fred Harvey, Lamy and Santa Fe, advising total number of passengers holding sleeping car accommodations to Lamy, desiring to make either of the tours.

Conductor Train 9 leaving La Junta will forward daily wire report to Fred Harvey, Lamy and Santa Fe, advising whether any detour passengers on his train.

Likewise, conductor Train 19 leaving La Junta will forward wire report daily to Fred Harvey, Lamy and Santa Fe, advising number of detour passengers.

Passengers on Trains 1, 2, 4, 14, 16, 20, 21, 24 and 92, make the detour from Albuquerque, hence following arrangements will apply:

Conductor of Train 1 will file daily wire report at Clovis addressed to Fred Harvey, Albuquerque and Santa Fe, showing number of passengers for the detour. In case Train 92 should have passengers for the detour, conductor of that train will likewise file wire report at Clovis.

Conductor of Train 21 passing Vaughn, will send daily report by wire to Fred Harvey, Albuquerque and Santa Fe, showing number of passengers for either of the tours.

Conductors of Trains 2, 4, 20 and 24 will forward daily wire report from Gallup to Fred Harvey, Albuquerque and Santa Fe, showing number of passengers for the detour.

Agent, El Paso Union Depot, will forward daily wire joint with Fred Harvey, Albuquerque and Santa Fe, advising number of detour passengers on Train 14 leaving El Paso. Conductor of this train will not render report covering any passengers for the detour picked up en route, especially from Train 1 at Belen, as conductors of Trains 1 and 92 on arrival Clovis will arrange for proper report of these passengers.

Conductor of Train 16 leaving El Paso will forward daily wire report to Fred Harvey, Albuquerque and Santa Fe, showing number of passengers for the detour. Conductor of this train, however, should not include passengers boarding that train at Belen from Train 21, as conductor passing Vaughn will arrange for report of such passengers.

The Indian Detours were really wired together.

11

THE WHERE OF IT — 1930

The market crash of October 28, 1929, had come so late in the year, the Indian Detours felt little immediate effect from the financial disaster in their 1930 bookings. There were 11,000 millionaires in the United States before the crash; there were still quite a few left who would continue their same lifestyle, which included vacation trips.

One of the millionaires contacted the Santa Fe office in May of 1930, asking for a driver he had had on a previous trip. Hester Jones was assigned as courier and during his private Land Cruise he talked incessantly about how he had worked all his life to become rich enough to take time off to enjoy the New Mexico scenery and no depression was going to rob him of the experience. When they put him back on the train, Driver Sayre told Hester he had spent three days controlling his urge to tell the man he hadn't worked nearly as hard, yet enjoyed the scenery every day.

While the monied dudes would remember the 1930 trips as being less well attended by Easterners they knew from the Society columns, the average dude would remember it was the year the flashlight bulb was invented. Now the camera toting Detourist could leave litterbug eggs behind him in Carlsbad Caverns and La Fonda's dining room as he made indoor pictures to add to his collection.

Unsettled conditions in Europe helped swell the Southwest tourist tide. Allied troops still occupied the Rhineland and the Saar, the Nazi Party was gaining notoriety and Italy was protesting the Treaty of Versailles. Things were even less settled in the Asian world, with Gandhi protesting British rule in India, revolts in Abyssinia erupting when Haile Selassie was proclaimed Emperor, and Mustafa Kemal's social changes, among them the renaming of Constantinople to Istanbul, bringing rumbles of discontent. The Southwest seemed a very peaceful place to visit compared to the rest of the world.

Despite the advances in aviation that came along quickly after Lindbergh's famous flight on May 20, 1927, the train was still the way to get around the United States. True, auto production had reached an all-time high in 1929 with 5,337,087 units being built, but it would take increasing pressures from the depression to make the family car overtake the train for transportation to distant destinations. It would be years before air travel was introduced for Europe-bound vacationers, and luxury cruise ships were losing their attraction for many.

One of the biggest changes in the Harveycar services in 1930 was a change of vehicle marque. The rigors of desert driving had proven one thing to Clarkson; Packards didn't have what it took. By the time the Packards had 25,000 miles on them, they were worn out, and 25,000 miles wasn't hard to rack up on Detours and Land Cruises. Clarkson had taken a long hard look at the 1929 repair records on the Packards at the Santa Fe garage, and a harder look at cars that would meet the Detour requirements. One car stood out on the Grand Canyon garage reports for size, reliable construction and especially for prestige.

The cars ordered in 1929 for the Grand Canyon fleet had been Cadillacs. Seven of them had been added to the existing vehicle fleet which included 3 Chevrolet roadsters, 4 Packards, one Studebaker, 13 Yellow Coaches, 4 closed and 13 open White Bender Sightseeing Coaches, 6 White and 2 Graham trucks.

Contact had been made with General Motors in 1929 to

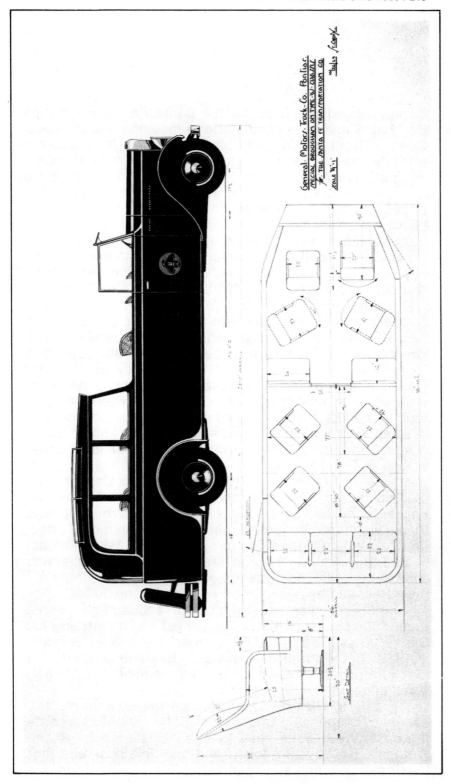

design a special vehicle for the Santa Fe Transportation Co. that would be a combination limousine and mini-bus. Open in front with a portable canvas top for inclement weather, the rear tonneau had a permanent roof and a Continental mount spare tire. The body was to be equipped with six swivel seats, four in the tonneau and two in the front compartment, a seat for driver and courier, a back bench seat for three people and two bench seats in the front compartment. The drawing even included the Harveycar insignia, but although it was planned to have Pontiac produce these vehicles, none were ever built. Nothing was purchased in 1930 other than Cadillacs.

Before the folders for 1930 were at the printers, Clarkson entered an order with the Cadillac dealer for the Santa Fe fleet of seven-passenger cars to be shipped to Las Vegas and to make their debut on the May 15th Taos tours. The price quoted was $3,344.38. They were mostly closed models. This was a reflection of cars in general, for while 90% of American cars sold in 1919 were the open touring models, by 1929 closed models accounted for 90% of sales. And by 1930 they had reliable heaters and the new wireless radios to help alleviate boredom on long drives across desert wastelands.

Meanwhile, the one Studebaker at the Canyon was ordered converted into a tow truck, as were two of the Packards that had been bought in 1926. Two White luggage trucks were ordered junked, one a 1920 2-ton model affectionately called 'Grand Canyon' and a 1925 3½-ton model named 'Big Jim'. A ¾-ton White bought in 1920 was also condemned. Clarkson was upholding his promise that only the safest and best was good enough for the dudes.

In a well planned program of acquainting people around the country with the Southwest and its attractions, Clarkson assigned five of the couriers to travel extensively in 1930. Riding the trains appealed to some couriers, the idea of a trip free except for the requirement to make personal appearances appealed to all.

Henrietta Gloff concentrated on the area where she had many friends and where many of her past dudes came from, the West Coast. In Los Angeles she spoke to the Women's Traffic Club, to the National Business and Professional Women's organization, and in Bullock's

Henrietta Gloff

Auditorium to an invited public. She went on to spend a month in San Francisco, talking to such groups as the Sunrisers, and then spending long days in the Santa Fe downtown office, talking to anyone tempted by the many newspaper articles and ads appearing daily.

The newspaper articles had one thing in common. They were turned out in duplicates, with only the area name to identify them, and they were mailed all over the United States. Word for word, the same article about Gloff in Los Angeles was tailored for Tucker in New York, Shuler in Pittsburgh and McFie in Chicago.

The girls talked before Rotary Clubs, to Music Clubs, Garden Clubs, Girl Scout groups, Kiwanians. Dorothy (Raper) Miller left her new husband behind in order to help Mary Tucker put on a real spread for 50 representatives of Buffalo travel bureaus and Railroad offices that started with a banquet and ended with a lecture and motion picture depicting the beauties of the Southwest.

A monthly magazine for chain hotels, showed an appealing picture of Mary Tucker, Indian bowl in hand, wearing her official regalia, inviting people to talk to her at the New York Santa Fe office on Fifth Avenue. The article was slightly ludicrous:

"And do you like being in New York City?", someone asked her. Turning her gaze to a large wall map of the pueblo country away off in the Southwest, she answered by asking: "Do you like talking about someone you love better than being with him?" Miss Tucker, nevertheless, is making herself as happy as possible for her from the wide open spaces to be in the high and narrow spaces of this New York town. She is living in Holley Chambers' apartment, with at least historic Washington Square below her.

The Baltimore & Ohio, enjoying fringe benefits from people East of Chicago who couldn't wait to take in the Indian Detours, was a bit more sophisticated in their coverage of Winifred Shuler's appearance at their Women's Music Club. After explaining she was one of some 35 such young women, they quoted her at great length in their publication.

"Half the world does not know how the other half lives," says Miss Schuler, "but we take it for granted they would like to know. For instance, how many people know that today we have hundreds of Indians as expert with the magic club as the boomerang throwers of Australia; that we have magicians among the Navajos who perform just as astonishing feats as the jugglers of India; that we have a Penitente Brotherhood among the native population of New Mexico that make religious processions and pilgrimages, including cross-bearing and flaggellation, a real flesh-and-blood Passion Play, events to the extent of crucifying one of their members; that we have Hopi priests who handle the deadliest of snakes; that we have Indians at Taos who, with their ancestors, have lived in five-story, two or three-hundred room apartment houses built of mud, for unknown centuries; that we have thousands of prehistoric ruins that in all probability housed more people than the entire population of three civilizations living there today.

"We have all of this in the great Southwest, besides all the scenic wonders such as the Grand Canyon of the Colorado, the greatest gorge in the world, the Carlsbad Caverns, so large that the Woolworth Tower could be placed in one of its many rooms and not be crowded; the petrified forest with its thousands of acres of reclining stone trees; the painted desert with its varied and brilliant colors that no words can describe; Canyon de Chelly with its red sandstone cliffs so high that ruins of entire villages look like bird's nests perched high on the sides, with its canyon so wide that there is space for Navajos to run their sheep and raise their corn; Chaco Canyon with its Pueblo Bonito (beautiful town), the most remarkable example of masonry to be found; Mesa Verde with its unknown number of ruins: Rainbow Bridge and Monument Valley, so unlike anything else in the world and so beautiful

Pottery selling from the Indian's and dude's viewpoint

that the sight of them opens new worlds for the beholder.

"This magic has been hidden in the Southwest for hundreds of years, but is now being opened up for the traveler by the Santa Fe Railroad Company, and Fred Harvey, through their motor detours into the Indian country. A motor service second to none in the world is available at all Santa Fe stations in New Mexico and Arizona, with fleet headquarters in the ancient capital of Santa Fe. Each car is accompanied by a driver, who is also a mechanician, and a courier who acts in the double capacity of hostess and guide. It is necessary in this little known country to have someone interpret the country as well as take care of all the bothersome details of travel."

The success of these emissaries proved to Clarkson this was a program which should be continued; a plan for more appearances of the couriers was put into effect.

New rates were in effect, too, still spiraling upwards. The Taos Three-Day Tour was now priced at $65.00, with children from five to twelve years old costing $32.50. Children under five were $6.75, but would not be assigned a seat, and surely many parents felt jolting around the roads of New Mexico even in a luxurious Cadillac would be a strain holding a child on a lap.

A trip combining the Frijoles trip with a tour of Puyé was added, costing $40 for adults and $20 for children. For

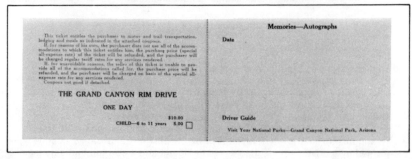

Cover and inside of a coupon book

Informational poster for Detourists

An autographed postcard of Jim White

tourists really on the run, a Day in Santa Fe cost $12.50 for adults and $6.25 for children.

The most important change was announced in bold type reading: "It is important to note that after May 15th, Lamy, New Mexico will be the official gateway for these Indian Detours and passengers will detrain and entrain at that point. No service from Albuquerque, New Mexico."

Because of the increasing numbers of options as well as regularly scheduled outings, coupon books were issued to everyone for everything. Eat a meal, sleep in a bed, ride in a car, enjoy a basket lunch, visit a museum that charged admission — it was all in the coupon book. And as an added attraction, the coupon book covers were a miniature postcard with hand-colored scenes. The back inside cover had a place for the autograph of courier and driver. It made an inexpensive souvenir that would advertise the trip after the dudes returned home.

The remaining millionaires were still bringing their private railroad cars across the country and the Santa Fe Railways reiterated in 1930 that it would allow the cars to be parked for sleeping purposes at either Lamy or Santa Fe, so long as the occupants were on the Tours or Land Cruises. And a rebate of $3.50 a day was made to those who slept on the train.

Harveycars, drivers and couriers were now stationed at Winslow, Arizona where tourists could bed down at La

Posada. This detraining arrangement made tours to the attractions of Arizona easier for those who didn't relish the auto trip from Santa Fe across the Indian country.

One trip greatly enhanced by the new arrangements was the tour to the Hopi Mesas. Perhaps no other Indian celebration impressed the dudes more than the Hopi Snake Dance, held every August. Because there were no accommodations at the villages, the accommodations were loaded on trucks and brought to the site. Large tents complete with cots, blankets, pillows, lanterns and wash basins made portable hotels, not up to the Harvey standards, but this was acceptable to the dudes. Tables and chairs were trucked out to make portable dining halls. Foodstuffs, beverages, cooking equipment, cooling devices, all assured the tourist they would eat unspoiled food, prepared in the Harvey Hotel kitchen, served, if not with silver candelabra as pictured in Sloan's etching of the Corn Dance, at least with napery. When the weather was too hot for the dudes to stay in tents, they slept in the school house at Keams Canyon.

There was even hot tea to bring a touch of grace to the meal, as Ruth Champion well remembers. The couriers were expected to serve the food which the Harvey chefs were busy cooking. With 60 people to wait on, there was always one in every crowd who called the courier over and asked if she could please 'make my tea a little weaker?'

Once two Boston ladies in Queen Mary hats took one deep breath as they started out of the coach, returned to their seats holding their noses and told courier Rainey Bartley they would have their meal served in the coach.

Whether the tourist was seeing the Snake Dance for the first time, or was a repeat viewer, the sight never ceased to amaze the city-bred travelers. The ceremony was held at Walpi and Mishongnovi on odd years and at Hotevilla, Chimopavi and Shipaulovi during the even years.

Driving to the mesa, the couriers told the legend of Ti-yo, a hero god who figured in many Hopi legends. His father was a chief and he had a brother and two sisters. He would sit at the edge of a deep hole in the Grand Canyon from which the Hopis believed man emerged from the underworld. Ti-yo wondered where the river water went on its endless journey and he finally asked his father's help in

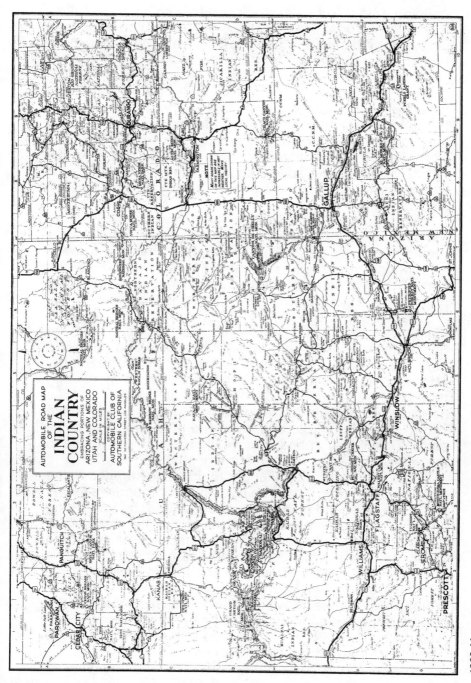

1929 Map

building a boat from a cottonwood tree so he could follow it. When the boat was finished, it was loaded with food prepared by his sisters and mother, while his father gave him gifts for the various earth and sky gods.

When Ti-yo's boat came to rest on the river bank, he climbed out and looked down a small hole at his feet. This was the home of Spider Woman who invited him to squeeze through the hole and join her in the sacred kiva. He gave her the gift his father had prepared for her and she said she would make herself invisible, perching on the top of his right ear to whisper advice as he journeyed on. She took with her some of her magic potion that calmed snakes and wild animals.

With Spider Woman guiding him, Ti-yo descended into the underworld, meeting snakes and bears which were turned docile by the potion squirted on them. In a lower kiva, whose entrance was guarded by the bears, he met the god of the six cardinal points and gave him a gift which prompted the god to promise him anything he wished for.

Passing further downward, Ti-yo calmed two snarling pumas to reach the house of the Woman of Hard Substance who lived in a kiva of turquoise and coral. He gave her one of his gifts and she welcomed him. Shortly afterward, as he sat talking to her, the Sun came rushing through the air and landed with a thud on the kiva roof. As he came into the kiva, Ti-yo gave him his gift and Sun told him to grasp his girdle and he would take him around the earth. Ti-yo hung on and was finally taken to the house in the west, where he was given many gifts.

Returning toward the upper regions, he stopped in the Snake house again where he remained for four days listening to the chief and being instructed on what songs to sing and how to paint their bodies so the rain would come. After giving him many gifts, the chief gave him two maidens who knew the charm which prevented death from rattlesnake bites. One girl was for Ti-yo and one for his brother.

Ti-yo spent four more days at the house of Spider Woman while she wove a special basket that would transport the two maidens and Ti-yo to his world on the surface of the earth. After he returned to his home, Ti-yo and his brother married the two maidens.

On the four following days after the wedding, snakes

came into the village from the underworld and ate corn in the kiva, returning to the valley each morning.

The legend concluded with the maidens reverting to their snakelike lives and bearing small snakes, who attacked the children of the village. Because the children all died of poison, their mothers forced the men of the village to migrate. In migrating, they taught the snake ritual to other clans.

The Hopi Snake Dance was explained as a dramatization of a ritual which had its origin in a myth. In 1923, the U.S. Government had tried to stop the ceremonies, using as an excuse the fact the Indians lost much time that could be better spent in working than in taking a nine-day vacation. They suggested the ceremony would be better done in the winter when work was over, either not realizing snakes hibernated in winter, or else hoping the ceremonies would automatically die out with the lack of snakes to be caught.

Despite the efforts of the government agents, the Snake Dance survived and the dudes watched in fascinated trepidation as the ritual was carried out. They saw only the final ritual, not the beginning, so they were given the foregoing action in a lecture before leaving for the Mesas. As the couriers told it:

> "First there is a gathering of rattlesnakes by loin-cloth wearing priests. Carrying a small bag of sacred meal and a digging stick, the only other piece of equipment is a buckskin bag into which the snakes are put as they are caught. The snakes are then dumped on the kiva floor and the priests select some to take home. Once home, the priest washes the snake in cold water in which yellow root medicine has been mixed. The priest then throws away his clothes and washes himself thoroughly.
>
> "After this is done, he fasts for a day and dances all night. He must feed the rattlesnakes before he feeds himself. This is the preliminary ritual and these rituals may vary slightly from clan to clan."

On the dance day, when the dudes were brought in to watch, the priests used gourds and rattles to imitate the sound of thunder. Women in ceremonial dress made a ring around a sacred rock and then the snake dancers appeared, two by two. The dancer on the left side held a rattlesnake in his mouth and one in each hand. The dancer on the right carried a ceremonial wand tipped in eagle feathers. With these, he tickled the head, neck and mouth of the snakes, an action which seemed to mesmerize them.

Hopi Snake Dance

As the snake carriers reached the east end of the enclosure, they spit the snakes onto the ground and went on to the sacred lodge at the east end. The women dipped their hands into shallow baskets they were carrying and scattered finely ground corn upon the dancers and the snakes, chanting prayers at the same time.

As soon as the dancers reached the lodge, they turned around and returned to the west end to pick up more writhing snakes, and repeated this until all the snakes that had been gathered were transported to the east end.

The priest then recited a prayer and the snake carriers seized bundles of snakes in their hands, running back to level ground below the mesa where they turned the snakes loose to the four directions. The purpose was to have the snakes carry their prayers to the underworld so the rain gods would answer them.

Purification rites in the kiva followed the release of the snakes, after the men had all taken an emetic and vomited over the sides of the mesa.

The universal question from the dudes was how the Indians could perform the Dance without being fatally bitten; to this the couriers were trained to answer that no one really knew. They were assured the emetic was a simple purification rite and had nothing to do with it, that the Indians did not defang the snakes, nor did they rub their bodies or hands with anything that might be an antidote, nor take one internally. It was suggested that perhaps the ritual with the tickling feathers might stupefy the snakes, yet there were cases when a snake could actually be seen hanging from his fangs buried deeply in an Indian's cheek. Some of the tourists watched wide-eyed, then joined the heave-ho over the side of the mesa without needing an emetic. And as though to point up the efficacy of the ceremony, the dudes were often caught in rainstorms before they could leave the mesa behind.

Clarkson ran into problems sending some of the tours into Arizona. When a coachload of dudes would sign up for the Grand Canyon cruise, he undoubtedly groaned as he smiled, for he knew the antagonism of the bus-line operators at the Canyon meant the dudes had to be transferred from the Harveycars to Canyon coaches before entering the Park and sightseeing along the rim.

Once, when a group had signed up for the Hopi Snake Dance, tour leader Chick Berchtold was stopped as he prepared to leave Winslow. The cars had been deadheaded from Santa Fe and carried New Mexico license plates. The Arizona Highway Department refused to allow the cars to move until they had Arizona plates as well. "There was no money allowance for that, and I made a fast collection from the other drivers and everyone I knew in town borrowing enough money to get the trip on the road without too much delay. Fortunately, it wasn't a weekend." After that incident, any cars likely to be in adjoining states were licensed in those states, and some of the cars that made trips to Mesa Verde, Navajo Country and into California looked like a well-branded horse.

The rates had not changed for the Hopi Pueblo Cruise in 1930. The Carlsbad Caverns Cruise and the Seven-Day Sierra Verde Circle Cruise had been added late in the Detour scheduling, and their prices were within reason. No changes were made in the rates for these trips either. Rates on the Cruises to Mesa Verde, Rainbow Bridge, Monument Valley, Canyon de Chelly, Painted Desert, Petrified Forest, Nava-Hopi land, Gallup and Zuni had gone up in price. One person now paid $70 a day, two persons

Ads such as this one brought people directly to the Grand Canyon by train

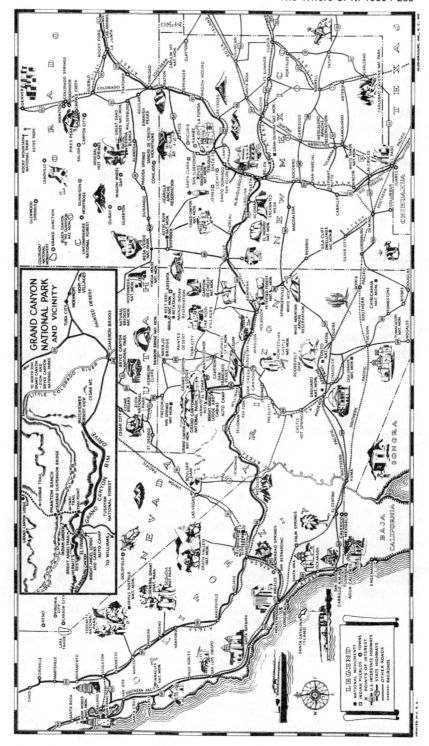

$80, three persons $90 and four $100. For many, who chose to take the trips by combining several destinations and staying out for as long as a month, the charges often amounted to the price of the car, but many people wanted to walk away from their transportation when the trip was over rather than drive their own car from Eastern points.

There were a few notes that appeared in the agents' bulletins which never found their way into the folders, but which explain why the New Mexico tours continued in popularity, increasing every year, while the Arizona tours never had that big a growth pattern. Train schedules showed train arrivals in Arizona were not conducive to detraining and sightseeing. The Chief arrived in Winslow at 1:25 A.M. hardly the time to begin a night's rest for a tiring tour. There were other trains, but the scheduling still presented a problem. The California Limited #3 arrived at 3:00 P.M., too late in the day to explore the Canyon and the Grand Canyon Limited #23 arrived at an even later time, 6:35 P.M. The Chief #20 arrived at 3:10 P.M. while the Grand Canyon Limited #24 gave a full day's sightseeing by arriving at 7:40 A.M. but meant the passenger had to get up in time to have breakfast at 6:00, or go hungry until lunchtime. A terse statement under 'Important Notes' reads: "Train #19, the Chief arrives Winslow 1:25 A.M. and is inconvenient."

The one convenient thing about Winslow was the hotel. Like many of the Harvey Houses, La Posada had been built in the 1880's, but in an effort to attract more people to Arizona, it had been completely rebuilt with 75 guest rooms and a dining and lunch room. Patterned after an old Spanish ranch, La Posada was an amazing oasis in an otherwise uninviting area.

From the hotel, a brand new trip was touted in 1930 — the Meteor Mountain Detour. Starting June 1st, the tour included the Petrified Forest, the Meteor Crater, three meals and an overnight stay for $17.50 per adult and $8.75 per child. Coupons could be purchased on the train by last minute deciders and a train courier informed interested parties that there were as many unknown factors as known ones about the origin, size and disposition of the object from outer space.

The known facts included the size, a diameter of 4,150 ft. at the rim, with a depth of 570 ft., and the information

Montage page of Arizona, Indians from Detour brochure

that there was no volcanic trace anywhere near the crater. So it had to be a meteor or group of meteorites, and the age of 22,000 years ago was more than an educated guess.

The dudes were told to look for the finely pulverized sandstone testifying to the force with which the object struck, and its discovery in 1871 by a scout for General Crook was talked about. The balance of fact and theory was saved for those who would take the trip and stand in awe on the rim, wondering if the estimated weight of 5,000,000 tons meant the meteor was still deeply buried in the center hole.

The combination of the two points of interest worked out well for the Harvey organization. Originally planned only as a Petrified Forest/Painted Desert Cruise, the addition of the Meteor Crater sparked new interest on the part of the train travelers. Their interest would be more expensive very shortly, for on August 7th, announcement was made that the Meteor Mountain-Petrified Forest cruise would now cost $25 for adults, $12.50 for children. To compensate for this, a change in train scheduling was made, arranging for more convenient hours of arrival and departure at Winslow.

Visitors' center at Bandelier National Monument

Indian bake ovens

Shaping the bread for baking

*Cover of the Nov.
1930 brochure*

With this change, the way opened up to offer the Natural Bridge tour at the Petrified Forest in the morning, a return for a leisurely lunch at La Posada, and a trip to the Meteor Mountain in the afternoon.

One of the most complete, costly and impressive folders that would ever be put out on the Indian Detours was published in November, 1930. With an artist's rendering of Indians, monoliths, Taos Pueblo, a Harveycar and gentle mountains in a composite picture on the orange/purple/black/tan/red and blue cover, this was the last folder that would carry the Harveycar insignia.

The folder was indexed and its crisp unembellished writing is strangely unlike past releases. Although no records exist of its authorship, either Birdseye changed his style or Clarkson changed writers.

All phases of the Indian Detour operation were spelled out and it provided a most comprehensive record of the areas covered on the Southwestern tours. A new style of

Following pages: Maps from the new brochure

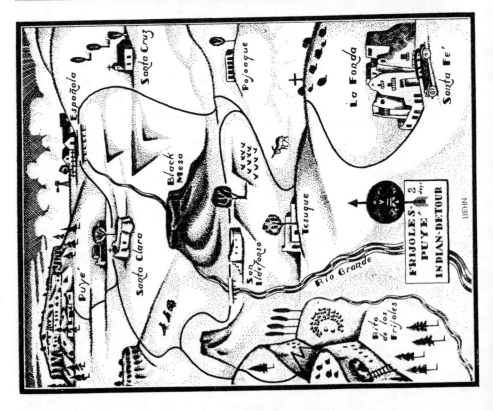

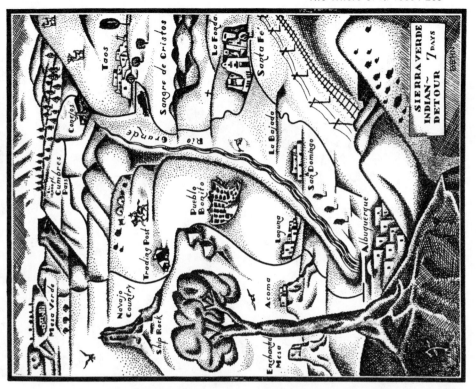

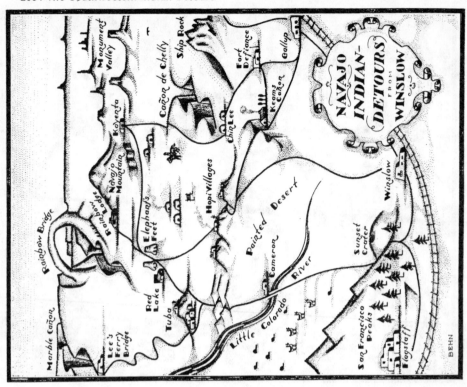

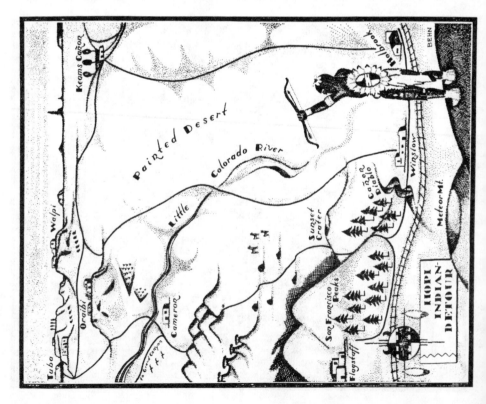

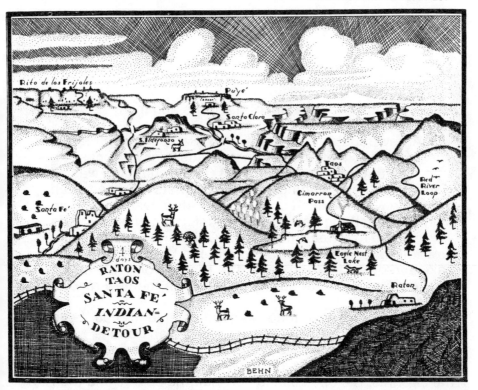

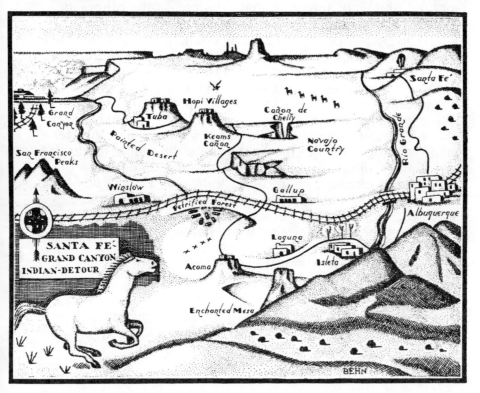

map was included for each of the tours and many new pictures had been used.

A new regular tour was added, Raton-Taos-Santa Fe. The completion of the Raton to Taos highway, passing smoothly through the magnificent Cimarron region was all Harvey had been waiting for. Past tourists who had seen the same New Mexican scenery year after year, now could plan on something new. Sentimentalists and history buffs who wanted to retrace more of the Old Santa Fe Trail, could now follow it from Cimarron to Moreno Valley, Eagle Nest Lake and over Cimarron Pass. The trip was only 100 miles; the new Cadillacs ate up the distance on the new road in one afternoon.

Before the new road was completed it had been necessary to drive the cars over a two-plank bridge when water filled a deep arroyo. Usually the dudes would take a look at the rushing water, the two boards little wider than the car tires, the open space between the boards and then get out and walk across to meet the car on the other side. Few ever realized they were much safer in the vehicle.

The whole tour took four days, taking in Taos and the Red River gorge, Puyé, Santa Clara and on to Santa Fe. The one fly in the pocketbook ointment was the charge. Because it was necessary to deadhead the cars from and to Raton, the back of the folder informed interested dudes there would be a 15¢ per mile surcharge. Referring back to page 26, the fine print mentioned 175 miles round trip for deadhead figuring, but they left it up to the reader to multiply the two figures out and find it was $26.25 extra for the privilege of having a new Harvey tour, plus $70 per day for one guest, $40 each for two, $30 each for three and $25 each for four or more guests. A real tongue-in-cheek appeared on the rate page under the heading

CHARGES: "A rather jolly feature of Harveycar service is that one is definitely apprised in advance of what may be expected in the way of expense."

Jolly or not, the Indian Detours were expanding their horizons.

12

THE CHANGEOVER: 1931-1932

For the first two months of 1931, the Harveycars and coaches made the usual Detour and Land Cruise runs, going out to the Zuni Reservation to see the Sword Swallowers Dance, or some of the ceremony of the New Year's Celebration. The latter was a movable holiday for the Indians, depending on the position of the sun. In 1931 it began on January 12th. The date was set by the Sun Priest who observed the sun through two forked sticks adorned with feathers and proclaimed it the proper time.

It was a ceremony designed to select the participants for the famous Shalako Dance which took place right after Thanksgiving Day and to be selected was a most coveted honor.

One of the Courier Instructional Bulletins was issued for informing the public of the ritual observed in the naming of the chosen ones. The couriers memorized the facts like a play script and read it back to the dudes on demand.

SUBJECT: HOW ZUNI CELEBRATES ITS NEW YEAR:

This day marks the beginning of a ten day fast called a "tesque", the first observance of which is a general planting of prayer plumes. For men and women in general, the "tesque" is over in *four* days; for office

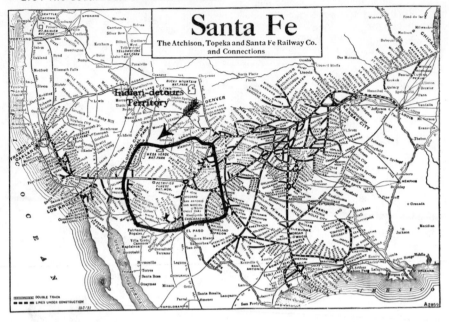

holders *eight* days are required; while the whole *ten* days are necessary to complete the work of the high priest or *cacique*.

Plumes, each consisting of four prayer feathers, have been made by the head of each family for himself, his wife and each unmarried child. Then upon this day set by the Sun Priest, each family goes to its own cornfield. The rest of the family watch as the father, or another head of the family, digs a hole in the ground, in which he plants his prayer feathers. Next his wife does likewise, with each child following in order of birth, one at a time, until all the plumes have been properly planted. During this ceremony the men offer prayers to the sun, while the women make their supplications to the moon. The villagers at large offer a common prayer, which is different from the much more elaborate one offered by the high priest.

The following prayers are offered during this ten-day observance: A prayer for the safe keeping of their best seeds, with a plea for a year of good crops. These best seeds have been previously collected and set aside in a pot.

Prayers for the safety and life of every kind of animal he or any of his family may own, are offered by the head of each family on the fourth day.

On the same day, the medicine men of eight clans offer prayers to the most fleet and powerful of the wild animals, such as the deer, buffalo, wild goats and bears, with added prayers that during the coming year their people may have the strength, swiftness and cunning possessed by these wild creatures.

A strict code of morals is prescribed for each Zuni during this ten-day ceremony. Each man must retire to his own room at night to sleep alone; and he must refrain from conversation with any woman during this retreat. He cannot smoke, nor make a light of any kind outside of his own house; nor may he throw ashes outside during this period.

One feature of the celebration is the choice by the Cacique of the participants in the next Shalako performance, such as the fire god Siatash, Mud Heads and Salimopeoa. The Salimopeoa are the spirits who were originally appointed to bring cereals to the Zuni (or Ah-shi-wi, as they call themselves), who prior to that time in their early mythology had subsisted upon the seeds of a grass. The Sa-la-mo-bi-yas went to the north, south, east, west, the zenith and the nadir to get these cereals and are represented in the colors always associated with these points: the Sa-la-mo-bi-ya of the east wear white; of the south wear red; of the west wear blue; of the north wear yellow; of the heavens wear all color; and of the earth wear black. Their masks are made of buckskin colored these different colors with clays and bordered about the neck with a ruff of feathers. Their nude bodies generally bear the same colors.

A council consisting of one member from each of six different clans must get together at some time during the "tesque" celebration and decide who shall build the Shalako houses for the next year. The performers of the Shalako must come from the clans whose members are appointed to construct the houses for that particular year.

After these selections are made, the chosen ones are brought before the Cacique for a lengthy lecture of instruction upon their duties and morals. A pledge is then exacted of each to live a life of peace and strictest morality during the sacred year, under penalty that he will be "kicked out" and another appointed in his place.

Indians replaced Couriers on Santa Fe trains to promote Detours

Each family that is to build a Shalako house, receives from the priest in charge of the most sacred kiva a plumage composed of a variety of symbolic feathers. This is taken home and kept until the next Shalako dance is over, when the Mud Heads come to take it and return it to the sacred kiva, where it remains until the succeeding "tesque", when it goes to a a reappointed home.

In February, the Cadillacs were busy transporting the dudes to the Buffalo Dance at Tesuque, the Deer Dance at Taos, and Eagle Dances at San Ildefonso, only this year there were lots fewer passengers. The Depression was affecting everyone at this point. Salaries for the drivers and couriers were down, but so were costs on the necessities as well as luxuries of life. And so were the receipts for the Santa Fe Transportation Company.

When Ford Harvey had died at Puyé in 1928, Byron S. Harvey, his brother, became president and head of the Harvey company with Ford's son Frederick his assistant. Byron had watched the early growth and recent decline of the Santa Fe Transportation Company and being a hard-headed businessman, had felt the returns certainly didn't justify the means.

The first rumor of an impending change was published in the Santa Fe New Mexican of March 7, 1931.

PLAN CHANGE OF CONTROL FOR DETOUR
Considering Several Plans for Future of Santa Fe Transportation Company

EXPECT STATEMENT SOON
Harveys Say no change in the Character of Service or in Company Personnel

Byron and Frederick Harvey today would neither affirm nor deny persistent reports here that Major R. Hunter Clarkson, and others will take over the ownership and operation of the Santa Fe Transportation company, motor bus division of the Fred Harvey system.

The Santa Fe Transportation company is the "Harvey Indian detour" system of scenic travels in New Mexico, Colorado and Arizona.

While neither of the Harveys would permit a quotation it was definitely understood, from a conversation with them, that several plans affecting the future of the Santa Fe Transportation company are being considered, but that no conclusions sufficiently definite to justify an announcement have yet been reached. As soon as it is possible a public statement will be issued by the company.

It was likewise understood that any plans in process of perfection do not contemplate any change in the personnel, in the character of the service now being rendered or in the company's relationship with the public.

The Harveys are in Santa Fe on a routine inspection trip of the properties of the Fred Harvey company and the Santa Fe Transportation company, and will continue west from here.

Major Hunter Clarkson, manager of the Santa Fe Transportation company, was reported to be either in Chicago for a conference with officials of the Santa Fe railroad, or to have left there to return to Santa Fe.

The Fred Harvey company and the Santa Fe Transportation company are separate corporations, but they work on a co-operative basis in the "Harvey Indian detour" projects.

For another week there was no confirmation from either side, and the tour business went on with employees wondering when they would be told something concrete. The announcement came on March 16th in simultaneous releases. The Albuquerque Journal ran a short notice as follows:

HARVEY SELLS BUS LINES

Clarkson to Take Over Detours, Allied Services

B. S. Harvey, president of the Harvey company, announced Monday that arrangements have been made to sell the equipment and good will of the Santa Fe Transportation company, operating the Indian detours and allied services, to R. Hunter Clarkson, who initiated the Indian detour project five years ago and has managed the operations up to the present time.

Clarkson's company will shortly take over the organization of the Santa Fe Transportation company, including supervisory staff, couriers and drivers, and the new company will continue to provide the same motor equipment, personnel and individualized service furnished on the various Indian detours, etc., under Harvey company management during the past five years. Headquarters will remain in Santa Fe.

Limousine "Couriercars" (formerly known as Harveycars) will be used in the two and three-day Indian detours and motor cruises.

La Fonda hotel at Santa Fe will remain under Harvey company management.

The motor operations of the Santa Fe Transportation company centered in Winslow, Ariz., will also be included in the transfer to the new company.

A longer coverage was given by the Santa Fe New Mexican, possibly because the majority of the people affected were in that area.

HARVEY MAKES ANNOUNCEMENT OF TRANSFER

Headquarters of Firm to Stay Here;
Character of Service Unchanged

KEEP ALL EMPLOYEES ON

Pay Roll Stays Same as Before;
New Company Called Hunter Clarkson, Inc.

The transfer of the Indian Detours and allied services, the Santa Fe

Transportation company, from the Harvey company to Maj. R. Hunter Clarkson was announced today.

In explaining the operation of the new company, Major Clarkson said that it would be continued on exactly the same basis as heretofore. The chief effect of the change will be to allow the management more leeway in the development of the corporation than was possible as a subsidiary of the Harvey company.

RENAME COMPANY

Major Clarkson said that the new company will be known as Hunter Clarkson, Inc. The automobiles will be known as Couriercars, and the insignia of the company will be changed to a conventionalized sketch of two eagle dancers. Otherwise there will be no change that can be recognized by the community.

The headquarters of the firm will continue to be in Santa Fe. The personnel and pay roll will be exactly what they always have been. The relation of the company with the Santa Fe railway and the Harveys will be unchanged. And the field of operation will be as before, limited to trips out of headquarters in Santa Fe and in Winslow, Ariz.

The company has completed arrangements which are calculated to materially increase tourist travel in this section. During the past year the company has had over 47,000 people to take the detour over the Santa Fe territory, and under the new arrangements, Major Clarkson said he would not be surprised to see this number doubled.

The official announcement issued today follows:

B. S. Harvey, president of the Harvey company, announces today that arrangements have been made to sell the equipment and good-will of the Santa Fe Transporation company, operating the Indian Detours and allied services, to R. Hunter Clarkson who initiated the Indian Detour project five years ago and has managed the operations up to the present time.

Mr. Clarkson's company will shortly take over the organization of the Santa Fe Transportation company, including supervisory staff, couriers and drivers, and the new company will continue to provide the same high standard of motor equipment, personnel and individualized service furnished on the various Indian Detours, etc., under Harvey company management during the past five years. Headquarters will remain in Santa Fe, N. M., as at present.

Limousine "Couriercars" (formerly known as Harveycars) will be used on the two and three-day Indian Detours and motor cruises.

La Fonda hotel at Santa Fe will remain under Harvey company management.

The motor operations of the Santa Fe Transportation company centered in Winslow, Ariz., will also be included in the transfer to the new company.

A brief item appeared in the Kansas City Times on the following day, released from the Harvey headquarter office.

HARVEY SELLS BUS LINES

Maj. Hunter Clarkson Buys Indian Tour Business

Byron S. Harvey, president of the Harvey Company, announced today that arrangements have been made to sell the Santa Fe Transportation Company, which has operated the Indian Tour busses of the Harvey service, to Maj. R. Hunter Clarkson.

New hat emblem

New car and coach insignia

> Clarkson, who has managed the transportation company from its inception, said the company would be reorganized under the name of Hunter Clarkson, Inc.
>
> The motor operations of the Santa Fe Transportation Company centering in Winslow, Ariz., Harvey said, will be included in the transfer.

Because of the operation in Arizona, the news was also picked up by the Arizona Republic on the same day.

Manager Buys Harvey Indian Detour Busses

> B. S. Harvey of Kansas City, president of the Harvey company, announced today that arrangements have been made to sell the Santa Fe Transportation company, which has operated the Indian detours busses of the Harvey service to Maj. R. Hunter Clarkson.
>
> Clarkson, who has managed the transportation company from its inception to the present time, said the company will be continued on its past basis but will be re-organized under the name of Hunter Clarkson, Inc.
>
> The motor operations of the Santa Fe Transportation company centering in Winslow, Ariz., Mr. Harvey said, will also be included in the tranfer to the new company.

The entire transfer couldn't have been as sudden as the public was led to believe, for within a week flyers were in the hands of Santa Fe agents announcing rate changes and nowhere did the customary Harveycar insignia appear as it always had on previous bulletins. Two of the trips, the two-day and three-day Indian-detours (now in a changed spelling form), had been reduced in rates, the former down $5 and the latter down $10. The popular but strenuous Frijoles visit had been eliminated on the two-day tour. The one-day tour had been raised $2.50 with the inclusion of Puyé.

The elimination of the Frijoles tour had been discussed before Clarkson took over. Because there was no road down into the ruins, all supplies had to be lowered with ropes. In fact, the tour car that took people around on the valley floor had been dismantled, let down in pieces and

The Couriercar garage
opposite La Fonda

reassembled. There were some mules available, but most of the dudes were expected to walk down and back, and depending on the progress of the tourists, this could badly delay the schedule for the rest of the day's tour. So it was no surprise when the bulletin omitted it.

ANNOUNCING: Important Rate Changes for Regular Indian-detours   Effective APRIL 1st, 1931

Your attention is drawn to certain important changes in rates effective *on and after April 1st, 1931,* for the regular Three-day, Two-day and One-day Indian-detours.

Rates for the Three-day and Two-day Indian-detours will be materially reduced. Routing of the Two-day Indian-detour will be altered to eliminate Frijoles Canyon and give guests the benefit of the exceedingly popular overnight trip to Taos, via the Puyé ruins.

Rate for the One-day Indian-detour ("A Day in Old Santa Fe") will be slightly increased and the itinerary vastly improved to include Santa Clara Indian pueblo and the luncheon drive to the Puyé cliff dwellings.

These reductions in rates will in no way affect the established high standards in accommodations, motor equipment, personnel and individualized service of the Indian-detours.

All Indian-detour Tickets Issued for Service April 1 or Later Should be Sold at New Rates.

Today the garage
is a shopping mall

Three-Day Indian-detour — New Rate — $55.00

Rate reduced from $65.00 to $55.00 per person, with half-fare in proportion. Otherwise no change in service or route. Charge covers nine meals, three nights' accommodations with private bath, 320 miles motor transportation. Limousine service throughout from Santa Fe. Itinerary includes Old Santa Fe, Frijoles Canyon, Puyé Cliff Dwellings and San Ildefonso, Santa Clara and Taos Indian pueblos.

Private Car Rates. Private car rates for the Three-day Indian-detour, including exclusive use of seven-passenger limousine, courier and driver, Lamy to Lamy, have been materially reduced. New rates as follows:

    1 person $150.25   2 persons $173.50   3 persons $196.75
    4 persons (4 full fares) $220.00   5 persons (5 full fares) $275.00
    Note: For half-fare add $12.00 to above. Two half-fares equal one full fare.

Two-Day Indian-detour — New Rate — $35.00

Rate reduced from $40.00 to $35.00 per person, with half fare in proportion. No change in type of service but routing altered to eliminate Frijoles Canyon and include Puyé cliff dwellings, Santa Clara Indian pueblo, Don Fernando de Taos and Taos Indian pueblo in delightful overnight trip. Charge includes six meals, two nights' accommodations with private bath, 220 miles motor transportation. Limousine service throughout from Santa Fe.

Private Car Rates. Private car rates for the Two-day Indian-detour, including exclusive use of seven-passenger limousine, courier and driver, Lamy to Lamy, have been materially reduced. New rates as follows:

    1 person $93.50   2 persons $109.00   3 persons $124.50
    4 persons (4 full fares) $140.00   5 persons (5 full fares) $175.00
    Note: For half-fare add $7.75 to above. Two half fares equal one full fare.

One-Day Indian-detour — New Rate — $15.00

Rate increased from $12.50 to $15.00 per person, with half fare in proportion. No change in type of service or motor transportation, which is by motor coach throughout, but itinerary extended to include luncheon drive to Puyé cliff dwellings and Santa Clara Indian pueblo. Charge covers three meals, one night's accommodation with private bath, all motor transportation.

Transportation Rate Only: Includes all motor transportation. Passengers make own arrangements at La Fonda for room and meals. $9.55 per person if rail ticket reads to Lamy, or $7.75 per person if rail ticket reads to Santa Fe, New Mexico. Both rates include luncheon at Puyé and entrance fee to Ruins.

Private Car Rates. Private car rates for the One-day Indian-detour, including exclusive use of seven-passenger limousine, courier and driver, Lamy to Lamy, will be as follows:

    1 person $56.75   2 persons $64.50   3 persons $72.25
    4 persons $80.00   5 persons $87.75
    Note: For half fare add $4.00 to the above. Two half fares equal one full fare.

Important

Please note that, effective April 1, 1931, limousines for all guests starting the *regular* three-day or two-day Indian-detours will depart from

La Fonda Hotel, Santa Fe, promptly at 9 a.m. daily. This hour is convenient for guests arriving at Lamy, New Mexico, on all principal Santa Fe
main line trains, eastbound or westbound. Scattered passengers arriving at Lamy from Santa Fe train No. 8, from El Paso and other southern
points, however, will not reach La Fonda until 10:08 a.m. It will therefore
be necessary for such guests to remain over at La Fonda until the
following morning before starting the first full day of their Indian-detour.
The additional expense involved in these scattered cases will amount to
the cost of either one or two meals, depending upon the train connection desired on completion of the Indian-detour.

All motor coaches for the trip to Santa Clara and the Puyé cliff
dwellings, included on the One-day Indian-detour, will leave La Fonda
Hotel, Santa Fe, promptly at 10:30 a.m. daily.

Indian-detours literature will be revised as rapidly as possible to
give full effect to the changes noted above.

It was obviously a stop-gap bulletin, as it promised a
revision would be available on all literature as soon as
possible. Meanwhile, the Santa Fe Transportation sign was
painted out on the garage opposite La Fonda, and 'Hunter
Clarkson, Inc.' took its place. A new insignia of a pair of
eagle dancers was designed for cars and hat emblems to
replace the 'big chicken' as the couriers and drivers called
the Harvey Thunderbird. A neon sign was made for the
garage, with the eagle dancers in brilliant colors, gyrating
as the sign pulsed.

Where previous folders destined for public consumption had been the type that folded vertically and could be
slipped into suit pockets, the new Couriercar folders were
an 8½ x 11 inches size and the first one was published on
April 20, 1931. Everything about it was crisp and new. The
type used was ultra modern, the Santa Fe logo had a new
stylized appearance, the cover picture was an up-to-date
one showing a young Indian boy in blue jeans with a sad-
dled horse. The folder was somewhat austere, with only
three printed pages, but the new rates were listed on the
first page, La Fonda was pictured and touted on the second
page and on the third page was a map of the tour routes.

One of the few small folders issued in the first year of
Clarkson's Couriercars was a coup for the Santa Fe. Clara
Elizabeth Laughlin, a prolific and interesting writer as well
as a woman of many talents, had established her own
Travel Service in Chicago, sending many of her clients on
the Indian Detours in the past. She was editor of a monthly
magazine devoted to traveling and had authored a series of
twelve books on travel entitled "So You're Going To . . ."

A common sight in Santa Fe

Rita Walker in a later Courier uniform

La Fonda after final remodeling

Two Chiefs pose at San Ildefonso

Community House Ruins at Frijoles

Headed for Flagstaff

covering various countries of the World. Having sent a number of friends to see the Southwest, she decided in March of 1931 to see it for herself.

Writing the report for her monthly magazine, she sent a copy to the Santa Fe Railroad head office, and arrangements were promptly made to incorporate her account of the trip into a folder to be used as promotional material.

THE INDIAN DETOURS — DISCOVERING AMERICA
By Clara E. Laughlin

. . . HAVE you ever discovered America? I did, last March. Columbus did, too, of course. But he didn't know what he had discovered — he thought it was India.

. . . LIKE him, we can take a westering trail. And like him, we may go home and tell of wonders seen. But there, except for the great joy of discovery, the similitude ends. For we may do our adventuring in a brief time (if need be) and in the lap of such luxury in travel that when I tried to tell about it in Europe, last summer, I could see that some, at least, of those who listened thought that I was "romancing."

. . .I HAD been to California, twice. I had even made stops en route, to see Salt Lake City, and Denver, and Portland, Seattle and Yellowstone Park. But I hadn't seen Grand Canyon, and I hadn't seen the Santa Fe country to which so many of my friends betake themselves for their holidays and about which they talk so ardently.

. . . I MEANT to go "some day." Certainly! When I "had time." But time, I find, is something most of us in these days never "have" — only as we make it.

. . . LAST March I went to Southern California in connection with the opening of our Los Angeles office, and to give some Travel Talks. I went "straight through" on THE CHIEF, and was almost sorry when I got to Pasadena; the journey was so restful and delightful.

. . . IT WAS on the way back that I discovered America. How many Americas *are* there? Many, I know. I have seen them nearly all. I have had great joy in nearly all I've seen — in the natural beauties, and in the different manners of living, and in the historic associations. Each of them is *America*. But each of them is a *transplantation* — the flowering in a New World of some "cutting" from an Old World stem.

. . . NOT until last March had I felt the full romance of our story as a nation. Because then I realized something of what our country was when the work of *"grafting"* began. Then I became aware that one who wishes to feel the epic of America *must* know what is left of primitive America in our great Southwest. Not to have that as a foundation is to leave the structure of our ideas about our country without a base.

. . . AND it is so *easy* to get!

. . . I HAD far too little time, nor could I "make" more, then. But as that is the case with many, perhaps my experience will serve you better than if I could recount months on horseback along the trails.

. . . IN GREAT and ever-greater numbers, Americans are "turning themselves loose" out in that magnificent, invigorating country, to stretch their lungs, their muscles, their *minds*, from the cramp of city living; are sending their children out there for an important part of their schooling; and, so charmed are they by the characteristics of that coun-

Above: The Santa Fe Limited leaving Pasadena for Lamy

Below: The Basket Dance at Santa Fe

try, they adapt themselves, while there, to its customs, and do not "easternize" it too greatly. I know this amuses the natives. But isn't it, after all, much better than going into a country and trying to make it conform to what we left behind us?

. . . THERE are such as I describe, and there are others who seek (in multitudes) the gorgeous playgrounds of California and do not leave their luxurious train between Chicago and the Pacific, except to "stretch their legs" for twenty minutes on an occasional station platform.

. . . THEY are, I'm sure, not indifferent to what there is to see en route. But they are in a hurry — just as I was in a hurry.

. . . I'M NOT qualified to write anything for those who wish to explore the Southwest in a more leisurely and thorough manner. For them, new books are multiplying rapidly, from the pens of authors who have lived in the places whereof they write (like Ruth Laughlin Barker, in her "Caballeros").

. . . ALL I have any qualification to do is to speak of what one may get in a very brief time (if he has no more) and a most perfectly organized manner, en route between Pasadena and Chicago, which will give him a great feeling for a section of his country that every good American ought to know.

. . . I'LL suggest it as a part of the eastward journey because so I took it. But it "works" as perfectly if taken on your westward way.

. . . I LEFT Pasadena on the Santa Fe Grand Canyon Limited at 1 p.m., and breakfasted at El Tovar, on the Canyon's rim, next morning. I could spend only one day there. This is tragically little. Yet, when that day was done I was drunk with glory. My mind was hung, forever, with pictures of incomparable grandeur. I had known, the sort of emotion we all need, once in a while, to show us what our capacity is when stretched to its utmost. I only drove along the southern rim for a short distance in each direction from El Tovar. I must imagine, as I am able, what sensations I might have had from the Canyon's deeps looking up. But when you're as full of glory as you can hold, what *more* could you be? To have the Canyon and the Painted Desert entered among one's spiritual possessions in a single day is to have touched sublimity indeed.

. . . LEAVING EL Tovar (a marvel of a hotel, where there seems no need to remind guests that all the water comes many miles in tank cars, and that all supplies must be brought from afar; yet there's another building which is greatly to surpass it, as I hear) after dinner in the evening, I found the sleeper in which I had left Pasadena, waiting, and resumed my journey. The next morning we were at Winslow, where again one leaves this most accommodating train for a motor drive through the Petrified Forest, rejoining the train at Holbrook, two and one-half hours later, after a seventy-mile trip which some travelers find a "high spot" on their journey; but I am bound to admit that I'm not enough of a geologist to get out of it what I should have. I got other things, though: the feeling of the desert, and the sense of age immemorial as witnessed by those marble stumps where the forest must have been cut down by some human hands — how many eons ago?

. . . THAT evening, towards six o'clock, I had to leave my friendly train. I was at Lamy, and a Hunter Clarkson motor-car was waiting to drive me to Santa Fe. Until I made that trip, it had not occurred to me that Santa Fe, the oldest seat of government in the United States, was not on a railway. There is, indeed, a little "spur" over which, I believe, some supplies are carried. But we, when we go there, leave rails and locomotives and accommodating "sleepers" behind, and set out to "discover America" — the America that conquistadores of Spain were conquering and colonizing for almost a century before the first English foot touched Jamestown. Before we leave Lamy, though, we have a veritable gem of a Harvey hotel to see — El Ortiz. The last dozen miles of the approach to Santa Fe is along the historic Santa Fe Trail of the Pack train and covered wagon and pony riders, the Indian fighters and the first overland mail. The old coaches that used to sway along the trail from Independence, Missouri, to Santa Fe, took two to three weeks for the journey, and the fare charged was $150 in gold.

. . . SANTA FE is a city of contrasts I must not try to speak of here. I was very full of Old Spain when I was there (my book, "So You're Going to Spain" being fresh from the press) and the sense I had of re-living her history in the New World was extraordinarily vivid. *La Fonda Hotel at Santa Fe is one of the most perfect combinations of taste and comfort, of luxury without violence to "fitness," I have ever seen, anywhere — just exactly what every traveler of discrimination would have "wished" there had he command of Aladdin magic. I'd like nothing better than to make a sojourn of some length there.*

. . . FROM Santa Fe, next morning, leaving it with great reluctance, I set out for Taos, along the Rio Grande; for the prehistoric cliff dwellings in the Puyé Canyon where the Harvey System maintains a delightful canyon cabin constructed of ancient stones, at which one rests, after climbing about the honeycomb cliffs, and enjoys a delicious lunch beside a log fire roaring in a boulder chimney.

. . . THENCE to Santa Clara pueblo, and on to Taos, where Kit Carson had his home from 1858 to 1866, and where he is buried. No one can estimate how many artists have painted pen-pictures and pictures on canvas, of Taos pueblo and its striking-looking citizens. Yet nothing quite prepares one for the reality upon which he comes when he visits the pueblo drenched in Western sunshine.

. . . I SHALL not try to describe it. I can't. I can only say that I found it immensely interesting and that it gave me so many things to think about I do not know how to tell what a foundation it put beneath all my feeling about America.

. . . IT WAS nearly noon, on the second day, when we left Taos — yet we were not too late for luncheon at La Fonda when the return trip to Santa Fe was ended. And there was a beautiful long afternoon for Santa Fe itself, and time for a leisurely dinner with friends. Then back to Lamy, and THE CHIEF, and Chicago early on the second morning. Leaving Pasadena on Wednesday, and arriving in Chicago Tuesday morning, I had seen enough of this Wonderland to give me a key to it so that, ever after, I may continue to explore it in books and "on the ground" with the feeling of one who is not quite a stranger.

. . . FOR the perfection of the Harvey hotels and the Hunter Clarkson service of cars and couriers, I have no words of praise that seem adequate to me. No place else in the world have I seen anything approximating the complete coordination of what is offered by the Santa Fe and these associate systems. At no point is anything lacking that can contribute to the luxurious comfort of the traveler, to the absence of uncertainty on his part, or to help him get quickly into such contacts as give him his best opportunity to understand what he is seeing, and to enjoy it to the utmost.

. . . THE girl couriers of Hunter Clarkson, Inc., are a model for the world — which, so far, praises them without stint but has not essayed to imitate them.

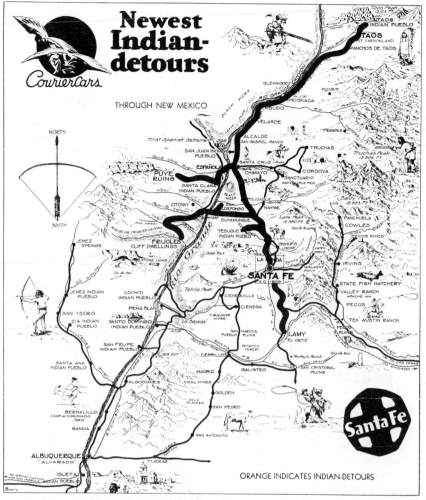

In addition to the One, Two and Three days Indian-detours there are a score of Couriercar Motor Cruises. to every off-the-beaten path corner of New Mexico and Arizona.

> ... AS ONE whose life is devoted to travel and to helping other people travel, *I have no hesitancy in saying that if there is anywhere else on the globe* a more complete care of the sight-seer, it has never come within my ken. Even were the country far less fascinating and beautiful, I'd feel rewarded for my stop-overs because they had taught me so much about what service can be — service to the traveling public.

Clarkson finally got it all together and on July 1st a new 23 page circular was sent to all travel and ticket agents. This was one of the first to come out without the Santa Fe Railroad doing the composing and printing. Instead, it bore the logo "Issued by Hunter Clarkson, Inc., Santa Fe, New Mexico, E. S. Bauer, Traffic Manager." The Santa Fe logo and the new Clarkson insignia decorated the top, and the words "Traffic-Circular No. 1" were followed by the title "Motor Services in New Mexico and Arizona."

Reading more like a book than a circular, the piece was indexed with railroad information, regular scheduled service, special cruises, private Couriercar cruises, general service information about Hunter Clarkson, Inc., hotels, climate, calendar of ceremonials and mileage charts.

The leading page read:

NEW — Indian-detours — rates
The Most Distinctive Motor Cruise Service In The World — Escorted by Courier

THE DELUXE WAY — by Couriercar — of visiting the hidden primitive Spanish Missions, old Mexican villages, colorful Indian pueblos, prehistoric cliff-dwellings and buried cities — all set in the matchless scenery and climate of the Southern Rockies.

Service is the equivalent of motoring with the finest of private facilities. Specially equipped Cruisers are used on the Three and Two-day detours limited to four guests to a single car.

3 DAYS $55.00 — Taos, Puyé, Frijoles Canyon, Old Santa Fe, San Il-defonso and Santa Clara Indian pueblos.

2 DAYS $35.00 — Taos, Puyé and Old Santa Fe. Santa Clara Indian pueblo.

1 DAY $15.00 — Motor Coach Service. Puyé, Old Santa Fe, and Santa Clara Indian pueblo.

One-Day Detour rate covering transportation *only*, allowing passengers to make own arrangements for room and meals at La Fonda, will be $9.55.

The individual rate includes every expense en route — motor transportation, courier service, meals, hotel accommodations with bath.

Eastbound or westbound, these distinctively new Indian-detours commence and end at Lamy, New Mexico, on your Santa Fe way to or from California.

After getting the various rules, privileges and no-nos out of the way, the circular devoted a separate page for each of the Indian-detours. Under the three-day tour, a new admonition was given concerning Frijoles:

Special Note — Actual descent into Frijoles Canyon and the subsequent ascent are most spectacular. Made afoot, of necessity, they entail a leisurely morning descent, and an afternoon climb, of several hundred feet in half a mile. A stimulating and pleasant exertion to those of normal health and strength, decision not to enter Frijoles Canyon because of age or disability should be made before departure of cars from La Fonda, when refund of $10.80 per person (full fare) will be made, and the day may be spent in Santa Fe or on other available Couriercar trips, as determined.

Door panel of Couriercar used at Carlsbad

The Land Cruises for Carlsbad Caverns, the three- or four-day Indian-detours and the seven-day Sierra Verde Circle Cruise, Petrified Forest Cruise and combination of Petrified Forest/Meteor Mountain Detour remained at the same rates; but a new tour was offered which combined the Petrified Forest/Meteor Mountain trip with a visit to the Hopi Pueblos, a 340 mile, two-day tour that cost $40.

The Santa Fe/Puyé/Taos two-day tour had proven popular and was retained with no increase in cost, and the daily rates of $70 per person were still in effect for anyone wanting to tailor their own vacation.

The Taos trip was enjoyed by the couriers and drivers as well as the dudes. Taos was known as a fun town during Prohibition, and with wide open gambling, the dudes spent freely, often including the guides in their invitations. The drivers knew where the speakeasys were, and one courier used to volunteer the name of a man in Pojoaque who made excellent rye whiskey. Kaye Montgomery was driver on one trip to Taos that involved several cars. One passenger asked one of the drivers where he could buy a jug. The driver took him to the doorway of the Don Fernando Hotel and pointed down the street to the church. Before he could say anything, the dude gasped, 'you don't mean to say I can get liquor in the church?' Montgomery answered for his friend: "No, he meant to say that's the only place you *can't* buy it."

One of the Taos tours ended up in a gambling hall because the Scotch couple on the tour wanted to see how 'one arm bandits' operated. The lady kept shoving quarters into one of the machines, consistently losing, while her husband kept wringing his hands and begging her to change to the nickel machine. Ruth Champion remembered their son was entranced with all the horses they saw along the road and since it was Spring, kept calling, "look, mother, another wee foal."

With his Scotch ancestry, Clarkson kept two things intact throughout his lifetime, his touch of burr and his kilts. The new circular had a page devoted to a listing of other places the Couriercars could go, among them several California locations — San Diego, Agua Caliente, Hollywood, Yosemite, Santa Barbara, a tour of the Missions, Palm Springs and Death Valley. When Sir Harry Lauder came for a visit in the Spring of 1931, Clarkson joined him in a Death Valley trip and was photographed with the famous Lauder, both men wearing kilts. The courier on the trip had guided Lauder on a previous trip to the Arizona Indian country, and had been called upon to explain the wearing of kilts to many of her Indian friends, who were a little shook up over seeing a man in a pleated skirt.

The last page of the circular listed the hotels involved in the tours, La Fonda, La Posada, Don Fernando. The effect of the Depression upon cost of away-from-home living was apparent in the prices. At La Fonda where single rooms with bath were $6.00 in 1929, they were now $3.00 and double rooms had come down from $8.00 to $5.00. Meal prices had been reduced correspondingly and breakfast was now $1.00, luncheon $1.25 and dinner $1.75. At La Posada, room rates were $3.50 for single, double $5.00, all with private bath. Don Fernando rates were $2.00 for bathless rooms, $3.00 with shower and $3.50 with bath, single or double.

Another service had been put into print. Realizing many dudes were spending entire vacations at dude ranches, Clarkson now offered 'taxi' service which would pick travelers up at the depots, deliver them to the ranches, and when the time came to go home, reverse the process, all for a fee.

In an effort to make the most income from the fleet of cars and buses, Clarkson also rented out his equipment for special trips that had nothing to do with the Detours or

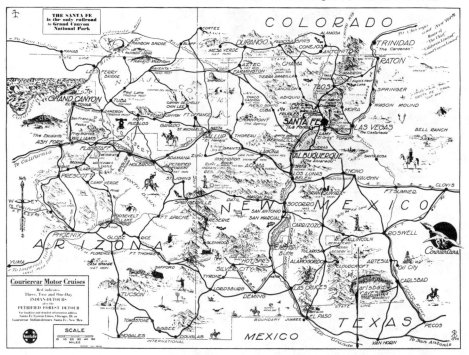

Land Cruises. One of his buses was hired, along with Driver Seery to transport a group of students from the University of New Mexico to the University of Arizona at Tucson for a track meet in 1931. On the way home, an overnight stop was made at a motel in Lordsburg. A canopy was about four inches too low to permit the bus to drive underneath, so Seery parked the bus as close as possible to the canopy for the night. The next morning he called for a count of heads and was assured everyone was on the bus, so he took off. At a rest stop in Hot Springs, (now Truth or Consequences), he asked where four of the boys were and was told they had been riding on the roof. Climbing up, he saw the boys stretched out on a mattress they had lugged out of the room and across the canopy of the motel. He wonders today how long the manager looked for that mattress.

With the cars traveling out-of-state on private Land Cruises, Clarkson saw the necessity for some of the drivers to acquaint themselves with driving on snowy mountain passes, and in 1931 a group of the drivers and couriers were assigned to two of the Cadillacs and taken on a driving tour over Wolf Creek Pass into Colorado's Rockies.

With such income producers as private tours, hiring

At Tesuque ladders led to the second floor

Climbing ladders was a Detour pastime

The only way to visit Frijoles was by ladder

Courier Margaret Wennips starts up Puyé ladder

out of buses and stage contracts for carrying mail, Clarkson managed to show a fair profit in 1931.

The political climate was deteriorating sufficiently in 1932 to make trips within this country more attractive than ever. No one really believed a paranoic paper hanger would really pose a serious threat to Hindenburg's presidency, but 1931 had been a particularly bad year for Germany and Austria with bank closures bringing about a depression that made the one in the United States look like a rehearsal for the real thing. Britain had gone off the gold standard and even such remote countries as Brazil were affected. By mid year, the Fascists were in power in Lithuania and Portugal. There was a stalemate in foreign travel — the Americans were not going to Europe, the Europeans were not coming to visit America, and the loss of foreign visitors meant Clarkson pitched his ads at the transcontinental travelers harder than ever.

There was one stumbling block. American tourists no longer spent freely, uncertain how long the Depression would last. Many people who were at first unaffected by the crash, found the delayed effects were just as serious financially. Clarkson had to cut corners, yet keep up the quality. But how?

He found the answer to this in reviewing what the tours included. A new bulletin was prepared for the one-, two- and three-day Indian-detours. In bold type, new prices appeared, with the one-day tour costing $12 instead of the previous $15; the two-day $26 as against $35 and the three-day at $39 down from $55. Also in bold type was how this was to be accomplished:

> Effective September 1, 1932, for the Fall and Winter seasons and until further notice, regular one-day, two-day and three-day Indian-detours rates will be cut. The New Rates will continue to include all motor transportation, Lamy to Lamy, New Mexico; hotel accommodations with private bath; courier service and admission fees — EVERYTHING in fact, WITH THE EXCEPTION OF MEALS.

In accord with the policy of no surprises, the prices of meals were given at La Fonda, Puyé, Frijoles, and Taos. It was explained on the flyer that many people preferred to take lighter meals, or skip some, and that the cost of the trip was thus tailored to individual desires.

Two days later another bulletin was released which called attention to a special hurry-up tour of Isleta. The information was released both in a flyer to traffic agents, and put into a very small folder designed for public consumption.

THE ISLETA Indian DETOUR — $1

• *Perhaps* you are racing cross-continent on the Santa Fe's Grand Canyon Limited — without time to spare for a real New Mexico stopover.

• *Even so,* if you like, you can step off the train for forty minutes of motoring, leg-stretching and sight-seeing in New Mexico's crisp, bracing air, without the slightest inconvenience, or the loss of a moment in reaching your destination.

• Here is how it may be done — beginning September 1, 1932:

• *The Westbound* Grand Canyon Limited (No. 23) pulls into Albuquerque at 11:40 a.m. (noon). It always pauses there for icing and a quick grooming. Isleta, one of the largest of those century-old inhabited Indian pueblos that dot the Rio Grande Valley, is not passed until 12:28 p.m. In this interval — between arrival of the train at Albuquerque and its departure from Isleta — the Isleta Detour will give you an agreeable break in the journey.

• *No. 23 arrives* Albuquerque, as stated, at 11:40 a.m. At 11:45 a.m., comfortable Pullman-windowed Couriercoaches depart with ISLETA DETOUR guests. The ensuing 25-minute drive slips out of the city, across the Rio Grande, down the irrigated valley, and ends 13 miles away in the 'dobe-lined heart of Isleta, with its 1,100 Indians. Here there is a quarter-hour to stroll about — around the brown plaza that Coronado's men first saw nearly 400 years ago; into the quaint old mission church; among the picture-puzzle "streets" and time-forgetting Indian homes.

• At 12:25 p.m. you reach tiny Isleta station. A few minutes later No. 23 renews the race westward . . . with a Fred Harvey luncheon beckoning from the inviting dining car.

• *Eastbound,* the ISLETA DETOUR fits in just as conveniently. The Grand Canyon Limited (No. 24) reaches Isleta at 2:47 p.m. At 2:50 you are off for fifteen minutes in the close-by pueblo. The Couriercoach drive that follows sets you down again at trainside, in Albuquerque, at 3:30. At 3:35 p.m. No. 24 pulls away for the East.

• *Costs* only $1.00 for adults; 50 cents for youngsters under twelve.

• It may be arranged for on the train itself, if you like, any time before arrival at Albuquerque or Isleta.

• *Every passenger on the Grand Canyon Limited* should make this trip . . . no delay, and only costs one dollar!

The Isleta tour was well received and will be remembered by one driver and courier. The purple gentian was blooming close by the road and one of the dudes asked if she could get out and inspect it closer. Obligingly Driver Seery pulled over. The dude stepped out and became the only strip-tease artist to take a Detour. Gathering bun-

ISLETA Indian DETOUR

Two folders.
Left: A reprint
Above: A new design

ches of the sweet blossoms, she was unaware bees had set up housekeeping in the flowers. As she sniffed the blooms, several bees transferred their attention from the throats of the flowers to the blouse of the dude. Stung and startled, she took off across the desert, yelling and stripping off her clothes as she went. Right behind her, but not gaining appreciably was Courier Wennips trying to pick up the scattered clothing without stopping. The fascinated tourists still in the car watched the girl in her undies finally come to a stop and eventually start back for the car carrying a bundle of clothes and wrapped Mary Martin style in the courier's jacket.

The first folder to revert to the vertical type designed for carrying in coat pockets was distributed in December of '32. The cover was faintly reminiscent of the final one to carry the Harveycar logo. Indians on horseback, cliffs rising above a canyon floor, Couriercar sedans on the dirt road and the double eagle dancer logo were rendered in grays, oranges and black. Most of the pictures used had been seen many times in Harvey folders. The text had changed little except for the new usage of 'Couriercar' and 'Indian-detours'. The only tours covered were the three Indian-detours and the Petrified Forest trip, and it was hoped people would give themselves a Christmas present by seeing the Southwest.

All of the pueblos featured Christmas celebrations. Not only did the pueblos have special dances for the season, but the Mexican villages held their las posadas. Some of the most beautiful dances were held on Christmas Eve at San Felipe and Santo Domingo pueblos. The dudes would be driven through the old mining town of Madrid with pastoral scenes, lights and las posadas pageants going on. They would then be taken to midnight Mass at the Pueblo church, and afterward would watch the Snow Bird or Parrot Dances. Afterwards the whole party was invited to eat with the Indians. One of the Indian hosts was Jo Esquibel, nicknamed 'La Fonda' because he would bring his beautiful jewelry to the Fonda lobby for the guests to inspect.

Although Clarkson had replaced the car and bus insignias promptly, whenever the vehicles would approach a Pueblo, the little children would run out yelling, 'here come the Harley car, the Harley car.' Few of them ever learned to say it properly, but they knew the cars meant treats. Driver Staab and other personnel would put small amounts of money aside and at Christmas time would buy bags of candy, nuts and fruit for the kids. Although the children never remembered the drivers' or couriers' names, they remembered the 'Harley' cars.

Long lasting friendships grew between the drivers and couriers and the Pueblo Indians. When a Detour car would arrive simultaneously with any other tour party, it was noticeable that the Indians would give their entire attention to the Detour group, inviting them into their homes and to share meals. Even on the Arizona mesas where the Hopis were ultra-reserved and not considered friendly by many tour agents, the Detourists were welcomed. One main reason for this was the thoughtfulness of Clarkson's people.

Staab was on a Petrified Forest tour and had stopped at one of the Hopi mesas. While the dudes inspected the pottery, he found some little girls playing hop scotch. Their brothers had etched the hop scotch chart in the rocky ground and the girls were using an old rock as a marker. Staab returned to his car and got some flat washers for them to use. Several months later he made the same trip and the washers were still being used by the same girls.

A Tribute to
NEW MEXICO

HUNDREDS *of years before white men set foot in America, red men of the Southwest were dwelling in six-story terraced apartments and enjoying a communal life whose simplicity and sincerity we can envy today.* ❡ *Here, in ages lost in the shadow of time, lived and loved and flourished a people whose origin is as mysterious as the reason for their vanishing from the face of the earth.* ❡ *Here, beside the tumbling Rio Grande, marched* Coronado *and his armored Spaniards, lured by fairy tales of gold and precious jewels, seeking the fabled wealth of the Seven Cities of Cibola and the Gran Quivira.* ❡ *Here Pueblo Indians, matching bow and arrow against powder and bullet, fought back later invaders in feats as desperately heroic as Marathon or Thermopylae.* ❡ *Here, nearer our own time, in these dim, deep canyons, on these sun-washed mesas, history was made. Here strode the mighty scout,* Kit Carson. *Here swept* Geronimo, *untamable Apache. Here Billy the Kid spread terror and met an outlaw's death.* ❡ *And here, in the dust of the plain, you still may see the deep ruts carved by horses' hoofs and wagon wheels in the blazing days of the Santa Fe Trail.* ❡ NEW MEXICO *abounds in colorful survivals. You wander through silent ruins of cities which may have been peopled when the Normans conquered England. Modern roads carry you to Taos, dreaming in the sun at the foot of snow-capped mountains; to Acoma, "City of the Sky"; to the Enchanted Mesa; to Zuñi, largest of the pueblos; to El Morro and its famous Inscription Rock; to the giant chambers of the Carlsbad Caverns; to Frijoles Canyon, with its amazing cliff dwellings; or to Chaco Canyon, where the story of Pueblo Bonito has been traced back more than a thousand years by a study of tree rings in the ancient timbers.* ❡ *What romance and poetry are in the very names! What unending variety in the landscape and climate! What enchantment of color! What unfathomed mysteries! No wonder that artists vie with archeologists in their enthusiasm, and that visitors come away with eager determination to return.* ❡ *Nor are the achievements of the present less inspiring than records and memories of the past. Albuquerque, Roswell, Gallup, Las Vegas, Raton, Silver City, Las Cruces—these are busy centers of industry and progress, while the very name of Santa Fe is a promise of safety and peace and healthfulness that await the traveler there.* ❡ NEW MEXICO! *Well have you been named "the Sunshine State." An empire you are, whose vast dominions have only begun to yield their wealth and glory. A vast population will one day build upon the foundation which the people of bygone ages have laid. And millions will enjoy your beauty and your bounty, which more travelers from every corner of the world are discovering every year. To you, second youngest of our Union of States, General Motors pays its tribute.*

*As broadcast by General Motors
to the Nation — February 15th 1932*

There was no cancellation of the various Land Cruises although they were not mentioned in the 1932 folder. Couriercars loaded up for the Gallup ceremonial as usual, and the Carlsbad Cavern Cruise remained one of the most popular ones. Without air-conditioning, the big sedans were hot in the summer. Montgomery had contacted Clarkson telling him the drivers were suffering from badly swollen legs due to the regulation about wearing high-laced boots and received permission for the drivers to change to cowboy boots for the desert trips in the summer.

The heat affected the passengers as well, and Staab was assigned the wives of four fishing enthusiasts who had sent them on the trip to New Mexico while they went to Alaska to fish. "The gals decided they wanted to go to Carlsbad, so we took off. It was a red hot trip. The summer had been real dry and extra hot. Coming back they started to sing in the back seat. We had no courier on that trip and I sang along with them. Finally I glanced back over my shoulder to ask them if they knew one of my favorite songs and they were all sitting there in their slips, swigging gin out of a community bottle. One of them explained they felt too hot in dresses, so they had simply taken them off. We drove 270 miles across the Malpais desert getting noisier and hotter, and just as we were coming into the outskirts of Albuquerque they put their dresses back on. That tour was one long party."

Lavish parties at La Fonda were hosted by Clarkson and his wife Louise in an effort to interest business and social leaders to not only take the trips themselves, but to talk friends and associates into joining them. Some of the big groups continued to book tours, calling all drivers, couriers and vehicles to duty. But this was now an unusual happening, not a regular thing.

The Indian-detours were losing their appeal.

13

THE WHO OF IT: THE DUDES

No story dealing with railroading would be complete without the name of Lucius Beebe appearing in it, and the story of the Indian Detours is no exception. He was a latecomer, going on the 1931 two-day trip to Puyé and Taos. Courier Rainey Bartley remembers him as a thoroughly charming man whose opulent traveling habits were left behind at the railroad station. He thoroughly enjoyed the dusty auto trip, climbed the shakey ladders into Puyé ruins and chatted easily with Taos artists and Indians alike.

There were people other than Beebe who arrived in their private coaches, one of them being Harry Guggenheim. For all her knowledge of geology, Dorothy Raper had little knowledge of mining men. Picking up an assignment slip on which had been written that she was to guide a private tour of the Guggenheim family, she spent two days showing them the usual sights. Then, thinking she would add a little extra treat, she asked if they would like to visit the mines. A shocked "oh, no!" puzzled her until she returned to the courier office and was told about her dudes.

Emma Weyerhauser of the lumbering company traveled to Santa Fe with a friend expressly to take the Land Cruise to Carlsbad. She immediately hit it off with Courier

Spanish and Indian Place-names

encountered in and about Old Santa Fe'
with their English pronunciations and
meanings

ACOMA: (Ah'-kome-ah)—'the people of the White Rock,' 'Acoma people.'

ALAMEDA: (Ah-lah-may'-dah)—a poplar grove or shaded walk.

ALBUQUERQUE: (Ahl-boo-kare'-kay)—named for Francisco Fernandez de la Cueva Enriquez, Duke of Albuquerque and 34th Viceroy of New Spain.

ALCALDE: (Ahl-kahl'-day)—mayor, judge, justice of the peace.

ALVARADO: (Ahl-vah-rah'-doh)—named for Hernando de Alvarado, chief of artillery under Coronado.

BERNALILLO: (Bare-nah-leel'-yoh)—'little Bernard.' Alcalde of Santa Fé in 1719.

CANYONCITO: (Kahn-yohn-see'-toh)—little canyon or gorge.

CASTAÑEDA: (Kahs-tahn-yay'-dah)—named for Pedro de Castañeda, principal historian of Coronado's expedition.

CHIMAYO: (Chee-my-yoh')—'excellent obsidian.'

CICUYÉ: (See-coo-yay')—a name applied by Coronado, exact meaning and derivation unknown.

COCHITI: (koh-chee-tee')—probable meaning, 'place of the rock kiva.'

CORDOVA: (Korr'-doh-vah)—named for Don Miguel Peralta de Cordoba, Baron de los Colorados.

CULEBRA: (Koo-lay'-brah)—a snake, especially rattle-snake.

EL ORTIZ: (Ayl Orr-teez')—named for an old and prominent New Mexico family.

EL RITO: (Ayl Ree'-toh)—the little river.

ESPAÑOLA: (Ays-pahn-yoh'-lah)—Spanish woman.

ESPIRITU SANTO: (Ays-peé-ree-too Sahn'-toh)—Holy Ghost.

EL RITO DE LOS FRIJOLES: (Ayl Ree'-toh day lohs Free-hoh'-lays) —'The Little River of the Beans.'

GLORIETA: (Glohr-ree-ay'-tah)—arbor or bower. Also feminine personal name.

GALISTEO: (Gah-lees-tay'-oh)—named for Nuestra Señora de los Remedios de Galisteo.

ISLETA: (Ees-lay'-tah)—islet, small island.

JEMEZ: (Hay'-mess)—name of an Indian tribe; the distance from the end of the thumb to the end of the forefinger, both extended.

LA BAJADA: (Lah Bah-hah'-dah)—the descent.

LAGUNA: (Lah-goo'-nah)—pond, lagoon.

LAS VEGAS: (Lahs Vay'-gahs)—the meadows or open plains.

LOS ALAMOS: (Lohs Ah'-lah-mohs)—the poplars.

LOS CERILLOS: (Lohs Say-reel'-yos)—the hillocks, little eminences.

LOS LUNAS: (Lohs Loo'-nahs)—named after the prominent Luna family.

MESA ENCANTADA: (May'-sah Ayn-kahn-tah'-dah)—enchanted mesa.

MANZANO: (Mahn-sah'-noh)—apple tree.

OTOWI: (Oh'-toh-wee)—'The Gap Where the Water Sinks.'

PAJARITO: (Pah-har-ree'-toh)—little bird.

PECOS: (Pay'-kohs)—probably from Latin 'pecus,' a flock; named for the Pecos Indians, expert sheep raisers and herders.

PEÑA BLANCA: (Pay'-nyah Blahn'-kah)—white rock.

PUYÉ: (Pooh-yay')—'Gathering Place of the Cottontail Rabbits.'

POJOAQUE: (Poh-whah'-kay)—Spanish version of a Tewa word, meaning 'water drinking place.'

RATON: (Rah-tone')—mouse.

RIO PUERCO: (Ree'-oh Poo-ere'-koh)—'rio,' river; 'Puerco,' pig; hence 'river of the pigs'—or, very dirty river.

RANCHOS DE TAOS: (Rahn'-chos day Tah'-os)—ranches of Taos.

SANDIA: (Sahn-dee'-ah)—watermelon.

SAN FELIPE: (Sahn Fay-lee'-pay)—St. Philip.

SANGRE DE CRISTO: (Sahn'-gray-day Krees'-toh)—blood of Christ.

SAN ILDEFONSO: (Sahn Eel-day-fohn'-soh)—St. Alphonsus.

SAN JOSÉ: (Sahn Hoh-say')—St. Joseph.

SANTA CLARA: (Sahn'-tah Klah'-rah)—St. Clara.

SANTA CRUZ: (Sahn'-tah Krooz)—holy cross.

SANTA FÉ: (Sahn'-tah Fay')—holy faith.

SANTO DOMINGO: (Sahn'-toh Doh-meen'-goh)—

TECOLOTE: (Tay-koh-loh'-tay)—from the Aztec 'tecolotl,' the ground owl.

TESUQUE: (Tay-soo'-kay)—Spanish corruption of old Tewa name meaning 'dry spotted place.' Why given is not known.

TRUCHAS: (Troo'-chahs)—trout.

TCHIREGE: (Ts-ree-gay')—'Place of the little bird.'

TSANKAWI: (Tsan-kah-wee)—'Place in the Pass of the Sharp Round Cactus.'

TYUONYI: (Tee-you-own'-yee)—probably 'The Treaty Signing Place.'

Pronunciation guide furnished the dudes

Einstein being made a Hopi Chief, Mrs. Einstein is to his left

Hildagarde Hawthorne at Frijoles

A composite poster made for a Mary Pickford tour

Ann Cooper, and after walking through the Caverns and returning to the hotel, invited Ann to have dinner with them. During the meal, the subject of souvenirs came up, especially the kind that are 'borrowed', such as towels with hotel names on them. Lamenting such practices, Ann assured Miss Weyerhauser couriers never filched so much as a match box without asking first. On returning to Santa Fe and unpacking, Ann found a Bible from the hotel that Miss Weyerhauser had tucked between her change of courier blouses.

A great deal of camaraderie existed between the dudes and their guides. It was one place where the greats of the world could be just people. Margaret Wennips especially liked Marconi and Einstein and being a linguist she was able to converse in their native tongues. She also found Will Rogers as much a charmer as his theatre audiences did, and when he would come to visit his son at Los Alamos School for Boys, she tried to arrange her schedule to fit in with his trips.

Hildagarde Hawthorne, grand-daughter of Nathaniel, had married a Sioux Indian and accompanied him on an Indian Detour when he wanted to study the Southwestern Indians and their culture as it contrasted with his.

Although no one can remember a U. S. President taking the tours, Vice-President Charles Dawes did so in 1929, influenced by the publicity the Southwest was enjoying.

Eleanor Roosevelt brought a huge entourage when she was First Lady, leaving behind a bill that would have bought several new Couriercars. No one knew exactly whom to send the bill to, so it was written off. Mrs. Vincent Astor insisted on paying for everything down to the last penny. A large number of tourists from South Africa, South America and New Zealand came with letters of credit worth thousands of dollars.

Many of the people who came had no idea what they would see. One professor of Archaeology at Cornell had been making yearly trips to Egypt to visit digs. His wife finally convinced him he should look at the digs of the Southwest, and he was assigned to Dorothy Raper. When she finished showing him the ancient civilizations of New Mexico, he admitted his amazement at what his native country had to offer.

FORM   I. D. E. O.
INDIAN-DETOUR EXCHANGE ORDER
Issued by the A. T. & S. F. Ry. Co.

| When sold for child five years of age and under twelve, punch one-half. When sold for child under five years of age, do not punch one-half, instead endorse across the face of coupon and stub "CHILD UNDER FIVE." As children under five do not require rail transportation, leave blank the provision for description of the rail ticket n connection with which this exchange order is sold and detach the gummed strip at the bottom of this order. | If One-Half ★ Punch Here |

AGENT'S STUB
NOT GOOD FOR PASSAGE
Amount Collected $..

Destination of Through Ticket

Via SANTA FE TRANSPORTATION CO.
FROM

ALBUQUERQUE ★
LAMY ★
SANTA FE ★

-------------------------------------- ★
VIA
PUYE TWO-DAY TOUR ★
TAOS-PUYE THREE-DAY TOUR ★

....
.... } ★
....

Issued in connection with
Form.. No..............................
Form.. No..............................
Issued by .... Ry.
At ....
Date of Sale..19........

Courier Kardell (left) and dudes at Puyé

INDIAN-DETOUR
Exchange Ticket Order

This coupon is to be exchanged at the office of the Santa Fe Transportation Co. in the El Ortiz Hotel at Lamy or Alvarado Hotel at Albuquerque, as designated by punch mark, for transportation of one passenger, via the

PUYE TWO-DAY TOUR ★
TAOS-PUYE THREE-DAY TOUR ★

....
.... } ★
....

(including meals and lodging)
FROM
ALBUQUERQUE ★
LAMY ★
SANTA FE ★

-------------------------------------- ★

| Amount Collected $.............................. | If One-Half ★ Punch Here |

Form I.D.E.O. | Not Good if Detached
Destination of Through Ticket

ARRIVING ON
Train No..
Issued in connection with contract
Form................................ No..............................

Issued by
The Atch., Top. & Santa Fe Ry. Co.

Driver Staab with dudes at Carlsbad Caverns

G U M
Attach to top of contract

Waiting for the Chief to arrive

Even on private Land Cruises, couriers were not supposed to accept tips. Howard Marmon of the car company brought his entire family on a holiday in New Mexico. With so many people, it was decided to use a Harveycoach instead of a car, and two couriers were assigned to the trip, Kay Angle in charge assisted by Zoe McGonagle. When the trip was over, Marmon handed each courier a note of thanks. Tucked inside Kay's were four $100 bills; in Zoe's $100. Talking it over, the couriers reasoned the sum was too large to be called a tip and should be called a present and not returned.

John D. Rockefeller, Jr., and his family were assigned to Courier Peggy Pollard. They had traveled first to the Grand Canyon, then decided to see the Nava-Hopi area. The entire family amazed the driver and courier with their stamina as they visited the mesas, rode horseback 14 miles to Rainbow Bridge, then crossed Lee's Ferry to the North Rim, extended their trip into Zion and Bryce and climbed on the train at Salt Lake City to return home.

The drivers and couriers preferred the Land Cruises because they got to know the people better. Most of the monied dudes, and their families, planned on spending at least two weeks on the Cruises, often deciding the night before where they would go the next day, often starting out for the Indian country and ending up two weeks later on the West Coast.

There were occasions when 'and family' included the family pets. Lily Pons was never without her poodles, toy-sized bundles of noise and energy. Although they would

Driver Ganz (left) and Driver Seery with dudes

stay the entire summer in Santa Fe, neither Lily nor her husband, Andre Kostelanetz, drove, always hiring a Harvey driver, preferably Norbert Staab.

With the privileges of the famous, Kostelanetz loved fly fishing but refused to wear wading boots. When on a fishing trip with Staab, getting to the other side of a stream always meant Staab had to carry Kostelanetz from one bank to the other on his back. Once when returning East, Lily wanted to say a personal 'thank you' to Clarkson; the poodles jumped out of the car as she left it. It took two hours to corral the dogs who chose opposite directions for their freedom dash, and the Santa Fe Chief was held up for a half-hour in Lamy so Andre, Lily and poodles could be reunited and sent on their way home. As Staab recalls them, "Andre was as wonderful as his music, and Lily as beautiful as her singing."

A dude makes friends with a Tesuque infant

That wasn't the only time a train was held up for a personage, as Rainey Bartley remembers. Taking a portrait-painting friend with her, she went to the Lamy station to meet a party of dudes. As the Harveycar approached the station, they saw the train was already in and an unusual amount of activity was going on. Recognizing a friend, Frieda Lawrence, widow of D. H. Lawrence, distraught and dashing back and forth on the platform, she went to see if she could help. The Lawrences had lived in Taos for a while, and his last wish had been to be buried in Taos. Dying overseas, his ashes were shipped to Lamy to be picked up by Frieda, but somehow they had disappeared between Chicago and Lamy. Putting her dudes in the car, Rainey went back to help and the ashes were finally located mixed in with the dudes' baggage. The train pulled out 20 minutes late.

The fact advertising for the Detours reached into foreign capitals meant many Asian visitors were welcomed at Santa Fe. After years of brushing the dust from her clothing after every outing, Anna Kardell was amazed to see the wife of Prince Faisel of India attired in a white chiffon sari emerge from a three-day trip in pristine condition.

Royalty failed to cause a stir in the Courier lounge. The guest list included Archduke Otto, Prince Peter of Greece, the Duke and Duchess of Alba, plus many Oriental dignitaries, English members of Parliament and French government heads.

Occasionally the financiers brought along their cooks, not completely trusting the menu when away from the Harvey Houses, and some of the small hotels and schoolhouses that housed the far-ranging Land Cruise tourists never smelled as good again.

Poets, painters and composers of both music and books found inspiration in their Detours. Oliver LaFarge won a Pulitzer Prize for "Laughing Boy"; Witter Bynner's poem is quoted elsewhere in this book; Sir Harry Lauder composed a song while touring Tesuque; Ferde Grofé wrote his 'Grand Canyon Suite' in 1931 after exploring the rim.

The Indian Detours had a long and distinguished guest list.

14

THE LEAN YEARS: 1933-1941

The Great Depression, as it was referred to in news clippings, had a far greater effect on the Indian Detours than Clarkson could ever have foreseen. Besides the very obvious fact money was tight and vacations were available only to those whose fortunes remained well above the norm, a greater threat to train travel and hence the Detours was felt by 1933; the American motorist had discovered the economy of family touring.

For the same amount of money spent for a train ticket from Chicago to Lamy for one passenger, a man could pack his family of four into his now reliable family car and drive to New Mexico, enjoying scenery and outdoor living in camp grounds along the way. Or, if he had a larger travel budget he could stay in cabin courts that were springing up along every transcontinental highway. Discovering the food in the Ma and Pa cafes along the road was usually beyond decent description, camping kits found their way into the luggage and the family often pulled into a pleasant spot off the road, rolled out bedrolls, stretched a canvas from the auto to stakes in the ground and spent a night eating in the open, communing with nature and saving money.

While most prices were going down, the Detour rates were bumped when Clarkson burned the midnight oil trying to make the venture show a profit. The one-, two- and three-day tours were raised from $12 to $14, $26 to $30, and $39 to $45 respectively. There were still no meals included, and the midday picnics, so enjoyed by the dudes, were a thing of the past. The driver and courier uniforms were beginning to look a little seedy, the cars were a little older, the working hours were longer with the salaries less, and the only things keeping their bloom were the Harvey Hotels with their unfailing standards.

The downhill slide was not entirely Clarkson's fault, but a good bit of it was because of his inability to balance his income and outgo. Used to lavish entertaining, good living and ignoring the inevitable bills, the Hunter Clarkson Company was quietly slipping into the red. Clarkson's brother Jim, who had taken a job as driver when he returned from one of his many trips to South America, joined Hunter in the office. Direct opposites when it came to financial responsibility, Clarkson furnished the charm and the bills,

Couriercars at the Vermillion Cliffs

while Jim furnished the budget and the payments. Without Jim's business ability, the Detours would never have survived the Depression years.

By 1933, all operations were concentrated in Santa Fe; Albuquerque was a forgotten mark on the Detour maps. Bulletins of that year emphasized there was a Hunter Clarkson Tours, Inc., office at La Posada in Winslow, Arizona, where requests for trips into the Indian country around the Petrified Forest would be handled. The trips to Arizona from Santa Fe had been phased out except for private Land Cruise trips.

Roger Birdseye's death early in 1933 had meant a new publicity chairman had to be found for the brochures, and Clarkson turned to the P.R. department of the Santa Fe. The November 1933 brochure was heavy on the editorial 'we', restrained in description and austere in coverage.

A lot of the couriers and drivers were laid off as business declined, some of them taking jobs in the local business and cultural fields in Santa Fe. The remaining employees doubled up on hours, mended their uniforms and hoped for the best. 1933 blended into 1934 and became 1935.

Remembering how business had improved when Clara Laughlin's travel story had been reprinted in a brochure, Clarkson contacted her sister at the New York Times in an effort to whip up some new publicity. Ruth Laughlin obliged and her article appeared in the August 18th edition of the paper, sounding much like a review of a brand new venture.

Girl Couriers in Southwest
College Graduates, They Explain to the Visiting Tenderfoot the Racial History of the Region

Feminine America is making its mark even in the Wild West. Cowboys and cow talk used to typify the Western cattlerange country, but now soft-voiced college girls explain the developments of the three races — Indian, Spanish and American — who have made Southwestern history an exciting story.

The toot of the motor car sounded the death-knell of the cow pony. Hundreds of miles of barbed wire fenced in the open range, cattle were parked in these restricted areas and cowboys were no longer needed to ride herd at night. The foreman driving over the ranch today covers as much territory as the cow pony traveled in a week. Of course, they are still cowboys, but many of them are only picturesque accessories to dude ranches, and young women are acting as spokesmen of the open spaces of the Southwest.

The Santa Fe Super Chief at Pasadena on May 14, 1936 on its initial trip Westbound

The Diesel electric Super Chief crossing the desert on its maiden voyage

T H E

Super CHIEF

FIRST EASTBOUND RUN, MAY 15th, 1936

BREAKFAST

FRUITS AND PRESERVES

Orange, one 15   Sliced Orange 20   Apple, one 10
Orange Marmalade 25   Apricot Jam 25
Preserved Figs 30; with Cream 35   Preserved Strawberries 25

CEREALS

Shredded Wheat Biscuits with Milk 20; with Cream 30
Rolled Oats with Milk 20; with Cream 30

STEAKS, CHOPS, ETC.

Small Sirloin a la Minute 1.25   Sirloin for one 1.60   Sirloin for two 2.75
Lamb Chop (1) 45   Lamb Chop, Extra Thick (1) 80
(to order—20 minutes)
Broiled Chicken, half 85   Fried Chicken, half 85
Calf's Liver and Bacon 70   Veal Cutlet, Plain or Breaded 65

POTATOES

French Fried 20   Hashed Browned or Lyonnaise 20   Au Gratin 25

BACON, HAM, ETC.

Bacon 65; half portion 40   Ham 70; half portion 40
Bacon and Eggs 70   Ham and Eggs 70

EGGS

Boiled or Fried Eggs 30   Scrambled Eggs 30
Shirred Eggs 30   Poached Eggs on Toast 45
Plain Omelette (3 Eggs) 50   Spanish or Mushroom Omelette 65

BREAD, ETC.

Hot Rolls 10   Corn Muffins 10   Raisin or Whole Wheat Bread Toast 15
Dry or Buttered Toast 15   Melba Toast 15   Milk Toast 30
Wheat Cakes with Maple Syrup 30

COFFEE, TEA, ETC.

Coffee, per pot 25   Kaffee Hag Coffee, per pot 25
Cocoa or Chocolate, Whipped Cream, per pot 20
Tea—Ceylon, Young Hyson, English Breakfast, Orange-Pekoe, per pot 20
Milk, per bottle 15   Malted Milk 20   Postum, per pot 15

An extra charge of twenty-five cents each will be made for all meals served outside of Dining Car

Guests will please call for checks before paying and compare amounts charged

SANTA FE DINING CAR SERVICE
Fred Harvey

These young women are the couriers of the Indian detour. Their range covers a third of the United States, a vast country of thousand-mile distances of mesas, mountains and deserts and thousand-year spans of history from prehistoric cave dwellings to Boulder Dam. The Indian detour centers in Santa Fe, N. M., which was the focus of Spanish and Indian life in this New World province for 300 years. Radiating from Santa Fe, the Indian detour trips run from two-day tours through forgotten Spanish villages, Indian Pueblos and cliff-dweller canyons to a month's cruise which may include Carlsbad Caverns in Southwestern New Mexico, Hopiland and the Grand Canyon in Arizona, Mesa Verde National Park in Colorado, Rainbow Bridge in Utah and Death Valley in California.

New York State could be fitted into almost any two counties in these Western States, whose population is so scattered that one may travel fifty miles without meeting another human being. This remote land is still the least known part of America, and for that reason travelers welcome the services of a courier to help them see it.

The idea of using young women as guides began a dozen years ago. The plan — a private enterprise — was taken over and enlarged by the Santa Fe Railroad until the rail companies were forced to eliminate extras. For the past three years it has been operated by a private company and has afforded an unusual profession for women.

There are many qualifications for the new profession. The couriers must be college graduates and pass examination in an intensive training course in history, archaeology, Indian and Spanish folklore and the geography and geology of the Southwest. This does not mean that learning is hammered into the unwary tourist, but that authentic information is available if the tourist is interested.

The courier must be first of all a tactful hostess, second a business woman who takes care of such details as paying hotel bills, making reservations, starting parties promptly, retrieving forgotten suitcases, packages and purses.

Adaptability is a prime requisite. The courier never knows what the next day may bring forth. On one trip she is in charge of a group of sorority girls who plan high jinks for the depths of Carlsbad Caverns. Next time there will be a somber group of Dunkards in little bonnets and long, black dresses.

The shadow of the cowboy is with the couriers. He is the driver behind the wheel, a picturesque figure in a ten-gallon hat, riding breeches, a blue velveteen shirt and an orange handkerchief with blowing ends. He has left off his spurs. His pleasant, sun-tanned face and general dependability add to the pleasure of a motor cruise. For many women, who still think of the West as cowboy country, these drivers are a perfect addition to the picture.

After a two-day trip, ladies of uncertain age but certain bank accounts often book a long motor cruise — provided the same handsome young driver operates the car. "He knows the roads so well," they explain. They don't mention the fact that a bold figure is still the right asset in a bold country and that his songs of the "Lone Prair-eee" around the camp fire at night are something to write home about.

Cowboys of the Billy-the-Kid era of fifty years ago would groan in their graves to think of a man nursemaiding a motor. Yet, with the genie of progress invading the West, a quiet motor is as essential as was the long-winded cow pony.

In 1935, eleven year old Les Thomas took the trip with his mother who headed her Dodge sedan down the road from Denver, Colorado. In Trinidad they slept on straw husk mattresses in a new Cabin Court for $4. Coffee shops were non-existent in this era, and it was necessary to drive up and down the main street of town to find a restaurant open for breakfast.

With a child's vivid memory, he remembers the dusty roads that led from Trinidad across Raton Pass and was impressed by the fact at the bottom of the long hill into New Mexico was a cemetery on one side for those drivers who didn't make it, and a motel on the other for those who did. Even the name comes back, The Swastika, a name that was painted out a year later when the Nazis made headlines.

After the long drive on graded but unpaved roads, the sight of Santa Fe was welcomed, and La Fonda was a real oasis after so many breakfasts of milk and stale doughnuts.

Returning from the Tesuque, Quivira, San Ildefonso Detour, his first purchase was a feathered headdress, and in this Les was typical of the dudes. As several drivers put it, "first the kids would get cowboy or Indian regalia and we knew the family would stay awhile. Then mother would buy some Indian jewelry and we knew she'd come back next year. If by the end of the vacation father bought cowboy boots and a 10 gallon hat, we knew he'd be back to live before too many years." In this case, it was the son who made the decision; Les Thomas built a home in the Southwest desert in 1956.

In 1936, Jim Clarkson opened his own tire shop and Studebaker car agency, severing connections with the Detours only nominally. He continued to help with the finances, still hampered by the free-spending habits of Hunter. Typical of gestures the Major made all too often, he saw to it the manager of La Fonda filled the rooms of Chicago dudes with American Beauty Roses to prove the desert was not all that sere. And he lavishly presented the same dudes with Indian jewelry — bracelets, necklaces, pins — whenever they celebrated a birthday on the tour. He made the ordinary tourist feel like a V.I.P., but to Jim it stood for Very Impractical Practices. Efforts to change

Ads such as this one brought many Oriental dudes to New Mexico

One of the late model Couriercoaches

such practices only led to arguments and Jim spent more and more time with his businesses than with Hunter's.

By 1937, the antithesis of the New Mexico and the Arizona tours was apparent. The Grand Canyon Tours, still using Harveycars, still adamant about not allowing Courier-cars to go beyond the entrance gates of the Park, were flourishing with such evening treats as color slide shows by Kolb Brothers, and a weekly showing of the latest Hollywood cowboy and Indian movies, most of them made in New Mexico and Arizona. Recognizing the value of drive-it-yourself vacationers, the camp ground had been enlarged and modernized, swelling the income possibilities.

The Clarkson tours were living a hand-to-mouth existence. The equipment was old and in need of replace-

Driver Staab at Taos in 1939. Courier Cooper inside car

ment. The inventory for 1937 showed Clarkson was stabling one 1927 Studebaker President truck, one 1927 Chevrolet International truck, six 1929 Cadillac sedans and one touring of the same vintage, four 1929 Yellow Coaches Model WA, five 1930 Yellow Coaches Model WB, one 1931 Express truck, one 1933 Yellow water truck, and one 1934 Chevrolet gas truck, one 1933 Chevrolet 50D truck, one 1934 and one 1935 Chevrolet truck, two 1935 Pontiac 6AA sedans and one 1935 Oldsmobile F-35 sedan.

The drivers spent their time repairing on the road and waiting for repairs in the garage. They made extra money by painting up as Indians and working on location as they drove the movie stars to and from the movie sets. They polished their shabby boots, re-creased their Stetson hats and made it through the next three years by driving freight line runs and carrying mail.

By 1941, the serious situation in Europe had precluded any foreign tourists. The dudes who had chosen the New Mexico desert over the Cornish seacoasts for a vacation a few years before, were now wearing air warden arm bands in London. The dudes who fled from the humid heat of the East Coast to the cool nights of Santa Fe were now scattered over the country in defense plants or in military training camps if their names had been pulled from the draft

Couriercars and Coaches at Carlsbad

fishbowl in October of 1940. The country was gearing for war. Once again, as in 1916, trains rumbled across the deserts through the night carrying tanks, trucks, ambulances, ammunition.

The 1941 New York automobile show featured lower, longer, broader more massive designs. Plymouth, Dodge and Ford had made production records, with four million, five million and 29 million cars respectively. An uneasy peace was being enjoyed, along with a sudden surge in the economy as war contracts were signed with embattled nations in Europe, and materiel was stockpiled just in case the U. S. was called upon to help or participate.

The drivers, couriers, hotel managers, even Indians discussed 'what if', and then in a few minutes on December 7th, it was no longer 'what if'; now it was 'what now.' Americans no longer had prohibition, they had gas rationing; they no longer faced a decision as to where to spend a vacation, they now had a war effort to support.

The prices of the various Detours in 1941 were the same as in 1933, with a new one-day tour offered that included Tesuque and a Santa Fe City drive for $10. The cars sat idle in the garage much of the time. A Mary Black of Washington, D.C., wrote to Clarkson after returning home, saying:

> "Perhaps the date of my trip was unfortunate as there were so few tourists for the special trip."

The date of her trip had nothing to do with it. With round-the-clock shifts, vacations for many were being postponed or taken close to home. There was no time to think of days in the sun.

The Indian-detours, through no fault of their own, were beyond help.

15

THE END

The amazing thing was not that the Indian Detours died, but that they didn't die sooner. Depression, a war, mismanagement, private motoring, all should have sounded the death knell long before the 1960's.

When war had been declared, the Major, now a U. S. citizen, had immediately gone to Washington and offered his services. His officer status in his native land helped him receive the same commendation in his adopted land; he was now a Major in the U. S. Army. Sent first to Casa Blanca, he was smuggled into Ischia. His talent at organization led to his being made commandant at the Port of Marseilles. A personal friend of Churchill, he enjoyed war, and did not return to the U. S. until everything was cleaned up to his satisfaction in 1956.

Two months after his return to Santa Fe, his wife died. Although his marriage was founded on British reserve, he was entirely devoted to Louise and her death meant a complete withdrawal from friends and business acquaintances. Moving to California, he went to work for Lockheed, leaving the entire business in brother Jim's hands, eventually giving it to him legally. He finally returned to his first love, ranching, buying property in San Diego County where he lived until his death.

Jim Clarkson in 1951

For a brief while, the Indian-detours were revived in 1947 with a new bulletin declaring they were back again. Rates had dropped approximately eight percent and the only trips offered were the one-, two- and three-day original tours. The surplus cars, tired and tireless were stabled at the Clarkson home in Tesuque, waiting for post-war automobile tire production to catch up with demand. The cars still in use could not be trusted on such journeys as Land Cruises, even had there been a demand for such trips.

Promotion of the tours was almost non-existent since Jim was more interested in his Studebaker agency and his tire shop than he was in whipping what he considered a dead horse. While he was a good credit risk, he was no gambler, and when Tanner Gray Lines offered to let him purchase their sightseeing tour franchise for $200, Jim refused it as too chancy. He could have combined the two businesses and made money. When offered a chance to invest in a ski-run transportation plan to augment the failing detour business, he turned his back on the opportunity.

The 1947 Brochure

In 1951 the employees of the detours, many of them with the company since its inception, arranged for a Silver Anniversary party. The invitations went out to more than 100 people to join the celebration on Tuesday, May 15th. The New Mexican in their May 20th edition reported on the affair. Everyone present was rooting for a rebirth of the tours.

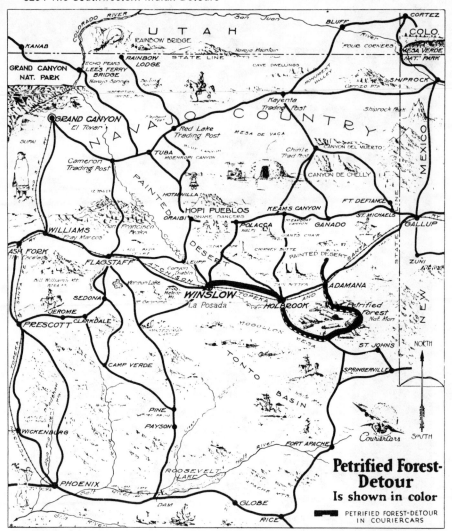

1941 Detour map

Indian Detour's Family Of Execs, Couriers, Drivers Have Silver Anniversary

It was 25 years ago on May 15 that the Indian Detours went into operation with a fleet of trucks, open and closed touring cars meeting the trains and taking tourists from all over the world over dusty New Mexico highways to the pueblos and cliff dwellings of an ancient civilization. It is conservatively estimated that a half million visitors have taken the tours in the quarter century; some say the estimate would be nearer one million. At any rate they are still coming from all over the world to see the Indian country via Indian Detours. When the silver anniversary was reached, the company decided it called for a bit of celebration and a dinner party was held last night at Arrowhead lodge for everyone who has been connected with the project and a number of friends who have known the detour business through the years.

1952 Couriercoaches at Santa Fe

James I. Clarkson, who heads the company today, presided as introductions brought reminiscenses after the assemblage of 100 guests had been wined and dined in the best Arrowhead fashion. He and Mrs. Clarkson headed one table. Carl Milam, termed the man who keeps the wheels rolling, and Miss Gladys Jenkyns, "the real boss of the outfit," presided at the second table for honor guests.

Ellis Bauer was introduced as "the oldest grad," associated in business with R. Hunter Clarkson, originator of the detours, before the

Silver program printed in red for the dinner

wheels began running. Wolcott Russel was listed from the earliest accounting department, as was a second banker not present, Quincy Appling. Lawrence Clardy was in it from the beginning and remains with the company today.

The couriers, who "made the service distinctive," came next, including Margaret Hubbell Rich and Ruth Heflin of the original class, Zoe Berchtold, Pamela Parsons, Edwards, Margaret Wennips Moses, Hester Jones, Consuelo Chaves Summers, Ruth Champion Montgomery, Eva Jane McChesney, Gladys Gilmour Temple and more.

Mr. and Mrs. Theodore Van Soelen were introduced because the idea of Indian Detours "was cooked up in their house." George M. Bloom, the bank president, Fletcher Catron, counselor, were other guests who spoke briefly. Then the David Coles were introduced as chief "boosters," Mr. Cole replied that he was still "just the boarding-house keeper."

Tommy Parker took a bow as the original driver and Sophia Kreasch for continuous bookkeeping.

Out of town guests included W. H. Jones, Santa Fe Railroad division superintendent at Las Vegas; G. C. Lyman, general freight and passenger agent and his chief clerk John Walters of Albuquerque. Whit Owen of the AT&SF received notice as the first traveling passenger agent for the detours. Others from the Santa Fe Railroad office attending were Mr. and Mrs. Mony Pesenti and Mr. and Mrs. David Benedetti.

John Gaw Meem, introduced because "he designed La Fonda," gave a brief tribute to Hunter Clarkson, then praised the courier system as an innovation he hoped could be resumed.

A Kenworth Couriercoach at Lamy

Above: Three Hopi women
Right: Dude at a roadside zoo

Double licensing was required by Arizona

For a brief period, the tours did rise Phoenix-bird style and a brand new 1953 folder detailed the usual one-, two- and three-day tour, plus a trip to the Grand Canyon with two choices. An inexpensive tour could be made by visiting Santa Clara, Chimayo and the sights of Santa Fe, then climbing back on the train and continuing to the Grand Canyon where the Fred Harvey cars would continue their sightseeing; or a six-day Land Cruise could be taken from Santa Fe at $388.25 which included Canyon de Chelly, the Petrified Forest, the Painted Desert, the Hopi mesas and the Canyon where the trip ended. A four-day Mesa Verde trip was also outlined, as well as a shortened three-day tour which eliminated a day's tour of Silverton, a drive over the Million Dollar Highway and an overnight at Durango. For $150, a three-day Land Cruise to Carlsbad was offered.

Simultaneously, an agents' bulletin was printed by the Santa Fe Railway repeating the tour information, and adding ticketing instructions and noting the fact La Fonda now had 70 additional rooms, concluding smugly, "the fine Fred Harvey standard of service, of course." A rundown of ceremonials was included and a listing of rental cars pointed out the train traveler was free to drive himself around to the points of interest if he preferred.

Jim had renamed the coach service The Indian-Detours Transportation Company, but retained the insignia of the eagle dancers. The drivers were now the couriers as well and much of the glamour that intrigued the dudes was gone. Instead of a chauffeured sightseeing drive, the service now was more like a hired-for-the-day taxi.

In 1968, Jim sold the interests of the company to Gray Line, who bought the rights to use the name Indian Detours along with the equipment. The name is in use by them at the present time.

But the Indian Detours, as they were known to people all over the world, with luxury motor cars and elegant coaches, with charming couriers and dashing drivers, with sincere welcomes to the pueblos, the personal friendliness of Taos artisans, pleasant picnics and fireside evenings, getting lost in the desert, getting stuck in the sand, returning each year to find the Southwest was virtually unchanged in the Detour areas, would not be enjoyed again.

The Indian Detours were ended.

List of Known Couriers and Office Personnel

Mildred Andrew (s)
Katherine Angle
Maria Baca
Jessie Barth
Zoe (McGonagle) Berchtold
Winifred (Shuler) Berninghaus
Rita Brady
Claire Bursum
Louise Bush
Hazel Connor (s)
Ann Cooper
Elizabeth De Huff
Frances De Huff
Erna Fergusson
*Henrietta Gloff
Emily Hahn
Ruth Heflin
Mary Louise Heller
Nel Hlavin
Gladys Jenkyns
Esther Jordan
Hester Jones
Anna (Coleman) Kardell (s)
Katherine Keleher (s)
Farona (Wendling) Konopak
Sophia Kreasch
Peggy Lewis (s)
Betty (Vogt) Long (s)
*Marcella (Matson) McCarthy
Eva Jane McChesney
*Amelia McFie
Janet McHendrie

Dorothy (Raper) Miller
Hazel Miller
Ruth (Champion) Montgomery
Margaret (Wennips) Moses
Carolyn Nelson (s)
Margaret Nelson
Helen (Dunn) Nickerson (s)
"Manya" (Norment) Wentworth
Pamela (Shackleford) Parsons
Agnes (Murray) Paxton
Ruth Perry
Peggy (Pierce) Pollard
Dorothy Pond (s)
Margaret (Hubbell) Rich
Miss Rockwolski
Kaye (Vogt) Sayre
Louise (Reisfar) Spalding (s)
Rita (Walker) Staab (s)
Lucille (Ridout) Stacy
Louise Studebaker
Consuelo Chavez Summers (s)
Gladys (Gilmore) Temple
*Anita (Rose) Waring
M. Wheelon
Margaret Williams (s)
Rainey (Bartley) Woolsey
Marguerite Wright

*Original Couriers
(s) Substitute Couriers

Name in ( ) is maiden name

List of Known Drivers and Office Personnel

Lester Adair
Quincy Appling
Ellis Bauer
Norbert Berchtold
Ed Blakey
"Buster" Brown
Frank Carroon
H. Case
Jack Cecil
L. L. Clardy
Willard Clark
Jim Clarkson
Wes Connor
Glen Conyers
Bruce Cooper
H. P. Curr
Albert Day
Tom Dozier
John Dunn
Francis Elmore
Jim English
Glenn Evans
Joe Fayette
Joe Flynn
Bill Foster
"Leather" Ganz
Gene Giers
Forrest "Slim" Good
Oren H. Goode
Bob Lewis
Eddie Luna
Tom Madden

Tony Martinez
Tony Mignardot
Karl Milam
"Spud" Milam
Charlie Miller
Julius Miller
Kaye Montgomery
Clarence Muralter
Russell Nelson
Tom Nickerson
John Nusbaum
Jack Ortiz
Thomas Parker
Hank Paxton
Andy Rich
Jose Ronquillo
Wolcott Russel
Frank Sayre
Charlie Seery
C. Shell
Lacy Shortridge
Jack Stacy
Norbert Staab
Howard Steel
Art Trauth
Eddy Von Nyvenheim
Ed Watts
Harold Webb
Dave Wheeler
Sam Young

ACKNOWLEDGMENTS

Many thanks to the National Park Service, the Carl Hayden Library at A.S.U. in Tempe, the Heard Museum, the Arizona Historical Society, The University of Arizona, Tucson, the curator of the State Records and Archives at the Capitol Building in Phoenix, and the Santa Fe Railways of both Chicago and Los Angeles, all of whom gave freely of substantiating material; to ex-couriers Ruth Montgomery, Hester Jones, Dorothy Wick Miller, Rainey Bartley Woolsey, Kay Sayre, Anna Kardell, Ann Cooper, Zoe Berchtold, Margaret Wennips Moses and ex-drivers Kaye Montgomery, Ellis Bauer, Tom Dozier, Bruce Cooper, Clarence Muralter, Wolcott Russel, Norbert Staab, Charles Seery, Chick Berchtold, all of whom fearlessly faced my tape recorder and entrusted me with their scrapbooks and photographs for copying; to Robert Hunter Clarkson who shared his family memoirs; to Mrs. Thomas Mabry, Judge E. L. Mechem, Mrs. Walter Mayer, Alice Bullock, La Fonda, and Sam Buchanan of the Taos County Historical Society all of whom helped put me in touch with participants; to Friendship Publications who researched bus history for me; to Dan Hammel of Dinon Photos in Phoenix who worked long hours to provide me with over 300 negatives and prints and most especially to W. E. Flohrschutz of the Santa Fe Railways who personally delivered archival material for photographing on more than one occasion.

PHOTO CREDITS AND SOURCES

ARIZONA DEPARTMENT OF LIBRARY ARCHIVES AND PUBLIC RECORDS: page 21 top and bottom.

ARIZONA STATE UNIVERSITY CARL HAYDEN COLLECTIONS: pages 60, 67, 72 top, 73 bottom, 89, 91, 92, 94, 97, 110, 122, 139, 173, 179, 191, 225, 238, 280 top, bottom left.

ELLIS BAUER: page 234.

ROBERT HUNTER CLARKSON: pages 43 right, 78 top left and right, 247, 276 top, 279 bottom right, 299 bottom right, 318, 321 bottom, 322.

TOM DOZIER: pages 101, 103 right, 126 top, 131 center and right, 135 top, 156, 197 top, 209 bottom, 213 top and center.

HEARD MUSEUM, PHOENIX: page 249 top.

ANNA KARDELL: pages 31, 48, 51, 55, 80, 119, 253, 262 bottom, 271, 299 bottom left, 301 top right, 303 bottom.

KRAUSHAAR GALLERIES, NEW YORK: page 161.

DOROTHY WICK MILLER: pages 78 bottom, 85.

MARGARET WENNIPS MOSES: pages 76, 83, 116, 241, 290 left and right, 299 top.

MOTOR BUS SOCIETY: page 175.

MUSEUM OF NEW MEXICO COLLECTIONS, SANTA FE: pages 24 top, 34, 37, 65, 66, 141 top and bottom, 198, 217 top and bottom, 223, 249 bottom, 262 top, 302, 306.

MUSEUM OF FINE ARTS, SANTA FE: page 43 left.

NATIONAL PARK SERVICE, JOHN C. O'BRIEN, GRAND CANYON: pages 38, 134 left and right, 163, 207 top, 209 top, 280 bottom right.

NEW MEXICO STATE RECORDS AND ARCHIVES, SANTA FE: pages 121, 199, 216 bottom, 282 bottom.

NORTHERN ARIZONA UNIVERSITY SPECIAL COLLECTIONS, FLAGSTAFF: pages 25, 28.

WOLCOTT RUSSEL: page 251.

SANTA FE RAILWAYS: pages 11, 12, 16, 23, 24 bottom, 29, 35, 38, 45, 53, 56, 57, 63, 68, 69, 71, 72 bottom, 87, 90, 115, 120, 129, 135 bottom, 144, 145, 148, 149, 153 bottom, 157 bottom, 164, 165, 166, 168, 171, 172, 178, 181, 182, 183, 186, 187, 188, 194 top, 203, 205, 207, 213 bottom, 216 top, 220, 232 top and bottom, 240, 258, 261, 262 center, 270, 279 top, 282, 285, 293 left, 298, 301, 308, 309, 310, 313, 314, 319, 320.

CHARLES SEERY: page 303 top.

NORBERT STAAB: pages 8, 49, 103 left, 107, 131 left, 206 bottom, 251 right, 275, 279 bottom left, 287, 301 bottom right, 324 bottom, 315, 321 top, 323 top right and bottom.

UNIVERSITY OF ARIZONA SPECIAL COLLECTIONS: pages 19, 27, 39 top.

THOMAS VANDEGRIFT: pages 49 top and bottom, 62, 245.

RAINEY BARTLEY WOOLSEY: page 40.

(Photos not credited are from the Author's collection)